A TRAILS BOOKS GUIDE

# WISCONSIN
# GOLF
# GETAWAYS

## A GUIDE TO MORE THAN 200
## GREAT COURSES AND FUN THINGS TO DO

JEFF MAYERS

JERRY POLING

TRAILS BOOKS
Black Earth, Wisconsin

Library of Congress Catalog Card Number: 2001087645
ISBN: 0-915024-91-8

Editor: Stan Stoga
Maps: Mapping Specialists
Design and Production: Impressions Book and Journal Services
Cover Design: John Huston
Cover Photo: Courtesy of Wilderness Woods Golf Course
at Wilderness Hotel & Golf Resort, Wisconsin Dells

Printed in the United States of America.

06 05 04 03 02 01 01  6 5 4 3 2 1

Trails Books, a division of Trails Media Group, Inc.
P.O. Box 317  •  Black Earth, WI 53515
(800) 236-8088  •  e-mail: info@wistrails.com
www.trailsbooks.com

*To everyone responsible for making Wisconsin a great place to golf.*

# Contents

# Introduction

Wisconsin truly does have it all when it comes to great golf. And it's gotten even better since 1994, when *Great Golf in Wisconsin*, the forerunner of this volume, was first published. Since then dozens of new golf courses have opened in the state, and it was our job to catalog the best, the unusual, the affordable.

In 1994, we took a detailed look at 25 of the state's best courses. This time, we took a different approach, trying to answer the question, "If I'm going to a certain travel destination, where should I play?"

*Wisconsin Golf Getaways* tells you where to play when you travel to 18 favorite travel destinations in Wisconsin—from the Lake Superior Shore to Milwaukee and everywhere in between. We've also included a section called "Across the Borders," guiding you to great golf just over the Wisconsin border in the Upper Peninsula of Michigan, northern Illinois, Iowa, and Minnesota.

You'll find courses by most of the world's current top course designers including: Pete Dye, Jack Nicklaus, Robert Trent Jones Jr., Arthur Hills, Arnold Palmer, Lee Trevino, Gary Player, Dick Nugent, Ken Killian, Bob Lohmann, Rick Jacobson, Lawrence and Roger Packard, and Andy North.

You'll find courses by some of the great designers of years past including: Robert Trent Jones Sr., Tom Bendelow, and Robert Bruce Harris. You'll find courses designed by regional architects, such as Art Johnson, Don Herfort and Joel Goldstrand. And you'll find courses designed by those who bought the land and built the courses, such as the incomparable Teal Wing Golf Club in Hayward.

Wisconsin's golf courses come in all lengths, too. That's why we included a section on nine-hole courses in each chapter. Sometimes, a nine-hole round is best for you and your family. Wisconsin has some of the best old-fashioned, family-owned nine-hole courses anywhere. Your travels through Wisconsin, with clubs in tow, would not be complete without a visit to Eagle Springs Golf Resort in the lake country of Waukesha County, where you can see the clubhouse with the apple tree growing through the roof and play the volcano hole. Intrigued? Read on.

Golf can be expensive. After you've paid all the bills—caddie fees and tips at Kohler Co.'s impressive Straits course on Lake Michigan—it'll probably cost you close to $220.

But golf doesn't have to be expensive. And Wisconsin still has plenty of good golf at low prices—despite the advent of many upscale, expensive courses. We've included a system that provides price ranges for greens fees, so you can judge the likely expenses before you call for the tee time. And we've included the phone numbers, directions, and Web sites, too. This green fees guide only includes the cart fee when such a fee is mandatory.

**$** means $25 per person or less
**$$** means $26 to $50
**$$$** means $51 to $75
**$$$$** means $76 and over.

Finally, we included tons of history and travel information—especially for those nongolfers who may be traveling along. So this is a great family travel resource whether you're playing golf or not.

Now, some thanks are in order. First, our thanks to three of the state's leading golf organizations—the Wisconsin State Golf Association, the Wisconsin Section of the PGA, and the Golf Course Owners of Wisconsin. You can read about their contributions to this great game at the beginning of the book.

And thanks to John Hughes, Rick Pledl, and *Wisconsin Golfer* magazine. John and Rick allowed us access to their files, including the many stories we've written for the magazine and its predecessor, *Wisconsin Golf.* John was a co-author of *Great Golf in Wisconsin,* and a lot of his work has been preserved here. Rick also provided important editing comments. Without John and Rick, this book wouldn't have been possible.

Dennis McCann, a *Milwaukee Journal Sentinel* and *Wisconsin Golfer* columnist, also deserves thanks for his suggested manuscript changes.

We hope you find *Wisconsin Golf Getaways* an invaluable resource as you travel the state. And please let us know if we missed anything, or whether the courses we cited have changed—for the good or the bad.

You can reach us through our publisher, Trails Books, P. O. Box 317, Black Earth, Wisconsin, 53515; www.wistrails.com.

Jeff Mayers
Jerry Poling

# I

# Great Golf Organizations in the State

## Wisconsin State Golf Association

The venerable Wisconsin State Golf Association (WSGA) is almost as old as golf itself in the Badger State. The nonprofit association of private and public golf courses was formed in 1901 and has its offices in Brookfield, a Milwaukee suburb. Its toll-free number is 888/786-4301. Its Web site is www.wsga.org, and the course directory information there was used frequently for our course information summaries. Its magazine is *Wisconsin Golfer*, based in Madison and edited by John Hughes (call 608/280-8800 for a subscription).

The association's impact on Wisconsin golf is huge. When you step off the measurement on a par-three tee, you do it from a round brass WSGA plate imprinted with the official yardage. When you submit your scores for handicap, the WSGA computes the number that allows you to compete in tournaments. It has one of the most

The first hole on the Palmer course, Geneva National Golf Club, Lake Geneva.

modern handicap systems in the country, and thousands of Wisconsin golfers take advantage of it for a small fee. When you play in a tournament, it could very well be a WSGA event. The organization sponsors 18 golf championships, including qualification for the U.S. Open. And when you peruse courses for their course ratings and slope, you have the WSGA to thank.

The WSGA also helps administer the Evans Scholarship program, which maintains houses at the University of Wisconsin–Madison and Marquette and has helped hundreds of young men and women get an education in golf and academics. In addition, the group maintains a hall of fame, a museum, and a library.

This book contains the course ratings and slopes for the top courses in the state, courtesy of the WSGA. Both course-difficulty ratings are meticulously computed using complex criteria. The condition or aesthetics of the course aren't included; scoring difficulty is the determining factor. Here's what those numbers mean.

## Course Rating

The course rating is a number, close to the total par for the course, that reflects the difficulty of a golf course under normal playing conditions for the scratch player. So, if a scratch golfer played 20 rounds at a certain course, the average of that player's 10 best rounds should equal the rating assigned by certified course raters. Yardage, the design of each hole, obstacles, prevailing wind, and other factors all play a role.

The highest course rating in the state, 76.7 from the black tees, belongs to the Straits course. Here are the rest of the top 10:

2. 74.9, Blackwolf Run, River course
3. 74.9, The Bog
4. 74.8, La Crosse Country Club (CC)
5. 74.8, Troy Burne Golf Club (GC)
6. 74.8, Blackwolf Run, Meadow Valleys course
7. 74.8, Lake Arrowhead GC, Lakes course
8. 74.7, Geneva National GC, Palmer course
9. 74.6, Cathedral Pines GC
10. 74.5, Country Club of Wisconsin

All but the La Crosse CC are open to the public.

## Slope

Slope is a number between 55 and 155 that indicates how difficult a golf course plays for all golfers with handicaps above scratch. An average slope is 113. Slope measures the difficulty of a course for average golfers in comparison to the difficulty for scratch golfers. So a course with a high slope rating will be proportionally more difficult for the average player.

The courses with the highest slope in the state, 151 (measured from the black tees), are Blackwolf Run's River course and The Straits. The rest of the top 10 are:

3. 143, Blackwolf Run, Meadow Valleys course
4. 142, The Bog
5. 142, University Ridge GC
6. 142, SentryWorld
7. 141, Cathedral Pines
8. 140, Lake Arrowhead GC, Lakes course
9. 140, NorthWood GC
10. 140, Geneva National GC, Palmer course

All of these courses are open to the public.

# Wisconsin Professional Golf Association

M ost golfers know about the Professional Golf Association (PGA), or at least they know it's the name of a major men's tournament. But there's also a Wisconsin Section of the Professional Golfers' Association of America, the WPGA. Headquartered in Milwaukee, the Wisconsin Section carries on the work of the PGA in Wisconsin. It's one of 41 section offices in the country that help the local PGA pro "meet the demands of today's marketplace and address vital issues such as pace of play, environmental concerns and accessibility," according to the PGA of America, which oversees a network serving more than twenty-five thousand members and apprentices. Its motto: "Making your golf game better, making golf a better game." When you take lessons, you should take them from somebody who is a PGA pro and has the PGA seal of approval.

The WPGA also sponsors many tournaments in the state, with special focus on juniors. In 2000, the Wisconsin Section announced the formation of the Wisconsin PGA Junior Foundation. Its stated goals are:

- To provide up to seven scholarships per year to high school seniors and college students based on academic achievement, community involvement and public service.
- To assist kids throughout the state in job training and placement in golf or a related field.
- To promote and administer junior golf tournaments throughout the state.
- To run clinics, exhibitions and camps to provide golf instruction.

Number 15 on the Meadow Valleys course at Blackwolf Run, Kohler, Wisconsin. Photo courtesy of Kohler Co.

For more information about these and other programs and to learn more about the WPGA, call 414/540-3820. Section information and the location of PGA pros in your area are available at its Web site, www.wisconsin.pga.com.

## Golf Course Owners of Wisconsin

The Golf Course Owners of Wisconsin Web site, wisconsin4golf.com, tells where their hearts are. Their acronym, GCOW, says a lot about where they're from. Yet most people would be hard-pressed to say they ever heard of the Golf Course Owners of Wisconsin. That's just fine with GCOW, so long as people keep playing and enjoying the state's public golf courses.

Since 1984, GCOW quietly has worked to make golf a better game in the state. A trade association composed of 165 of the state's more than three hundred daily-fee golf courses, GCOW exists to help its member courses deal with a variety of issues, but the group's ultimate goal is to make golf a better game in America's Dairyland. "Our mission is to get more golfers in the game, promote more tournaments, encourage clinics, reach the average golfer," says John Marxen, the group's president and manager at Two Oaks North golf course in Wautoma. Since about 1990, Dick Roellig has been the GCOW executive director. He believes that the daily-fee courses are the backbone of the state's golf industry. "We always say that nothing happens until the golf course is built," Roellig says.

GCOW works in association with the Wisconsin State Golf Association, the Wisconsin Professional Golfers Association and the Wisconsin Golf Foundation, Marxen said. GCOW is a chapter of the National Golf Course Owners Association. The group has a comprehensive state golf course guide on its Web site, with a link to the Wisconsin Travel Guide. The Web site also has links to major state golf organizations.

When it isn't promoting golf, GCOW is providing help to course owners on such issues as labor laws, state legislation, the environment, and promotion and marketing, Marxen says. If you were considering building a course in Wisconsin, you'd be wise to make one of your first calls to GCOW. Its main office is in Mauston, which you can call at 800/348-2721. Find the Web site at www.wisconsin4golf.com.

The quality of Wisconsin courses and the number of courses and players reached new heights in the 1990s, thanks in part to the efforts of GCOW members. "People come to Wisconsin actually for golf now," Marxen said. Many of them come to play well-known courses but are pleasantly surprised to find numerous other links that are challenging, in excellent condition, and affordable, he says. Wisconsin once was known mostly for its pastures. Now people are roaming its fairways, too. Soon it may challenge golf destination states like Florida or South Carolina, Marxen proudly says: "We're gaining on them."

On, Wisconsin!

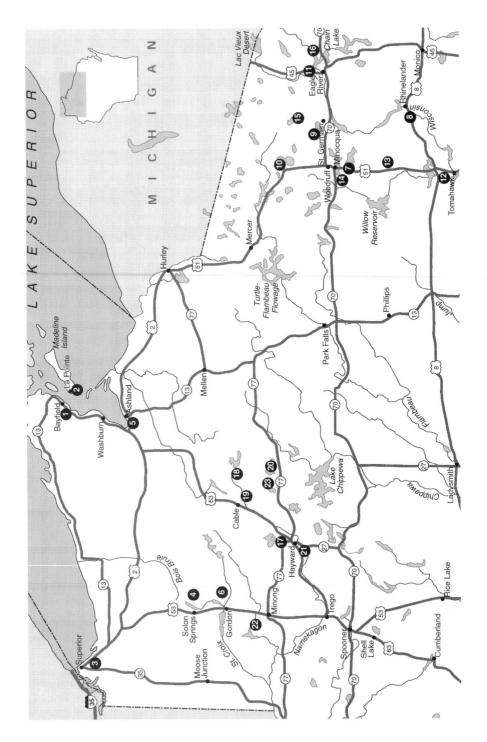

# II

# North Woods

1. Apostle Highlands Golf Course, Bayfield
2. Madeline Island Golf Club, Madeline Island
3. Nemadji Golf Course, Superior
4. Hidden Greens North, Solon Springs
5. Chequamegon Bay, Ashland
6. Forest Point Resort and Golf Course, Gordon
7. Timber Ridge Golf Club, Minocqua
8. NorthWood Golf Course, Rhinelander
9. St. Germain Golf Club, St. Germain
10. Trout Lake Golf and Country Club, Arbor Vitae
11. Eagle River Golf Course, Eagle River
12. Inshalla Country Club, Tomahawk
13. Pinewood Country Club, Harshaw
14. Wildwood Golf Course, Minocqua
15. Plum Lake Golf Course, Sayner
16. Lake Forest Golf Course, Eagle River
17. Hayward Golf and Tennis Club, Hayward
18. Forest Ridges at Lakewoods, Cable
19. Telemark Golf Club, Cable
20. Teal Wing Golf Club, Hayward
21. Hayward National, Hayward
22. Black Bear Golf Club, Minong
23. Spider Lake Golf Course, Hayward

# 1

# Lake Superior Shore

Take a boat around the Bayfield peninsula between Ashland and Superior and you'll have to travel about a hundred miles, a tiny slice of Lake Superior's 2,726 miles of shoreline. But don't tell the people of Wisconsin, especially those from Ashland, Bayfield, Superior, and bays in between, that their slice of Superior is insignificant. To them, it's the top of the world, the northernmost and most pristine part of the state, the gateway to the Great Lakes and the 22 Apostle Islands. It's nirvana, utopia, and to the residents of one hamlet, Cornucopia.

The summers and sometimes even the summer days can be short, depending on how the north wind blows off the frigid lake, but when June, July, and August arrive, the local residents celebrate the season. Average high temperatures of 65 to 71 °F are perfect for any outdoor sport, golf among them. Golf may not be the major reason why Madeline Island swells from 180 year-round residents to 2,500 in the summer months or why Bayfield becomes one of the busiest tourist cities in the state, but enough good golf courses exist that it can be a reason to head north or at least a reason to pack the clubs.

At Apostle Highlands in Bayfield, your first shot must carry Lake Superior. Well, not the big lake but a large pond shaped like the lake and built to scale, with a lighthouse. No mulligans if you don't reach Canada.

Along Wisconsin's Lake Superior shore, golfers can play on an island, play 500 feet above an island, have views of Chequamegon Bay, or play through forests. They can do it without having to make a tee time a week in advance and without spending half the vacation budget on two greens fees and a riding cart. Golfers also can have the time of their life while learning about the French and Indian history of Madeline Island, why Bayfield was named in 1997 the best small town in the Midwest, just how many quadrillion gallons of water Lake Superior holds, why many of the brownstone buildings in Ashland and Bayfield look like the brownstones in New York and Chicago, why Calvin Coolidge once set up a summer White House on the Bois Brule River, and how the area's ore docks helped the United States win two world wars.

From Ashland to Superior and around the Apostle archipelago, it's one memorable trip around Wisconsin's scenic tip. So pack a sweater, and head north.

# Apostle Highlands Golf Course
*Bayfield*

B y the eye-opening third hole at Apostle Highlands, nothing else seems to matter. Sailboats leave little white wakes 500 feet below on Lake Superior. That dark green thing in the lake is 14-mile long Madeline Island and those bright green spots on it, the Madeline Island Golf Club. Those hills in the distance are the Porcupine Mountains of Michigan. The sky never seemed so blue or the heavens so close.

Apostle Highlands is the course where stress goes for a vacation. Some golfers, of course, still play for score but give up on that idea once they stand on the third tee—or on any of the 13 holes that seemingly float above the lake—and realize that whatever it is they're feeling is bigger than bogeys and birdies.

It's not that golfers can't score at Apostle Highlands, a fair course with wide fairways but some challenging elevation changes. At 6,332 yards from the back tees, pars and birdies can be had, if you can get your head out of the clouds, which, depending on the weather pattern, may actually be possible.

Building one of Wisconsin's most scenic courses wasn't owner Stan Stevenson's vision. Stevenson owned much of the land and decided in the 1980s to have it logged off. The result was an eyesore that Stevenson wanted to rectify. Stevenson was a plumber by trade who left Chicago in 1968, eventually bought a lumber yard in Bayfield, and began building homes. Faced with unsightly cut-over land high over Lake Superior, Stevenson, then a nongolfer, first thought of hous-

Apostle Highlands, with the third hole overlooking Lake Superior.

ing. Then two men from Ashland proposed a golf course. "It came through the back door. It was more accidental," Stevenson says.

Home sites are being sold around the course, and an occasional homeowner can be seen or heard. But on a course where golfers stare zombie-like at the vast expanse of water and woods below them, nothing seems to matter. "I never envisioned it would turn out the way it is," Stevenson says. "It just blows you away. We get comments like that all the time. We think we have a good course, but overall not many courses can offer what we can." The front nine opened in 1990, but when Stevenson and partners acquired another 80 acres for the back nine, which opened in 1995, the course went from good to grand. More swaths of cleared land opened broader views of the lake. "That really changed the golf course. The views became spectacular," Stevenson says.

Stevenson is proud that Lake Superior not only can be seen on 13 holes but that it can be seen as far as the eye can see. The down-to-the-lake third and 12th holes give golfers more trouble than they should, partly because it's disconcerting to hit a ball that looks like it's headed for the world's largest freshwater hazard. The 383-yard third and 517-yard 12th holes aren't long because they play precipitously downhill, but choosing the right club and staying focused becomes the challenge. A good tee shot on the third hole is about 230 yards to a ridgeline, where the green is visible. The 12th is a dogleg par-five around two rock-filled washes, making position the key.

Golfers don't have to worry about actually hitting into Lake Superior—more than a mile away—except on the first hole. A Lake Superior–shaped pond was created by course designer Bill Korpella on the first hole, a 524-yard par-five. Those on the blue tees hit from the Bayfield Peninsula, past the Keweenaw Peninsula, and into Canada, otherwise known as the fairway. The white tees are near Isle Royale, which has a working miniature lighthouse. Golfers have been known to guffaw that they just drove a ball clear across Lake Superior, while others have been known to mention the Edmund Fitzgerald as their ball disappears.

Like Apostle Highlands' third hole, the fifth and sixth holes are vista par-fours that go downhill toward the lake and don't play as long as their 417 and 454 yards. The front nine then works its way back up to the clubhouse. While playing eight and nine uphill, make sure to look back for more views.

On the back nine, holes 10 and 11 stay on the highlands before 12 through 15 loop down and back up the hillside, all with great lake views. Although the lake isn't visible on 16 through 18, the sequence of par-five, par-three, par-four through the woods is one of the best on the course. Suddenly, it's possible to concentrate on golf again. On the 383-yard 18th, it's possible to cut the corner over big trees but at the risk of plunging into a pond that's not far from miniature Lake Superior—and looks suspiciously like Lake Erie.

Apostle Highlands pro Barry Hansen likes the course because it's not overly difficult. "It's playable for most every golfer. There's not one hole that will make or break you. It's a sporty course," Hansen says. "If you're not careful with club selection, you can drive it into trouble. You don't need your driver a lot." The toughest part of the course may be the greens, Hansen says, because they tend to break toward Lake Superior even when it appears they shouldn't. The 12th green, for example, slants severely away from the lake (or so it seems) but doesn't have a severe break. At the top of the green, putts begin to break uphill toward the lake. "Your eye will fool you. There are numerous putts that break uphill. That gets people going," Hansen says with a laugh.

Numerous boulder-filled washes provide extra hazards as well as drainage routes for rainwater to rush down the hillside. Truckloads of excavated rock were sold to landscapers when the land was cleared. Because of its elevation, climate, and proximity to the Big Refrigerator, a.k.a. Lake Superior, the condition of the course ranges from very good to average.

Facing east, Apostle Highlands is a great place to play in the morning as the sun rises over the lake. It's also not bad when the sun sets. "The pink sunsets and the evening shadows, they just change the whole course," Stevenson says.

Apostle Highlands can look and play like a different course every day, depending on the wind, the clouds, and the time of day or year. As you can well imagine, fall is spectacular. And so is the view from the deck after a round, no matter what your score.

*6,332 yards/par-72/70.5 rating/124 slope*
*Architect: Bill Korpella*
*Fees: $$*
*Call: 877/222-4053 or 715/779-5960; Web site: www.win.bright.net/~aposhigh*
*Directions: One mile south of Bayfield on Highway 13, turn on County J.*

# Madeline Island Golf Club
*Madeline Island*

Few people would dispute that Madeline Island Golf Club is one of the most memorable in Wisconsin. How many other places can golfers take a ferry to an island and play golf? Or play on double greens and fairways designed by one of the biggest names in golf course architecture, the late Robert Trent Jones Sr.?

Madeline Island Golf Club, with breathtaking views of Lake Superior, is one of only two island courses in Wisconsin. The other is Deer Run Golf Club and Resort on Washington Island off the tip of Door County in Lake Michigan.

The setting can't be beat, and sometimes the course can't either. In 1968, Madeline Island Golf Club opened to much fanfare. Owner Theodore Gary hired bagpipers from New York and flew in friends from the Twin Cities for the weekend. Not counting the soiree, about $4 million was spent on the nine-hole layout by Gary, a wealthy Twin Cities resident and golf enthusiast who spent summers on Madeline Island and wanted a top-notch course for his entertainment. Gary hired an expensive architect, Jones, who had to ferry topsoil for the greens across the bay to the rocky island. The native clay soil made a good base for the fairways, says Jerry Dunn, Madeline Island pro.

Dunn was among the hundreds of local laborers who helped build the course, starting in 1965. "They had an unbelievable number of local laborers picking rocks and sticks and making brush piles. It was a monumental task carving that out of the woods," Dunn says. His job in 1965 was to burn the trees and brush that were cleared from the fairways-to-be, and in 1966 he helped install the irrigation system. Dunn, then a promising 20-year-old amateur golfer, was introduced to Jones Sr. one day when Jones was checking the construction. Jones' son, Robert Trent Jones Jr., also a renowned architect, assisted his father at Madeline Island, Dunn says.

Jones Sr. designed a course that some people like to compare to St. Andrew's in Scotland, although that may be stretching it. Madeline Island Golf Club does have some similarities to the Old Course with deep bunkers, double greens, and a seaside setting. However, trees play a prominent role at Madeline Island, unlike St. Andrews. Madeline Island Golf Club starts near a marina and an old Native American cemetery but winds into a heavily forested hillside, where views of Lake Superior are a stunning reminder that this isn't an average round of golf.

Madeline Island is a nine-hole course, but it's much more than that. The second time around, golfers can play separate back-nine tees, fairways, and pins that are adjacent to the front-nine holes. Seven of the double-size greens have two pins, one for the front nine and one for the back nine. The flags are red on the front nine and white on the back. Make sure you know which ones you're playing.

The design itself must have been a complex endeavor. For example, the first hole is 399 yards to a pin on the right side of the wide green. The second time around, as the 10th hole, it's 444 yards to a pin on the left side of the green. The back nine is on the same course, essentially, but it seems much harder. The second hole is 109 yards over a pond to the left side of the green, but as the 11th hole, it's 181 yards to the right-side pin. And so it goes. Holes seven and 16 are the only ones that have separate fairways. Three holes have common teeing areas before the fairways split, so check the scorecard before taking aim.

Tourists think the course looks easy because the first few holes are open. "When they play and they see that their score doesn't look very good, then they see that Robert Trent Jones spent some time here," Dunn says. "The thing that belies the yardage total is the fact that the par-threes are short and the par-fives are short, and the par-fours are, by and large, narrow and long with nasty approach shots." Dunn calls holes 10 through 12 the "toughest stretch of holes you'll run into anywhere." They include the 444-yard 10th downhill, 181-yard 11th over water, and 431-yard 12th uphill. The final hole—much like the course—isn't conventional. It's a par-three down a steep hill to a shallow green guarded by a pond in front and sand in back—not an easy way to finish, especially if you take a peek at Lake Superior on your downswing.

With so many things to do on Madeline Island, the golf course often isn't busy. And if the ferry is running late don't worry, because the pro shop is used to golfers missing their tee times for just that reason. However, because you're paying for the ferry ride across, call for a tee time or to make sure no special events or busy days are tying up the course. It doesn't hurt to ask about the condition of the course, either, as the extreme northern climate and short summers limit the growing season. The course, which has mostly bent-grass fairways, has worked in recent years to improve spotty conditioning.

*6,366 yards/par-71/71.0 rating/131 slope*
*Architect: Robert Trent Jones Sr.*
*Fees: $$*
*Call: 715/747-3212*
*Directions: A 15-minute ferry ride from Bayfield to Madeline Island, and the course is to the right of the ferry dock near the marina off Old Fort Road.*

# Nemadji Golf Course
*Superior*

When people think of Superior, Wisconsin, they most likely envision people ice fishing, playing hockey, or skiing. But summer sports? They don't have summer up there, do they? The city by the lake is more than 320 miles from Madison and nearly 400 miles north of Milwaukee. Don't underestimate the hardy souls of the north. Superior not only has summer, but it has so many golfers that its 36-hole municipal course, Nemadji, is one of the busiest in Wisconsin. In 1998, nearly eighty thousand rounds of golf were played at Nemadji, and that's on a course where the season is up to two months shorter than the southern part of the state.

When the weather gets nice, Superior golfers hit the links. In addition to the eighty thousand rounds, Nemadji has up to a hundred business outings a summer, more than a thousand members, and more than two hundred children in a junior program. The course has three teaching pros, a chipping and nine-hole putting course, and a three-hole par-three course for children. From groups of kids to young adults, seniors, women, and couples, everyone seems to play in Superior. The game's popularity in the city may have something to do with the course. Superior residents have had an 18-hole municipal course since 1932. Nemadji expanded to 27 holes in 1984 and to 36 holes with the East course, designed by Roger Packard, in 1991. With four nine-hole courses, everyone gets to play.

Nemadji pro and manager Mark Carlson estimates that only 10 percent of Nemadji's rounds are played by tourists. With two excellent nine-hole courses, reasonable rates, and a well-managed, well-conditioned course, more visitors would be wise to give it a try. In 2000, Nemadji was in the process of converting all its traps from brown to white sand.

The best 18 holes are the East and North courses, which have woods, water, and interesting terrain. The South and West courses are mostly flat and fairly open, although renovations on the West course during 2000 and for several years thereafter "will make it a very nice course," superintendent Steve Flagstad says. "The West course greens are the toughest."

Packard's East course may be the best nine. At 3,339 yards from the tips, it can challenge and charm most any golfer. Holes four through six cross a road into woods and hills. The fourth and fifth are short, strategic par-fours that play uphill and dogleg to the left at the end with trees lining the fairways. The sixth is a 179-yard shot with about a 50-foot drop. The eighth and ninth are risk-reward par-fours, 378 and 380 yards, respectively, with ponds near the green that make long hitters think twice. Golfers who don't want to take a chance of making a triple bogey go for eagle—a carved wooden eagle, that is, that makes a nice target at the corner of the dogleg on number eight. It's one of five animal carvings that adorn the East nine. The North course has some of Nemadji's original holes. It starts with three open, flat holes before entering a woods. The West course has the most water and the most sand.

Even with 36 holes, be sure to reserve a tee time at Nemadji, where the golfers come in swarms when the weather warms up. And be sure to tuck a jacket or sweater in your golf bag. Golfers can't see Lake Superior from the course, but they can feel it. When the wind comes off the lake, look out. "It can be 90 degrees and 20 minutes later be 45 degrees," Flagstad says.

Nemadji usually opens in mid-April and closes the last Saturday in October, although the weather in May, June, September, and October often can be chilly.

*North/South: 6,362 yards/par-71/69.7 rating/120 slope*
*East/West: 6,701 yards/par-72/72.7 rating/133 slope*
*Architects: Stanley Pelchar (original design); Don Herfort and Roger Packard (additions)*
*Fees: $$*
*Call: 715/394-0266; Web site: www.downsdd.com/nemadji.html*
*Directions: Off Highway 35 (Tower Avenue) in Superior, turn west on North 58th Street and go 1 mile.*

# Hidden Greens North
*Solon Springs*

One look at Hidden Greens North, and it's easy to see why owner Bob Baldwin chose the name Hidden Greens, or so it seems. The course itself is virtually hidden, several miles down a county highway in the thick woods of northern Wisconsin. Most of the greens are hidden, too. The par-fours and par-fives usually dogleg, with the greens nestled around some bend in the fairway or above or below a knoll. Part of the romance of the course is standing on the tee, peering down a lane of green fairway through the forest and wondering, "Where's the green?"

Baldwin didn't have any of the course's geographical characteristics in mind when he named it Hidden Greens North. Out of gratitude, the Solon Springs course is named after another course, Hidden Greens in Hastings, Minnesota. Baldwin worked there for about 10 years before he decided to head north and build his own course, with the help of Lenny Swanson and Alan Swanson, the Hastings course owners. All three of them own the Solon Springs course, although Baldwin has the option to buy it. About a mile from popular St. Croix Lake, the land where Hidden Greens North lies originally was owned in the 1800s by a railroad and then a farmer who let his cows cross County A to pasture on the land. Baldwin and the Swansons are the third owners. Baldwin not only got the name of his course right, he got the course right, which was no easy task considering his mission. Baldwin designed the course and its greens and oversaw their construction, and now he is the manager and greens keeper at Hidden Greens North.

The clubhouse and number nine at Hidden Greens North.

Baldwin's toughest job was not only carving the fairways from the heavily forested land but keeping them playable for the vacationing golfers from nearby St. Croix Lake, the Eau Claire Lakes chain, Hayward, Superior, Duluth, and other tourist pockets of northern Wisconsin. St. Croix Lake is the headwater of the St. Croix River. "This was a solid woods," Baldwin says of the land, where he first marked fairways using a 150-foot-long yellow nylon rope and ribbons. A logger on a bulldozer then followed Baldwin's lead through the woods. The result was a tranquil course, one where golfers won't hear many sounds except for birds in song, clubheads knocking balls, or balls hitting trees. The fairways all are tree lined, but Baldwin says the average width is 30 to 35 yards. Knowing that typical golfers don't like to lose their balls, Baldwin also thinned the forest beyond the fairways and maintains a well-groomed rough. "We are constantly mowing our roughs," Baldwin says.

At 6,100 yards, the secret to Hidden Greens North isn't hitting long but playing smartly. The holes meander through a lovely forest of jack pine, red pine, white pine, birch, spruce, poplar, scrub oak, burr oak, and other varieties of trees. Rolling terrain, large greens, and three water holes add to the beauty. The course was built without sand traps and probably doesn't need any, but Baldwin said he most likely will build some.

Each nine makes a large loop through the forest, hole after hole of quiet and greens tucked into cleared corners of the woods. Both nines are par-36, each with two par-threes and two par-fives. The greens are big targets—averaging 5,000 to 6,000 square feet—many of them fairly level and with a moderate speed, something Baldwin favors in order to keep them playable during busy summer months. The tight front nine isn't easy, but the back is harder. It starts with a hidden green—the 10th—that sits atop a hill on the 328-yard hole. The prettiest and toughest par-three on the course is the 12th, 189 yards downhill to a wide green framed by spruce and pine trees.

Baldwin's marquee hole, and the one he worked hardest on, is the par-four 15th, a dogleg right. The perfect drive is 230 yards to the bottom of a hill. The approach shot then must angle right across about 75 yards of water, which laps 10 feet from the large green. Golfers cross a small walk-bridge to reach the green. The tee shot through trees is demanding and the approach shot scary, but the 15th is a championship hole and a gorgeous one. Before Baldwin shaped the hole, only a ravine marsh existed. He dug out a 15-foot-high bank of sand to create the level fairway and green area. Then he dredged the wetland to create a broad forest pond. Much of the sand he removed was used to build the course's tee boxes. Don't let down after the 15th. The par-five 16th hole also can make or break a round. It's a birdie hole at just 463 yards, but the fairway bends left all the way through the forest. A clump of four 60-foot-high poplar trees on the right and a wetland on the left leave a narrow opening to the green.

Baldwin knows that his course, with all the trees, is challenging. "There are always people who think it's narrow, but it's also very fair." It's also true to its name—Hidden Greens North really is Up North and really does have hidden greens.

*6,100 yards/par-72/70.2 rating/125 slope*
*Architect: Bob Baldwin*
*Fees: $*
*Call: 800/933-6105 or 715/378-2300*
*Directions: Off Highway 53, go 5 miles east of Solon Springs on County A.*

# Chequamegon Bay Golf Course (formerly Ashland Elks)
*Ashland*

It used to be just another nine-hole course that was popular with Ashland-area residents. Vacationing golfers either didn't know the existence of the Ashland

Elks course (the former name of the course) or didn't bother to play it if they did. Now golfers are forced to make a decision. On their way north to the Apostle Islands, Bayfield, Superior, or points between, do they drive a few extra miles along the southern shore of Chequamegon Bay and play the remodeled and newly named course? The sporty old course has been intermingled with the championship-level new holes to complete a course that's worth stopping by.

Architect Garrett Gill of River Falls, Wisconsin, carved five of the new holes through a forested hillside with treetop views of the bay, and he designed four holes in a lowland area through more trees and past three ponds. The weakness of the course is five original holes that run through open, flat land. The front nine plays up the hillside and the back nine on lower ground. "Garrett Gill wanted to make sure the new holes fit with the old holes," Chequamegon Bay pro John Mesich says.

The most exciting new holes easily are on Gill's hill. Holes three through seven are scenic and challenging. Each one offers a pretty bay view. The third hole is 394 yards across a ravine and uphill. The 410-yard fourth then plunges straight back down the slope through birch, pine, spruce, and poplar trees. The fifth hole is just 357 yards, but it's uphill with the tee shot needing to carry a ravine. Gill left a tall, lone pine standing behind the green. Landing above the cup on number five isn't a good idea, but it lets you look back toward the bay, the best view on the course.

Most of Gill's new holes force golfers to make a decision on club selection or shot placement. Several finishing holes are good examples. The 15th plays short, 317 yards and slightly downhill, but Mesich recommends an iron off the tee to keep it in the narrow fairway. The 16th is 527 yards, but a pond comes into play at about 230 yards, and a deep ravine guards the green. The 18th plays 531 yards past two ponds.

The original nine opened in 1925. It was designed by pro Sandy Campbell, a native of Scotland. He laid out two par-fives (1 and 9) and a par-four (10) on rolling terrain that still give golfers fits. "We have a lot of undulation in our fairways. There are not too many level lies on the entire course," Mesich says. "When we built the new nine, we kept that in mind."

*6,531 yards/par-72/71.8 rating/128 slope*
*Architects: Sandy Campbell (original nine); Garrett Gill (second nine)*
*Fees: $$*
*Call: 715/682-8004*
*Directions: Highway 2 to Highway 112, then go south to Highway 137. Go*
*    west 0.25 mile.*

**Best Nine-Hole Course**

# Forest Point Resort and Golf Course
*Gordon*

Vacationers in the Eau Claire Lakes area near Gordon used to go to Forest Point because it was more novelty than golf course. It was one of the last courses in the state with sand greens. "They didn't believe anything like that existed," owner Dave Babcock says. Now golfers go to Forest Point because it's real golf. The old sand greens course was just 2,200 yards and a par-33, but it has become a regulation-length course with all the trappings of a fun place to play—water, trees, a waterfall, and, of course, sand.

Forest Point opened in 1932. Owner Harold Fowler, a World War I veteran, was told by his doctor to give up farming. A friend laid out the course, and Fowler was in business. Dave and Andrea Babcock bought the course in about 1975 but didn't convert the greens from sand to grass until 1995. They also redesigned about six holes. Now Forest Point is a par-36, 2,840-yard course from the back tees.

Forest Point takes a horseshoe-shaped route through the forest. All of the holes are tree lined. On the first hole, a 356-yard par-four, water wraps about two-thirds of the way around the left side of the green. Forest Point has one of the largest greens, 12,000 square feet, and one of the smallest, 1,000 square feet, in the state.

Golfers whose rounds come apart on the par-four, 245-yard fifth hole can blame the heavens. The hole features what Babcock calls a "meteor pond. You can tell by the way the dirt has been thrown up that it was hit by a meteor. I didn't realize it until I started talking to other people about it." The meteor landed in a bad place—in the middle of the fairway. After the round, some Forest Point golfers look for meteors or shooting stars in the North Woods while staying at one of Forest Point's seven log cabins. The Babcocks plan to add another nine holes on 90 wooded acres nearby.

*2,840 yards/par-36/68.2 rating/115 slope*
*Architects: Dave Babcock and Steve Babcock*
*Fees: $*
*Call: 715/376-2322; Web site: www.forestpoint.com*
*Directions: On Highway 53, turn east at Gordon to County Y and follow the signs. Or take Highway 27 north of Hayward 17 miles, then left on Denver Road.*

## More Fun Things to Do

Be it Superior, Bayfield, Madeline Island, Washburn, Ashland, or dozens of other small cities along the shore, commercial, cultural, recreational, and educational opportunities abound. In other words, the area is a great place to have some fun.

A good place to stop before exploring is the Northern Great Lakes Visitor Center near Ashland (intersection of Highway 2 and County G, (715/685-9983). It has a storehouse of information about the history of the region and what to do and see. It also has a theater, exhibits, programs, nature trails, and a breezy, five-story observation deck that resembles a lighthouse.

On Lake Superior, you can see the light. Eight lighthouses are open for tours between Ashland and Superior, including six in the Apostle Islands. One of the best ways to see them is to use the Apostle Island Cruise Service out of Bayfield (800/323-7619), which offers evening lighthouse cruises in the summer.

Boats of all kinds are available. Charter sailboats and fishing boats can be rented in Superior, La Pointe, Bayfield, and Ashland. If you want something more intimate, try a sea kayak. Instruction for beginners is available. Canoeing is excellent on several rivers, including the Bois Brule, Montreal West Branch, and Turtle.

The Madeline Island Ferry Line is proof that half the fun in life is getting there. The busy boats ferry people and vehicles on a refreshing, 20-minute ride from Bayfield to Madeline Island. The golf course isn't the island's only attraction. Big Bay State Park (715/747-6425) has lake caves that can be explored along 9 miles of trails and a 1.5-mile-long beach. The Madeline Island Historical Museum (715/747-2415) is on the site of an old trading post for the American Fur Company. The museum, operated by the State Historical Society, tells the 350-year-old history of the island. You can drive around the island, but many people bring or rent bikes to see the sights—including a large population of white-tailed deer—firsthand. A bus tour of the island also is available. Big Bay Town Park has camping, fishing, and a beach.

Three other state parks and a state forest are in the area:

- Amnicon Falls State Park (715/398-3000) near Superior has a series of waterfalls and a covered footbridge over the Amnicon River.
- Pattison State Park (715/339-3111) south of Superior has Big Manitou Falls, the state's highest waterfall at 165 feet, as well as the eighth-highest, the tandem Little Manitou, 30 feet.
- Copper Falls State Park (715/274-5123) has 40-foot Copper Falls and Brownstone Falls.
- The Brule River State Forest (715/372-4866) near Brule has excellent trout fishing and first-rate canoeing, from slow-moving water to whitewater

rapids. Ten canoe landings are on the river, two of them at pretty but primitive state forest campgrounds, the Bois Brule and Copper Range, both among pine trees. The Turtle-Flambeau Flowage in southern Iron County has 19,000 acres of water and 220 miles of natural shoreline.

Bayfield is the jumping-off point for exploring the islands. The Apostle Islands National Lakeshore Visitors Center (715/779-3397) in Bayfield has information about getting to the islands and free history presentations. The ferry line, cruise boats to the outer islands, and watercraft rental all originate in Bayfield. Bayfield also is known for its eclectic restaurants, shopping, bed and breakfasts, including the acclaimed Old Rittenhouse Inn, galleries, and festivals. The city comes alive in the summer and fall with sailboat races, music and arts festivals, the Lighthouse Celebration, and the October Apple Festival, which draws fifty thousand visitors.

Near Bayfield, the Big Top Chautauqua (888/244-8368, June through September) has local variety shows under a big tent. North of Bayfield in Red Cliff, the Red Cliff Band of the Lake Superior Chippewa operates the Isle Vista Casino (800/226-8478) and a campground and marina. For more gaming, try Fond-du-Luth Casino in downtown Duluth or Black Bear Casino in Carlton, Minnesota.

Other attractions include: Fairlawn Mansion and Museum in Superior; S.S. Meteor Museum in Superior, a tour of an 1896 ship made in Superior; Ashland Area Historical Museum (715/682-4911); Washburn Historical Museum and Cultural Center (715/373-5591); and the Western Bayfield County Museum (715/372-4359) in Iron River.

Across the bay from Superior, Duluth has attractions such as the Lakewalk, Duluth Dukes minor league baseball, the Great Lakes Aquarium, Playfront (a giant playground), the Marine Museum near the lift bridge, Glensheen Mansion, the William A. Irvin floating ship museum, The Depot railroad museum, the Lake Superior and Mississippi Railroad, and Lake Superior Zoo. Or just grab a sweater, stroll along the bustling lakefront or boardwalk and see ships from around the world pass under the lift bridge. If you want to know more about the shipping industry and see the bay, take a harbor boat tour.

In Ashland, don't forget to drive by a structure that makes some skyscrapers look small. The old Soo Line Ore Dock on Water Street is 1,800 feet long, the largest shipping dock in the world. If stood on end, it would dwarf New York's Empire State Building by 600 feet. The dock, which took nine years to build, is no longer in use but is an ever-present reminder of the mining and shipping industry that helped build Ashland.

Short golf courses in the area include par-31 Norwood (715/374-3210) at Lake Nebagamon, par-65 Poplar (715/364-2689), and par-31 Pattison Park (715/394-0266).

## For More Information

Apostle Islands National Lakeshore: 715/779-3397; www.nps.gov/apis

Ashland: Chamber of Commerce 800/284-9484 or 715/682-2500; www.visit
    ashland.com or www.travelashlandcounty.com

Bayfield: Chamber of Commerce 715/779-3335 or 800/447-4094; www.bayfield.org

Bayfield County: Tourism and Recreation 800/742-6338 or 715/373-6125;
    www.travelbayfieldcounty.com

Iron River: Chamber of Commerce 715/372-8558; www.iracc.com

Madeline Island: Chamber of Commerce 715/747-2801; 888/475-3386; www
    .madelineisland.com

Superior: Superior Douglas County Visitors Center 800/942-5313; www.visit
    superior.com

Washburn: Chamber of Commerce 800/253-44955 or 715/373-5017; www.win
    .bright.net/~washburn/

# 2

# Eagle River, Minocqua, and Rhinelander

When people talk about the idyllic North Woods of Wisconsin, they usually refer to a broad area where forests and lakes replace silos and silage on the horizon and a place where the pace of life is slower and the state of mind more relaxed. It's the area where the call of a loon on a moonlit lake replaces the whine of an engine on a six-lane highway.

Real Wisconsinites know the place and the feeling. To them, the North Woods means only one thing—that upper third of the state where tall trees, tiny cities, and thousands of amoeba-shaped freshwater lakes dot the map. In the Badger State, the epitome of the North Woods can be found in the Eagle River–Minocqua–Rhinelander area. With more than thirty-two hundred lakes, streams, and rivers and thousands of acres of forest land, this is the North Woods to the more than two hundred thousand tourists who seek to get away from it all.

Up north, visitors can canoe a wild river, camp in a quiet forest, or catch a trophy muskie or walleye. They can take a walk in the woods, see a bear or an eagle, have a piece of fudge on Main Street, or watch the sun set over a lake. It's a place where trucks loaded with fresh-cut logs rumble through town, where giant fish are mounted in the restaurants and gas stations, where lawn ornaments are bears carved from tree stumps.

Minocqua, virtually surrounded by a chain of five lakes, is called the "Island City." Eagle River is on a chain of 29 lakes, believed to be the largest such chain in the world. People have been coming here to fish for so many years that there's now a tour of historic boathouses.

For most of the last century, required gear for a North Woods vacation included a tent, a boat, a fishing pole, and reservations at a mom-and-pop resort. People today also pack their golf clubs, or if they don't, they probably wish they had once they see the many quality courses. "This wasn't a golf destination. People looked at Lake Geneva and the [Wisconsin] Dells. Golf is becoming another reason to come here," says Brian Baldwin, pro at the St. Germain Golf Club. "Ten to 15 years ago there wasn't any golf here, and now there's a lot. When you have quality facilities, people will come."

The North Woods cities may be small, some—like St. Germain—even unincorporated, but the golf courses have a big-time feel. A first-rate course can be played five days straight with little driving in between. Most importantly, the courses have a North Woods feel. Numerous holes are carved from dense forest, over bogs, and around ponds and rivers, giving them a fantasy quality. On many courses, golfers enter the woods on the first tee and don't emerge until the 18th green. Now that's getting away from it all!

# Timber Ridge Golf Club
*Minocqua*

Roger Packard, together with former U.S. Open champion Andy North of Madison, Wisconsin, has designed many well-known golf courses, including Trappers Turn in Wisconsin Dells. Before they teamed up, Packard (the son of designer Lawrence Packard) spent years designing courses on his own. For almost 20 years, his solo gem in northern Wisconsin received little attention. Timber Ridge opened in 1979, but because it was a private course way Up North in Minocqua, few people heard about it or had the chance to play it.

Then, in 1997, Timber Ridge opened to the public, and another Packard course became a popular destination for Wisconsin golfers. It still may not be well known among the golfing public, but in 1996 it held the Wisconsin PGA championship, a sure sign of respect. "Roger Packard designed it as a North Woods, private atmosphere. But he made a perfect public resort course—it's the perfect location and layout for an upscale course," says John Hietala, Timber Ridge pro.

The beauty of Timber Ridge is two-fold. First, it's a public course that still feels like a private club. It has about two hundred members and all the amenities that they have come to expect. Second, it's a woods course, but chances are you won't lose many golf balls at Timber Ridge. Big red and white pine trees stand guard over the fairways and greens, but they're often skinny enough to allow for a recovery shot. In short, Timber Ridge is the most playable championship course in the north.

Timber Ridge is plenty tough, but it's also forgiving. For example, all of the par-fives can be reached in two shots, but all of them require taking a risk. Also, the greens are fast and have plenty of undulation, but they are large and receptive to approach shots. "The par-fives make this golf course. They're tempting, challenging, and rewarding for the shot maker but punishing if you miss," Hietala says. "There aren't a lot of low scores here."

Timber Ridge was built on land that once was a pine plantation. The best holes cut through remnants of that land while traversing ridges and crossing four ponds.

On the front nine, the course begins to shape up on the third hole, a shaded 408-yard par-four doglegging slightly to the right through tall pines, which also guard the green. The green on the par-three, 178-yard fifth sits in a bowl of pines atop a hill, with the fairway slanting sharply to the left toward the woods. Don't hit it fat. The 524-yard seventh is a good example of Packard's tempting par-fives—the daring player can cut off 50 yards and shoot for an opening to the green between trees and a waste area (eventually to be a pond).

Several picturesque holes make the back nine memorable. The 543-yard, par-five 11th doglegs through big pines again, as does the 12th, 385 yards. Watch out for the pond on the corner of 12. Another pond and gaping bunkers swallow errant shots on the 139-yard 13th.

The two holes that most golfers go home talking about are 14 and 16. The 14th is just 327 yards, but Packard left a 40-foot pine tree—don't try hitting over it, no matter what brand of distance ball you're playing—about 200 yards out, forcing players to choose the right or left side of the wide fairway. The 16th is Timber Ridge's postcard hole—a 170-yard par-three slightly downhill. A pond lies about 20 yards short of the green, and Packard added a touch of Pete Dye–style aesthetics when he slanted railroad ties on end to make a rustic wall about 10 yards short of the green. The dark beams also form a high lip on the long bunker, which runs the left side of the green. Packard saved two long par-fours, the 451-yard 17th and 423-yard 18th, for the finishing holes. Golfers come out of the woods there and finally have room to whale away on a couple of tee shots.

*6,627 yards/par-72/71.8 rating/127 slope*
*Architect: Roger Packard*
*Fees: $$$*
*Call: 715/356-9502; Web site: www.timberridgegolfclub.com*
*Directions: Four miles south of Minocqua on Highway 51.*

# NorthWood Golf Course
*Rhinelander*

In these parts, NorthWood Golf Course is Number One all the way around. It's the longest course, 6,724 yards; has the highest rating, 73.1; and the highest slope, 140 (making it among the toughest in Wisconsin). It's also the tightest course, having been cut entirely from maple, birch, and pine trees once owned by Wausau Paper Company. Given that, it also may be the most scenic. For a pure Wisconsin golf challenge, NorthWood is one course you won't want to miss.

With 18 complementary holes, each one a test of navigational skills—a.k.a., golf course management—NorthWood lives up to its name.

Most people wouldn't classify NorthWood as a benevolent course, but benevolence is how it came to be. The city of Rhinelander had discussed building a course for almost 20 years. Finally, former Rhinelander Country Club superintendent Paul Cooper, with backing from the mayor, spoke to Wausau Paper Company, parent of Rhinelander Paper. After three months of talks, the company agreed to donate land for a course.

When Minneapolis architect Don Herfort designed the course, he was told to pick 260 acres from an 800-acre plot of land. Herfort saw 18 holes hiding in the hilly forest, then exposed them without ruining the Up North feel. Each hole seems to blend with the land chosen for it. The result was a course that looked natural and played fair when it opened in 1989, and it has continued to get better.

That said, no course in the North Woods in Wisconsin will eat more golf balls than NorthWood. The fairways have wide landing areas, and the greens are generously large, but off-line often is off the course at NorthWood. Because Herfort left thick woods bordering most fairways, most balls that go in the woods stay there. If you do find your Titleist, gladly take your unplayable lie penalty and move on.

So how can NorthWood be tamed? A little forest at a time. It's a classic position course requiring well-placed tee shots and patience. If you can't hit the ball straight, it could be a long day. Play for position on the par-fives and keep the driver in the bag on the shorter par-fours. And when you can, peek over the fairway knolls and around the doglegs to see what's ahead. On four holes, water hazards come into play but aren't easily seen.

The front nine is the hilliest at NorthWood and 40 yards longer than the back nine. Fortunately, many of the front-nine holes play downhill from the tee. A good example is four, a pretty 402-yard par-four that descends a hill. The approach shot is downhill to a green perched on a hillside with a pond lurking on the left. The fifth also is a downhill par-four, 366 yards, with the green nestled in a bowl of trees around a corner. On the seventh hole, a 507-yard par-five, don't ricochet off the boulder in the middle of the fairway, and don't pull or snap-hook the ball left into the water.

The back nine is more scenic than the front, mostly because of a bog that was dredged to make a finger lake. The bog creeps into play on holes 11, 12, and 17. The 11th is a lovely, 142-yard par-three from an elevated tee over the pond. The green is shallow, and the pond is cut only about 10 feet from the front of the green. Nearby is a 30-foot, man-made waterfall that calms your nerves before setting sail with your Top-Flite over the water.

The best hole on the course may be 17, over the pond. It's a 400-yard dogleg left par-four. A well-placed tee shot through trees to the corner is only half the trouble. The pond creeps in on the left, so don't try to cut off too much. It's possible to lay up right of the pond on the approach—if you're playing for a bogey. Reaching the green in regulation requires a short- to mid-iron over the pond, which again hugs the edge of the green.

The second best hole on the back nine is 16, a 527-yard par-five. From a hilltop tee, golfers can see the green a quarter-mile straight ahead. But it's an obstacle course to the finish. Trees line the first 300 yards of the down-the-chute fairway. Then golfers must decide whether to attempt to clear a 30-yard-wide pond on their second shot or play right of it. Beyond the pond, a large fairway bunker on the right presents another hurdle for those who have laid up. The green is nestled amongst more trees.

A round at NorthWood is the real thing—pure golf in the North Woods.

*6,724 yards/par-72/73.1 rating/140 slope*
*Architect: Don Herfort*
*Fees: $$*
*Call: 715/282-6565*
*Directions: Three miles west of Rhinelander on Highway 8.*


# St. Germain Golf Club
*St. Germain*

In the late 1600s, a French soldier named Jean Francois St. Germaine (then spelled with an *e* at the end) settled in northeastern Wisconsin. He married a Native American woman and for years oversaw trading between the Native Americans and the French voyageurs. The Town of St. Germain in Vilas County eventually was named after the soldier, and a tall statue of Chief St. Germaine—in honor of all Native Americans—now stands at the corner of Highways 155 and 70.

A few miles down Highway 70, some of the pristine northland eventually fell into the hands of a paper company, Four Timbers Venture Group. Part of the land, 600 acres, was sold to the Town of St. Germain to build a golf course and promote tourism, town chairman Brian Sherren says. Only about fifteen hundred people live in the township, but the area swells by tens of thousands of people each summer. In 1993, the town opened nine holes at a cost of $1.2 million. Two years later, a second nine was added for another $1 million.

The result today is a scenic, 18-hole course that even the old trader Jean St. Germaine would be proud of. It has trees, water, deer, and other critters—all the good things that kept him in Vilas County more than three hundred years ago. After all, the name *St. Germain* means "forest."

Number six at St. Germain Golf Club.

The allure of the North Woods has been the drawing card for St. Germain Golf Club, a retreat best imagined as ribbons of bluegrass carpet woven between fibrous woods. "Once you tee off, it's just you and nature from that point on," says St. Germain pro Brian Baldwin. "There are no homes [along the course]. That's what brings people back—they're from the city and they are in the North Woods."

From the stunning log clubhouse (privately owned and operated), St. Germain appears to be a flat course. As it winds near the Northern Highland American Legion State Forest, the land begins to roll into and out of ravines and along ridges. The result is a course that takes golfers on a gentle ride through an enchanted forest.

St. Germain has so many trees that chances are you won't even notice the hundreds blown down in a 1999 wind storm. More than enough raw lumber remains to make the course a championship test and a test of your nerves. Well-placed ponds, trees and bunkers—and greens that average more than 100 feet deep—keep golfers on the toes of their soft spikes hole after hole.

The first test comes on holes four through seven, when the land begins to roll. The signature hole comes at the 373-yard fifth. From an elevated tee, golfers must negotiate two ponds, one straight ahead, to a plateau fairway. Another pond on the right keeps golfers from cutting the corner of the sharp dogleg right. It's a beautiful but unnerving tee shot. Then it's a mid-iron to an elevated green. The front nine finishes with another intimidating hole. It's only 374 yards, but the number nine tee shot must carry a ravine, and golfers must choose a right or left route around a grove of pines. With a pond left of the green, choosing the left fairway route may be best so your approach shot can be aimed away from the pond.

All the back-nine holes are cut from the same forest as the front. The best holes come at the finish, 15 through 18. The 15th, although only 352 yards, is a tight dogleg to a green tucked behind tall trees. The 16th is a narrow 379-yarder and the 17th a sharp dogleg 379 yards around a pond. The 18th can be the toughest hole on the course—a 506-yard par-five. The double dogleg hole has trees, sand and water—a three-shot par-five, and all three shots must be on target. "Obviously, it's a tight course. Position off the tee will determine your success," Baldwin says.

If you haven't had enough of the trees—or if you just want to make your peace with them—stop in after the round at the Whitetail Inn and relax among huge hewn logs and dine below massive antler light fixtures. On your way out of town, don't forget to pay your respects to Chief St. Germaine.

*6,651 yards/par-72/72.2 rating/130 slope*
*Architects: Gilmore Graves (original nine); Don Stepanek (second nine)*
*Fees: $$*
*Call: 715/542-2614; Web site: www.stgermain-golfclub.com*
*Directions: Three miles west of St. Germain on Highway 70.*

# Trout Lake Golf and Country Club
*Arbor Vitae*

First, the bad news. Trout Lake golf course isn't actually on Trout Lake, only near it, and the lake doesn't come into play. A body of water called the Trout River does figure into four holes, but there aren't any trout in the river or the lake. Now the good news. Trout Lake Golf and Country Club is every bit as pretty and peaceful as it sounds. If you're looking for serenity on a golf course, head 10 miles north of Minocqua on Highway 51, turn on a gravel road through the woods until you see a homey, log-cabin clubhouse overlooking a fairway and a river. The only time you'll be sorry is when it's time to leave.

Like a cozy resort, relaxed Trout Lake golf course is easy to fall in love with, a course where you wish you could linger, one you'll yearn to return to when it's vacation time again. Maybe it's the lakeside setting or the maturity of the course.

Maybe it's the peaceful screened porch on the clubhouse, shaded by pine boughs, that overlooks the 18th fairway. Maybe it's the shallow Trout River, as lazy as a North Woods summer day.

The golf course is good too, a tough par-72. But at Trout Lake scores just don't seem to matter. "We try to make it as fun and challenging as possible. There's the old clubhouse, the dirt road, no houses. People like to have a beer on the porch after the round and watch golfers play the 18th hole," says Phil Coon, one of three owners of the course. Coon also owns nearby Coon's Franklin Resort.

In the late 1920s, Phil's grandfather bought the land from the Wright Brothers logging company. Part of it was a company farm and part of it woods. Workers came in with horses and plows and built 18 holes by hand. Except for minor changes, those 18 holes are the same ones golfers still play today. The clubhouse is the original farmhouse, although it was remodeled in the mid 1990s.

Playing Trout Lake is like going back in time. The greens are small and undulating. Some of the bunkers are deep. And the course is an out-and-back design—similar to St. Andrew's in Scotland. The middle of the course is farthest away from the clubhouse, and the holes follow a clockwise route around the edge of the forest. Virtually all the trouble at Trout Lake is woods on the left side of the fairway while the right side—to a slicer's delight—is always the open part of the course on the old farmland. "If you're a hooker, you're in trouble," Phil Coon says. Of course, if you slice too much, the course will play much longer. Or, if you play smart, you just might be able to cut off a chunk of Trout Lake's 6,175 yards. Out of nine dogleg holes, eight bend to the left. The most severe is the 513-yard, par-five fifth hole—a horseshoe that has golfers peeking around the corner to find the green hidden near a tamarack swamp. It's the one-handicap hole. The toughest par on the front side is the 431-yard, par-four sixth hole. Woods and water guard the left side—of course—of the fairway, which runs gently downhill to a narrow green.

The middle six holes are the tightest, with woods on both sides of the fairways. The best of those may be 11 and 12. The 11th is 391 yards downhill and the only dogleg right on the course—through trees all the way. The 12th is only 298 yards, but it's tree lined and up a slanting fairway to a small, severely sloping green. Many of Trout Lake's greens are half the size of modern putting surfaces, and most have banked edges or severe slants that make holding the green and chipping an adventure. If you miss the green, miss it short and straight.

On the par-four 18th, only 260 yards, most golfers step up to the tee in front of the Trout River and take dead aim at the green. With bunkers on both sides of the green and a depression in front, getting home in one looks easier than it is. Yet the fun is in the trying, especially since a few fellow golfers usually are watching from the clubhouse porch along the 18th fairway. "Eighteen is a classic. Everybody loves that chance to drive the green. People would like to play it over and over if they could. Sometimes we do when it's not busy," Coon says. The 18th hole is symbolic of the entire Trout Lake course—one that you wish you could play over and over.

*6,175 yards/par-72/69.9 rating/124 slope*
*Fees: $$*
*Call: 715/385-2189; Web site: www.troutlakegolf.com*
*Directions: Ten miles north of Minocqua/Woodruff on Highway 51.*

# Eagle River Golf Course
*Eagle River*

To winter lovers in Wisconsin, the words "Eagle River" mean one thing: the World's Championship Snowmobile Derby race. It's the one time each year when the tiny city (population 1,400) gets statewide and national exposure. Snow lovers may find it hard to believe, but golf in Eagle River has been around longer, much longer, than the snowmobile derby. In fact, golf in Eagle River even predates the invention of the snowmobile. In 1925, Carl Eliason of nearby Sayner, Wisconsin, invented the snowmobile. In the early 1920s, the first nine holes of the Eagle River Golf Course opened on what was a dairy farm.

These days, the city golf course is doing just as well as the snowmobile. Eagle River has a scenic 18-hole municipal course to entice summer vacationers, as well as the local snowmobilers who need to while away the hot months. With many tree-lined, bluegrass fairways and rolling hills, golfers might even imagine they're on a North Woods snowmobile trail.

Like many area courses, straight shots are good shots at Eagle River. "You have to have good course management. Some holes require what we call position golf," says Brad Missling, Eagle River pro. He also warns that you "have to be a good putter because of the undulation of the greens. It's tough to make a lot of putts out here."

The first five holes at Eagle River aren't tree lined, but the city plans to remodel them, possibly starting in 2001, to bring a pond and marsh into play, including making an island green on the third hole. "We want to make those holes tie in with the rest of the course," Missling says. The rest of the course offers few breaks, beginning with the 375-yard sixth hole, a sharp dogleg to the right through trees. Then it's hole after hole of demanding tee and approach shots. The 11th is a good example. At 375 yards from an elevated tee, golfers must find a narrow strip of fairway doglegging left around a pond. Once past that hazard, the approach must carry another pond to a wide but shallow green. The 11th hole— the course's signature hole—is part of the new nine, which opened in 1988.

Holes 14 through 17 are par-fours that track through the woods and help make the course one of this region's elite. Par this stretch and the memory will keep you warm all winter. The 15th, for example, is 398 yards—maybe the second prettiest hole—slightly downhill with trees framing the entire hole. The 16th, called the saddle hole by Eagle River's 275 members, is 401 yards doglegging downhill between two grassy banks that often carom marginal shots back into play. The perfect drive is a draw off the left bank, which will kick your ball to the bottom of the hill, 100 yards from the green. No shortcuts on the 17th; it plays all of its 455 yards from the back tees.

Holes 12 and 13, a par-five and par-three, respectively, may be the least aesthetically pleasing on the course because they come out of the woods next to the snowmobile derby half-mile oval and an elementary school. Unattractive as they are, 12 and 13 still seem to fit. What would a trip to Eagle River be without a taste of snowmobiling?

*6,112 yards/par-71/69.4 rating/121 slope*
*Architect: Don Herfort (expansion and remodeling in 1988)*
*Fees: $$*
*Call: 800/280-1477 or 715/479-8111; Web site: www.eaglerivergolfcourse.com*
*Directions: Highway 45 north in Eagle River past the Eagle River bridge. Turn*
*    east on McKinley Boulevard.*

## Other Area Courses

# Inshalla Country Club
*Tomahawk*

This short course has undergone a major renovation over the last few years, and by the 2003 season it's due to stretch from the old distance of 5,599 yards to more than 6,400 yards at par-70, 35 on each side. In the meantime, the course will play at more than 6,100 yards—thanks to the front-nine renovation that lengthened par-threes (one up to 200 yards), added sand traps, and created the course's first true par-five, the 540-yard sixth that snakes through wooded terrain.

Woods and water dominate this family-owned course, which gets its name from an Arabic word said to mean "God willing." It opened as a nine-hole course in 1964 on the inspiration of John F. Hein, a former oil company engineer. It went to 18 holes in the spring of 1989 largely on the determination of his son, John Hein Jr., also an engineer. Hein Jr. also has managed the latest expansion, spurred by the desire to install a driving range, make room for home sites, and repair damage from a tornado.

John said his father used to say, "Someday we'll have a country club, *inshalla.*" The dream has come true, and it's getting even better. The best holes at Inshalla used to come right after one another on the back nine. Number 15 is a 168-yard par-three, and 16 is a 328-yard par-four; both make use of a slender man-made pond. Par demands accurate, delicate golf shots. These fine holes will remain intact, inshalla.

*5,874 yards/par-70/66.6 rating/109 slope*
*Architects: John F. Hein (original nine); John Hein Jr. (renovation and expansion)*
*Fees: $$*
*Call: 715/453-3130*
*Directions: Go 2 miles north of Tomahawk on Business Highway 51 to County U, then go 0.5 mile to Clear Lake Road.*

# Pinewood Country Club
*Harshaw*

For a one-stop North Woods getaway, Pinewood may be your place. The woodsy, hilly course features a trout stream—Bearskin Creek—and a few ponds but no sand traps. It's not a bad place to learn the game. In fact, the club has a golf learning center. The Pinewood recreation complex also has mountain biking trails, cottages, and a 2,700-foot airstrip for small planes. The first nine opened in 1962 and the second nine in 1970. The most memorable hole on the front nine is the 96-yard third—straight downhill. The back nine is carved from a stand of pine trees.

*6,165 yards/par-72/69.8 rating/123 slope*
*Fees: $$*
*Call: 888/674-6396*
*Directions: Thirteen miles south of Minocqua on Highway 51 turn east on Rocky Run Road, then left on Lakewood Road.*

# Wildwood Golf Course
*Minocqua*

At just 5,689 yards, Wildwood isn't a championship test of golf, but with nine ponds and the winding Tomahawk River, it can be plenty challenging. While Wildwood—next to Peck's Wildwood Wildlife Park—has plenty of short holes, there's also the behemoth 630-yard, par-five fifth hole on which ponds come into play on the first and second shots. Wildwood is an easy walking course, and golfers can choose a nine- or 18-hole greens fee.

*5,869 yards/par-72/68.6 rating/115 slope*
*Architects: Jim and Greg Peck*
*Fees: $$*
*Call: 715/356-3477*
*Directions: Two miles west of Minocqua on Highway 70.*

## AUTHORS' FAVORITES: WATER VIEWS

The Straits, north of Kohler. The Lake Michigan shoreline, thanks to Pete Dye, bears a striking resemblance to the Irish coast.

Apostle Highlands, Bayfield. Five hundred feet above Lake Superior and the Apostles, it doesn't get any better than this.

Madeline Island, La Pointe. It starts—and ends—with a refreshing ferry ride to the only inhabited Apostle Island. And Robert Trent Jones made sure the first five holes overlook the marina and Chequamegon Bay.

Peninsula Park, Door County. From the earliest settlement days, a great piece of property overlooking Green Bay.

Lawsonia Woodlands. The newer course at venerable Lawsonia provides dramatic golf and a couple of striking views of Green Lake.

Deer Run Golf Resort, Washington Island. The course is not on par with the Madeline Island track, but the ferry ride is worth it.

Abbey Springs, Fontana. The views of Lake Geneva make you forget you just duffed your drive.

Shoop Park, Racine. A lighthouse on Lake Michigan, too.

Naga-Waukee Golf Course, Pewaukee. The inland lake views get you thinking that sailing is the preferred après-golf activity.

## Best Nine-Hole Courses

# Plum Lake Golf Course

*Sayner*

If you're looking for a laid-back round far from the maddening crowd, Plum Lake Golf Course is the spot. On the shores of Plum Lake near the tiny town of Sayner, golfers play nine holes then retire to a cozy lakeside porch that wraps around the 1923 clubhouse. Several national magazine articles have been written about the clubhouse and some of its antique furnishings.

The setting is hard to beat, and so is the history. Plum Lake is one of the state's oldest nine-hole courses. It was built in 1909 by a few prestigious men. Among the charter members was Charles A. Goodyear, the same businessman who helped start the Goodyear Tire Company. Also on the original member list were Louis James, the 1902 U.S. Amateur golf champion, and his father, Fred, who helped design the course. What were they doing in northern Wisconsin? Plum Lake, circa 1910, was the last stop Up North for railroad passengers who had boarded in Chicago. Long ago, Chicago's wealthy residents headed to Wisconsin in the summer to fish and—once horses and plows cleared the woods—to play golf. The old railroad bed now is the maintenance road for the golf course.

Plum Lake doesn't come into play on the golf course (the lake frontage is used for social functions), but it does provide a lovely backdrop for the 3,067-yard course. Like any old course, this one has charm if not architectural correctness. Golfers can't see the green on the 150-yard fourth hole, but a 15-foot flagstick helps for direction. The green sits about 20 feet below the fairway in what locals call the "sugar bowl." All shots funnel into the bowl, making for a quick and easy hole. On the ninth hole, tee shots fly over a hill to a fairway that falls about 40 feet. After finding their shots, golfers ring a bell to signal the next group through.

Plum Lake, hearkening back to its exclusive beginnings, still has one private-club perk. Between 2:30 and 4:30 each summer day, only the members can tee off.

*3,067 yards/par-36/69.3 rating/126 slope*
*Architect: Fred James*
*Fees: $$*
*Call: 715/542-2598*
*Directions: One mile east of County N and Highway 155 in Sayner.*

# Lake Forest Golf Course
*Eagle River*

Except for a few hole modifications in the middle 1980s, golfers have been playing the same Lake Forest Golf Course since 1917. That means you can tee it up on the same holes as President Eisenhower and actresses Elizabeth Taylor and Joan Crawford, all of whom played the course at one time or another decades ago while they were up north on vacations.

Lake Forest isn't long—2,819 yards—or difficult, but it's a fun place to get in nine holes when the fish aren't biting or if you want to take a break from the Jet Ski. About half of the holes are wooded, and the 179-yard fourth hole requires a tee shot over a pond.

*2,819 yards/par-36/66.8 rating/115 slope*
*Fees: $$*
*Call: 715/479-4211*
*Directions: Go east 4.5 miles from Eagle River on Highway 70, then turn left on Range Line Road.*

## More Fun Things to Do

With thousands of tourists and cabin owners pouring into the area each summer, this part of the state learned long ago how to cater to vacationers. Most people have a hard time choosing what not to do. Do you pass up the shops of downtown Minocqua, Eagle River, or Rhinelander? Which of the thousands of lakes do you choose for a boat ride or a fishing excursion? Many people, of course, come to the area simply to do nothing. Why not lie in a hammock along a lakeshore, an especially inviting idea after a round of golf?

Golf can be just the beginning of an action-filled day in the North Woods. The Lac du Flambeau Reservation has excellent displays of Native American culture at the George W. Brown, Jr., Ojibwa Museum and Cultural Center (715/588-3333) and at the Wa Swa Goning authentic Ojibwa village. The museum has a four-seasons diorama, a 24-foot Ojibwa dugout canoe, a fur trading post, a world record sturgeon, and programs and performances. Nearby is the Lake of the Torches Resort and Casino (888/599-9200), if you haven't lost too many bets on the golf course.

The North Lakeland Discovery Center (715/543-2085) in Manitowish Waters has weekly educational programs and activities. The Bearskin-Hiawatha State Trail (715/385-2727) stretches 25 miles between Minocqua and Tomahawk and cuts through part of Timber Ridge golf course. Ride the Lumberjack Special

Steam Train and visit the Camp Five Museum (800/774-3414), an 1870s logging camp in Laona.

The Thunder Marsh Wildlife Area (715/365-2632), 3 miles north of Three Lakes, has 3,000 acres of spruce and tamarack forest with many unusual varieties of birds, including such royal species as the ruby-crowned kinglet and the king-fisher.

Other attractions include the Tomahawk Area Historical Center (715/453-2741); the Logging Museum Complex in Pioneer Park in Rhinelander; Vilas County Historical Museum (715/542-3388) in Sayner; Carl's Wood Art Museum in Eagle River; the International Snowmobile Racing Hall of Fame and Museum (715/542-4488), free, in St. Germain; Holt and Balcolm Logging Camp (715/276-7561) in Lakewood; Lakewood Fish Hatchery in Lakewood; Trees for Tomorrow Natural Resources and Education Center in Eagle River (715/479-2396); and the Minocqua Museum.

Traditional hotels, motels, and beds and breakfasts make lodging easy, but if you're looking for something more rustic, check out the weekly cabin rates at one of the hundreds of lakeside resorts. The Northern Highland/American Legion State Forest has 18 family campgrounds with nearly nine hundred campsites, and numerous private campgrounds also are in the area. Children can find all the mini-golf, go-carts, batting cages, water slides, arcades, and horse riding they can handle. Wisconsin Dells it isn't, but more family attractions are being added each year.

For family golf, try the 19th Hole (715/542-4042), a manicured, nine-hole, par-three golf course that's only 737 yards long. It's adjacent to a mini-golf and directly across Highway 70 from the St. Germain Golf Club. Big Stone Golf & Sports Bar (715/546-2880) in Three Lakes is an executive-style par-34 course.

If your children want a more up-north experience, see one of the Scheer's Lumberjack Shows (715/356-4050) in Woodruff; kids can cross-cut logs with the pros at the matinee. In Eagle River, try the fishing pond and see a mini–log cabin at the Northwoods Children's Museum (715/479-4623), which has 14 hands-on exhibits. Or take a tour of the Art Oehmcke State Fish Hatchery (715/358-9215) in Woodruff.

## For More Information

Eagle River Area: Information Bureau 800/359-6315 or 715/479-8575; www .eagleriver.org

Hazelhurst: Information Center 715/356-7350

Oneida County: Visitors Bureau 800/236-3006; www.oneidacounty-wi.org

Manitowish Waters: Chamber of Commerce 715/543-8488; www.manitowish waters.org

Minocqua/Arbor Vitae/Woodruff Area: Chamber of Commerce 800/446-6784 or 715/356-5266; www.minocqua.org

Rhinelander Area: Chamber of Commerce 800/236-4386 or 715/365-7464; www.rhinelanderchamber.com

Sayner/Star Lake: Chamber of Commerce 888/722-3789 or 715/542-3789

St. Germain: 800/727-7203 or 715/477-2205; www.st-germain.com

Tomahawk: 800/569-2160 or 715/453-5334; www.gototomahawk.com

# 3

# Hayward and Cable Area

Since the 1800s, people in the Hayward-Cable area have been thinking big. That tendency probably was passed down from the old lumberjacks, whose job was to log off virtually the entire North Woods by hand. Their icon was the mythical Paul Bunyan, a mountain of an outdoorsman. Generations later, life in northwestern Wisconsin hasn't changed all that much. The area is beautiful again with second-growth forests and still-clear lakes, although the burly lumbermen have been replaced by a new breed of northern adventure-seeker—thousands of cabin owners and vacationers. They still live big and have big ideas, even though the main cities, Hayward with two thousand people and Cable with eight hundred, are small.

Did you say big? In the Hayward-Cable area, you can explore the state's largest wilderness lake (the Chippewa Flowage), enter the nation's largest cross-country ski race (American Birkebeiner) or the largest off-road bike race (Chequamegon Fat Tire Festival), see a world record muskie (at the Moccasin Bar), enjoy the Midwest's largest powwow (Lac Courte Oreilles Honor the Earth Pow Wow), feel like Jonah himself and stand in the mouth of a 4.5-story high fiberglass muskie (at the National Fresh Water Fishing Hall of Fame) or watch logs roll, muscles flex, and wood chips fly at the Lumberjack World Championships (held in Hayward since 1960). You even can imagine what it was like to think big hundreds of years ago by canoeing the Namekagon River, like explorers Jonathan Carver and Henry Schoolcraft in 1767 and 1831, respectively.

As more and more people have discovered the Hayward-Cable area, so have the golf courses continued to improve. Before 1970, only a few nine-hole courses dotted the landscape. Before the 1990s ended, the area had five 18-hole layouts, including three that were built in the 1990s. Another 18-hole course, Black Bear near Minong, was scheduled to open in 2001.

The golf courses are plenty challenging, and they have some holes that seem out of this world. Towering pine trees, thick woods, glacial ridges, marshes, ravines, and spring-fed forest ponds are just some of the obstacles you'll encounter. At times you'll wish you had a cross-cut saw to clear a path to the green.

If you play at sunrise or sunset, you'll also see white-tailed deer and an occasional bear, fox, or raccoon scurrying across the fairway. And if you're listening, you'll hear songbirds and see eagles and hawks that will bring to life the still woods and blue skies of the sparsely populated north country.

As in most resort areas, tee times are recommended during the summer months. Yet you can expect leisurely, quiet rounds of golf far from any metropolitan areas. Interstates, housing developments and high-rise buildings are miles away. With the fairways winding trail-like through the forests, golf is a quiet venture in an area that likes to think big.

# Hayward Golf and Tennis Club
*Hayward*

It's the oldest major course in the Hayward area, and for many golfers it's still the best. The Hayward Golf and Tennis Club opened in 1924, but it doesn't look or play anything like an antiquated course—the greens are large and fast, the bent-grass fairways smooth, the holes strategically designed. And unlike many North Woods layouts, golfers usually can find their ball when it strays off the fairway. "We hear it all the time—it's such a fun course to play," pro Dave Blake says. People love to play Hayward G&TC because the layout always is in good condition and is fair and challenging for all levels of golfers. "The condition in this neck of the woods is very impressive," Blake says.

That's why Blake and his coworkers have one of the busiest courses in northwestern Wisconsin, accommodating nearly forty thousand rounds of golf a summer. It's not unusual for an entire day's worth of tee times to be reserved. Despite a continuous line of golfers, play at Hayward G&TC usually isn't slow because golfers can easily see their ball in short rough, and the trees aren't thick on the parkland-style course.

Unlike many North Woods courses, everything but the terrain makes Hayward G&TC a great place to play. The front nine is mostly flat and the back nine only gently rolling. A variety of doglegs, fairway bunkers, ponds and mature trees keep the holes intriguing. Some of the credit goes to architect Ken Killian. In 1998, he rebuilt many of the bunkers, added some traps, remodeled several holes, and made other changes. The course now has about 50 sand and grass bunkers and four water hazards. The original 1924 nine-hole course had been changed several times, and a second nine was built in 1970. "Killian gave the course visual challenge. There's much more decision-making now," Blake says.

The newer front nine starts with five benign holes before it kicks into gear. The sixth hole is ranked the toughest on the course, a 444-yard par-four around two fairway bunkers. Holes eight and nine are the most fun on the front. Eight demands a shot 189 yards over a pond with a beach bunker. Depending on the tee, you will have to carry the pond or skirt the side of it. Either way, you're usually hitting into the prevailing west wind, Blake says. The ninth is a 531-yard dogleg. If you can drive over the fairway bunkers on the left, you'll have a shot at reaching the green in two.

The older back nine has more character and is more challenging. "The back nine is very strong. You need each club, and there's some rolling terrain," Blake says. The 451-yard 10th hole is rated the second-toughest on the course, although only because it's long. The 392-yard 11th, with a new Killian-built green along the edge of some red pines, is more interesting. Distinguishing characteristics on the 212-yard 12th and 500-yard 13th are grass bunkers near the greens.

The course's postcard hole is 14, a 164-yard par-three over a pretty cattail pond. The wide green, guarded by three bunkers, slopes sharply toward the water. The pond ends about 10 yards short of the green, so it's not so much an obstacle as it is a decoration. The 14th is the work of Killian, who put in the pond after sinking the entire hole about 10 feet and using the excavation to create mounding. Killian changed the 15th hole from a straight par-four into a dogleg left, 516-yard par-five. With out of bounds defined by thick trees on the left, it's one of the few holes where you could lose a ball.

The 16th hole is a great place to make birdie—if you don't get too greedy. The safe shot is an iron or fairway wood to the corner of the dogleg and a half-wedge up to the green. Some golfers can't resist trying to carry a grove of red pines to reach the green in one. But hit it high and long, or the tall trees will knock down any weak shot and leave you scrambling for par. Holes 16 through 18 are why Blake says "we have some great par-fours. That's the meat of the golf course." After the 395-yard 17th over a ravine—a tight but fair hole that Killian didn't change—the finale is a 391-yard par-four (it was a par-five, pre-Killian). It doglegs left over a knoll. Approach shots must carry a pond and then two bunkers.

Be sure to make a tee time well in advance at Hayward G&TC. If you feel like walking, this is your course. In fact, at only a half mile from downtown, you could even walk to the course.

*6,685 yards/par-72/ 71.8 rating/125 slope*
*Architects: Art Johnson (second nine); Ken Killian (redesign)*
*Fees: $$*
*Call: 715/634-2760; Web site: www.haywardgolf.com*
*Directions: One-half mile north of downtown Hayward on Wittwer Street.*

The 13th hole, Forest Ridges at Lakewoods.

## Forest Ridges at Lakewoods
*Cable*

Have you ever played a golf course where you enjoyed the setting so much that you didn't worry much about your score? Breathtaking Forest Ridges, east of Cable, is one of those places. Owners Phil and Kathy Rasmussen once said they wanted their design to be considered the Pebble Beach of the North Woods. Although few people would compare Forest Ridges to the famous California course that held the 2000 U.S. Open, it's not hard to see what they mean. At Forest Ridges, much like Pebble Beach, the setting is paramount. Pebble Beach has the

Pacific Ocean. Forest Ridges has the Chequamegon National Forest. They both have holes where golfers stand on the tees and say, "Wow!"

With 11 carries over ravines and three over water, with target fairways that climb and descend glacial ridges, Forest Ridges is equal parts scenic tour and golf course. It's not for the beginning golfer or for someone who despises losing a few balls or shooting several shots higher than normal. Forest Ridges is for golfers who want a thrilling shot, a new challenge, every hole.

When Minnesota architect Joel Goldstrand, a globe-trotting designer who has done many Midwest courses, took on Forest Ridges in the early 1990s, he knew that coping with the landscape would be tough. There isn't a flat hole on the course—nothing even close to it. It's 200 acres of uneven glacial terrain. "It's the most exciting-looking golf course I've ever done. The land is so irregular that it was very difficult to create enough good landing areas," Goldstrand said. The word *chequamegon* is thought to have meant originally "long point or strip of land." It's a fitting description for many of Forest Ridges' holes—long points and strips of land are the tiny landing areas, and everything else either is forest, ravine, pothole, or bog.

Forest Ridges is adjacent to Lakewoods Lodge, one of the oldest and best known in northern Wisconsin. Vacationers have been going to Lakewoods on Lake Namekagon since 1907, many of them in the winter to cross-country ski and snowmobile on miles of nearby trails. Lakewoods several times has been named the top snowmobiling resort in the nation. In the summer, fishing and boating opportunities draw visitors to Lakewoods, but the Rasmussens thought a golf course would complete their resort. The $2 million course opened in 1994.

The course was almost unplayably tight when it opened, but it has become friendlier after years of creating wider landing areas and margins between the fairways and forest. Still, expect some cruel bounces or lost balls on shots that just miss the fairway or green. Remember, the interior forest views are worth half the price of admission here.

Five par-threes are Forest Ridges' camera holes, one-shot beauties that will leave you searching for adjectives before you hit and, possibly, expletives after-ward. The second hole has a 60-foot drop to the green; it's 137 yards of fun. Two holes later, you stand 70 feet above the green on the fourth tee. Check out the view of lovely Lake Namekagon on the horizon. It's 192 yards to a figure-eight green with a ridge in the middle.

The best of the par-threes are yet to come. The seventh hole has only a 50-foot drop, but there is no fairway, just tee, marsh, and green. It's a pure thrill ride—from the 183-yard tee shot to the winding path down the hill and across the marsh to the wide green, which looks like a front lawn under the shade of mature pine trees. Five tees are set in the hillside, each one about 10 feet farther down the hill. Had enough? The par-three 11th is downhill 169 yards over Mirror Lake with a view of the lodge in the background. And the 13th is the grand finale of the par-threes. Say a little prayer before you hit this shot. The tee sits on a ridge that's over 50 feet above Erik's Pocket, a bottomless bog lake. The green sits in a cove of pines on the opposite bank 181 yards away. It's a hit-or-miss hole, one where even if you do miss you say it was fun trying.

The bogged-down 13th is a good example of how Forest Ridges acknowledges its course may be too demanding for some golfers. The front tees were put on the opposite side of the lake, still requiring a carry shot but not a long one. The long carry over Erik's Pocket simply is too far for some recreational golfers. On all Forest Ridges holes that require a carry, a drop area is provided on the far side with a one-shot penalty. Without that bit of benevolence, some golfers could empty their bag of balls before reaching land.

The 13th, with its all-or-nothing shot, is symbolic of the course. Many other such shots await. The 381-yard third hole requires a perfect tee shot to a triangle-shaped landing area above a ravine. Another ravine swallows anything to the right on the 333-yard sixth hole, which plays sharply uphill to a two-level green. On the 360-yard 15th, your assignment, should you choose to accept it, is: Drive over a forest pond and hit your approach uphill to a green called the "Snowman" because it has three stepladder levels. Each level gets higher and narrower. From front to back, it's about 140 feet. Careful, or you might record a snowman on the scorecard.

It doesn't end there. On the lovely 16th hole, 350 yards downhill, approach shots must carry a marsh to a boomerang-shaped green with a Norway pine growing at the curve. No, the pine is not the flagstick, although it's not a bad target. Log-backed sand traps enhance the visual beauty of the 16th. At just over 6,000 yards from the back tees, Lakewoods's difficulty isn't length but numerous demanding shots that are a joy to try but nearly impossible to pull off all the way around. Some golfers find them too tough. Others revel in the unusual challenge.

You may lose your golf game at Forest Ridges, but you won't get lost, not with global positioning satellites guiding you around the course. The graphics system mounted on the carts diagrams each hole, tells you how far you are from the green, and keeps score electronically. It also puts you in touch with 911—in case you fall into one of those ravines and can't get up.

*6,069 yards/par-71/70.9 rating/137 slope*
*Architect: Joel Goldstrand*
*Fees: $$$ (includes motorized cart)*
*Call: 715/794-2561 or 800/255-5937; Web site: www.lakewoodsresort.com*
*Directions: Eight miles east of Cable on County M.*

# Telemark Golf Course
*Cable*

For years, it was one of the best-known vacation destinations of northern Wisconsin. Telemark Golf Course, much like its well-known nearby namesake, the ski lodge, was a picture of the North Woods—a bring-your-camera course of forest vistas with towering white pines, spindly jack pines, cathedral spruce, and shimmering aspen.

The first nine opened in 1968 and the second nine in the mid 1970s. It was the summer playground for a downhill resort that also hosted six thousand skiers in North America's largest cross-country ski race each February, the American Birkebeiner.

Then Telemark Lodge ran into financial trouble several times during the 1980s and 1990s. The course alternately was either playable or not, depending on the money flow at the lodge. In the early 1990s, the course almost closed as playing conditions worsened and golfers quit coming. Golfers complained that weeds were growing on the greens and that they found grass several inches high on the tee boxes.

The clubhouse and finishing hole at Telemark Golf Club.

In 1993, Rich and Judy Titus bought the course and began bringing it back to its original splendor. After years of neglect, it was a long process making the holes playable again, but as the 1990s ended, they had turned the corner. They built a new cedar chalet clubhouse in 1995, with a deck overlooking the lovely 18th hole. Trees and foliage were brushed back, leaving more room for error. Holes were reshaped. The bluegrass fairways were restored. Tee boxes were improved and enlarged. They cleared land and built a driving range with a spectacular view of the forest.

"It's been a real collective effort to figure out what changes to make," says pro Rick Christ, who works with the Tituses and their son Brian, the superintendent. "We want to have the course in excellent condition and at the same time make it more playable for all levels." The first hole, for example, is a pretty, downhill par-four of 372 yards through the trees, but the old tight fairway has been widened, making a much friendlier opening hole—and faster play. The Christ family has extra incentive to keep Telemark well groomed. They also own the nearby Spider Lake Golf Resort, a nine-hole course with lodging. They sell golf packages for the two facilities.

Outside of a much-improved ninth hole through the woods (the old one finished in the open near the base of the ski hill), Telemark's layout is essentially the same. The front nine starts on somewhat open land near the lodge before turning into the woods for good on the fifth hole. The entire back nine is through trees. "The trees—that's the signature of this course," says Christ, who grew up in Hayward and was a pro in Colorado before returning in 1997. "I've played golf all across the country, and every hole here has unique characteristics. I never feel like I've played that hole before."

Holes five through nine are an excellent finish to the front nine. The 364-yard fifth may be the most memorable. The sloping fairway is wedged between a wooded hillside on the left and a wetland on the right. The small green is tucked into a cove of trees. The back nine keeps getting prettier, starting with another downhill par-four through sky-piercing white pines, the trees that made the North Woods famous. From the forest floor, it's an uphill shot to the green. "Ten is a beautiful golf hole. I appreciate it more all the time," Christ says.

Original designer Art Johnson of Madison let nature do his work on the back nine. The holes flow like water through the woods. Johnson seemingly put a tee box wherever he had a great view. Seven of the nine holes play downhill. The 516-yard 11th couldn't be prettier—slightly downhill over a rolling fairway that narrows near a two-level green. A shallow, spring-fed pond lurks on the right. Playing this isolated hole feels like vacation.

If you can par 13 through 15, a trio of tough par-fours, pat yourself on the back. At 388, 347, and 387 yards, they aren't long but dogleg through trees and require accurate tee shots. You must carry a forest pond on the 157-yard 16th, but the view on this hole will keep you relaxed. Don't be deceived by the water—the hole plays its distance, even though it looks much shorter.

An excellent par-five awaits at 17—482 yards bending right on a tight fairway. The second shot must negotiate a large white pine—the "guardian pine"—near the middle of the narrow fairway. Be careful on the green—the steepest one on the course. The 18th is only 339 yards, and a little draw or hook off the tee can take you to the bottom of a hill and leave only a pitch to the elevated green. "Sixteen through 18 are three of the best finishing holes of any course around I've seen," Christ says. "Eighteen gives you all kinds of options. It's a great finishing hole."

The key to playing well at Telemark is "not to try to hit the ball too far, to play under control. The course doesn't play that long," Christ says. The good news at Telemark is that people are playing the course again and loving it.

*6,407 yards/par-72/70.6 rating/128 slope*
*Architect: Art Johnson*
*Fees: $$*
*Call: 715/798-3104; Web site: www.cable4fun.com/golf27.htm*
*Directions: Two miles east of Cable on County M, turn at Telemark Road.*

# Teal Wing Golf Club
*Hayward*

Their slope ratings, 140 to 150, are higher than your blood pressure. Their names can give you chills—Whistling Straits, Blackwolf Run, University Ridge, SentryWorld, The Bog. They're all 6,800 yards or longer. They were designed by famous architects. And most are in or near metropolitan areas. They are Wisconsin's toughest golf courses.

Hovering near the top of that elite list is one gentle-sounding course that seems out of place, Teal Wing Golf Club. It has an impressive slope of 139, the same as a course that Gary Player designed at Geneva National in Lake Geneva. However, Teal Wing was designed partly by Tim and Prudence Ross, a pair of middle-aged nongolfers who spent much of their life operating a resort. Their course is only 6,379 yards long, and it's hours from the nearest metropolitan area—even 20 miles from Hayward. Teal Wing Golf Club is out of the way and ... out of the ordinary.

You want tough? "I truly believe yard for yard [Teal Wing] is the hardest in the state," says Bill Linneman of the Wisconsin State Golf Association. If it were another 500 yards longer, it might be the number one–ranked course in Wisconsin in terms of difficulty, Linneman added. Tim Ross wanted it tough: "Golfers don't drive a hundred miles to play an easy course."

The secret lies in Teal Wing's many trees—ancient hemlock, pine, poplar, birch, maple—thick stands of them on a peninsula between the Teal River and Teal Lake, the land where the Rosses, Wisconsin's oldest inn-keeping family, have been entertaining guests since 1921. The origin of the resort dates to 1904.

For most of the century, Ross' Teal Lake Lodge built its reputation on rustic, lakeside cabins, home-cooked meals, famous pan-fried walleye, and trophy muskie fishing on Teal Lake and adjoining Lost Land Lake. In the early 1990s, family members reasoned that if they didn't find some use for their highly valued wooded land above the lake that it might fall prey to developers. The Rosses and their children Ben and Victoria didn't want that. Tim is the third generation of his family to run the resort.

You don't have to stay at one of the 24 log cabins—all along the lake—to play the course, although if you ever get a look at the Big Pine cabin, its screened porch shaded by heavy-limbed hemlock trees hard by the lakeshore, you'll want to.

The lodge's original dinner bell and main building still are used, including the honey-colored log dining room, old stone fireplace, and impressive mounted fish. When the course opened in 1997, most of the trees remained, too. The Rosses saw to that. They cut down thousands of trees to clear the fairways, but they didn't take any more than absolutely necessary. "Prudence and I walked every inch of this land," Tim Ross says. "We chose which trees we wanted to save," Prudence Ross says. "We made [the course] fit the land."

Lake Breeze Golf Course in Winneconne has a green shaped like the state of Wisconsin. So does Christmas Mountain in the Dells.

Gary Player or even Tiger Woods might find this course a challenge from the back tees. Linneman, a one-handicap golfer, shot 84 and lost seven balls the first time he played. One local pro visited the course, intent on using his length off the tee to humble some of the short holes. The pro didn't break 100, and the course broke his ego. "It's a strategic course," Tim Ross says. "You've got to think. If you try to overpower it, it will jump up and bite you."

In addition to a challenging course, the Rosses tried to build a course that disturbed as little of their beloved family forest as possible, even if it meant excruciatingly tight holes. The uncompromising result was Teal Wing. Building the course wasn't an easy task. Tim and Prudence first marked their holes in the forest with strings and balloons, partly so that they could find their way out. A longtime employee, George Fletcher, cleared and shaped the fairways with one bulldozer. With little or no topsoil anchoring the trees, the Rosses bought a 41-

Teal Wing Golf Club, number 17.

acre farm 8 miles away and for three months trucked in all the black dirt for the fairways at an extra cost of $150,000. The Rosses worked with the Department of Natural Resources and the Audubon International Signature Course program to make sure their course was as natural as possible. Logged-off trees were used for course building projects, such as the clubhouse. They didn't fill any wetlands and barely even disturbed any, using 55-gallon food drums to build floating bridges. Most importantly, course construction didn't touch an ancient stand of hemlock trees at the center of the course. A cart path winds through the enchanting forest between the 10th and 11th holes, but not one hemlock was cut down. "It's one of the largest stands [of hemlocks] left in the north country," Tim Ross says.

The Rosses suggested the layout for most of the holes, but one of Tim's old college friends, Pete Miller, a former superintendent at Firestone Country Club in Akron, Ohio, came in to finalize the plans. The greens were built by the late Jim Holmes, who once had the same job for the legendary Robert Trent Jones. Holmes also was one of the first agronomists for the United States Golf Association. Many years ago, Holmes gave aspiring architect Pete Dye his first job.

Teal Wing opened to considerable media attention, some of it from national golf periodicals, because the Rosses were their own general contractors. Much like Forest Ridges (137 slope at just over 6,000 yards), Teal Wing is very tight, although the terrain is flatter and more forgiving. The Rosses also have worked each year to brush back the forest edges. Teal Wing has five sets of tees (down to

4,029 yards), but landing areas can be narrow and some doglegs easy to hit through unless you take less than driver. So check your yardages before teeing off, and bring a camera. And if you have nonplaying friends or family members, bring them along. The Rosses have four-seat carts and keep extra putters for tag-a-longs. Nongolfing lodge guests often take out carts just to tour the course.

Teal Wing is divided into the River Nine and the Hemlock Nine. Water is a factor on 10 holes, but golfers have to carry it only four times. All the holes are tree lined, and all but three of the par-fours and par-fives are doglegs.

The River Nine, the front, winds down a hillside away from the lake and lodge toward the lazy Teal River. If the first three holes haven't tested your ability to hit an accurate tee shot, four will. It's 389 yards through a tunnel of trees and over a knoll to a green in a hollow. The fifth is 186 yards over a marsh to a wide but severely sloping green, one of many that designer Jim Holmes artfully used to carpet the forest floor. Holmes said the greens were the best he ever did. "You get the feeling these greens were intended to be here," Prudence Ross says. Holes six through nine finish along the river. The gorgeous ninth tee overlooks the usually placid stretch of river, once the site of a logging operation. It's a 445-yard, uphill par-five, but hitting the green in two is a challenge because the Rosses left a 150-foot tall maple tree at the crest of the hill.

The back nine isn't any easier, with marshes, water, and, of course, more forest. The prettiest hole is the 15th, 149 yards from an elevated tee to an L-shaped green guarded on three sides by a pond and on the fourth side by sand. The par-four 17th, running downhill through birch trees to a subtle green in a clearing, is another beauty. The 544-yard 18th has a boulder in the middle of the fairway (too big to remove, the Rosses say) and one last chance to negotiate the giants of the North Woods.

By themselves, many of Teal Wing's holes would be the best holes on many courses in Wisconsin. That includes the one-handicap hole, the second, a 522-yard par-five that plays downhill and doglegs to the right past a pond to a wide, picturesque Holmes green that melts into the landscape. As a collection, Teal Wing's demanding holes can be nerve-wracking. What's the tonic? Take a few extra balls, play it safe off the tee, enjoy the North Woods, and revel in the fact that—even though Teal Wing wasn't designed by Pete Dye or Gary Player—you just played one of Wisconsin's toughest and prettiest golf courses.

*6,379 yards/par-72/72.1 rating/139 slope*
*Architects: Pete Miller, Tim Ross, Prudence Ross, and Jim Holmes*
*Fees: $$*
*Call: 715/462-9051 or 715/462-3631; Web site: www.tealwing.com*
*Directions: Twenty miles northeast of Hayward on Highway 77.*

# Hayward National
*Hayward*

Hayward National was part of the 1990s golf course boom in the Hayward-Cable area, joining Forest Ridges and Teal Wing as new 18-hole designs. Yet if you don't remember the name Hayward National, your mind isn't playing tricks. The course opened in the early 1990s as Spring Creek Golf Club and expanded to 18 holes in 1997, when it changed names to Hayward National. With a brick clubhouse that opened in 2000 and work continuing on a five-hole learning center as part of the practice area, Hayward National continues to improve and mature.

At 6,327 yards on mostly level terrain, it's a good test for recreational golfers. The front nine is especially forgiving. It was cut from a 40-year-old red pine plantation, but the fairways and roughs are wide. The sixth hole, a 163-yard par-three that runs along a marsh, gives golfers a taste of what's to come on the back nine. An irrigation pond also can catch tee shots on the 407-yard eighth hole and the par-five, 457-yard ninth. The back nine has few red pines but much more character. All but the 10th and 18th holes play through a marsh created by Spring Creek, which flows through the course but is barely visible amongst the thick wetland vegetation.

Hayward National prides itself on smooth greens. They are especially attractive targets on the back nine, where they look like oases near the matted and reedy marsh. One such hole is 13, which is 142 yards over a pond to a large green that juts into the marsh. The ever-present marsh runs the entire length of the 435-yard 14th hole, and a bowl of wetland restricts drives on the left side of the fairway as well.

The 16th and 17th holes require carries over the marsh. Be careful on 16, 326 yards. Most golfers choose a fairway wood or iron to reach a small landing area. A shot too far carries into a stand of red pines. The narrow fairway then turns left. Approach shots again must carry the marsh, which surrounds the green.

Hayward National isn't long or particularly demanding, but it offers a pleasant escape into two natural worlds, one of pines and one in a wetland.

*6,327 yards/par-71/71.0 rating/123 slope*
*Architect: Gary Pietz*
*Fees: $$*
*Call: 715/634-6727 or 715/634-1595; Web site: www.haywardnational.com*
*Directions: From downtown Hayward, south 3 miles on Highway 27.*

## Black Bear Golf Club
*Minong*

Scheduled to open in the spring of 2001, Black Bear will feature wide fairways on wooded land that once was a boys' camp. Architect and owner Gary Pietz, who also designed Hayward National, cut the course from stands of oak and red pine on slightly rolling land. Ponds will come into play on four holes, including the 14th, a 410-yard par-four. It is a slight dogleg right with a tough approach shot to a large green guarded by water.

*6,500 yards/par-72*
*Architect: Gary Pietz*
*Fees: $$*
*Directions: Highway 53 to Highway 77, go west 0.75 mile to County I, then north 0.75 mile to Nancy Lake Road, then left 3.4 miles to the course.*

**Best Nine-Hole Course**

## Spider Lake Golf Course
*Hayward*

Golfers at Spider Lake can enjoy the beauty of the North Woods without having to worry about it; or to paraphrase the old saying, they can see the forest without the trees. Almost. The first and ninth holes at the par-36 course play through a stand of red pine trees, but most other holes have wide fairways, a few rows of pines, and little chance to lose a ball.

"Should you stray, typically you're not in much trouble. It's a really nice walking course," says Rick Christ, who doubles as the pro at Spider Lake and Telemark Golf Course, which are separated by about 10 miles of Chequamegon National Forest.

The course is next to Clear Lake on the Spider Lake chain of lakes. Golfers have pleasant views of the surrounding forest and Clear Lake, but neither come into play.

*3,300 yards/par-36/not rated*
*Fees: $*
*Call: 715/462-3200; Web site: www.cable4fun.com/golf27.htm*
*Directions: Thirteen miles east of Hayward on Highway 77 to Murphy Boulevard, north about 2 miles to clubhouse entrance.*

## More Fun Things to Do

Don't forget to bring your fishing pole and tackle box. With dozens of lakes in the area and the 15,300-acre Chippewa Flowage—a destination lake if there ever was one—the fish always are biting somewhere near Hayward. The area has a reputation for world-class muskie; the biggest ever, at 69 pounds, 11 ounces, was caught by Cal Johnson in the Chippewa Flowage in 1949. It's mounted as part of a fish and wildlife display at the Moccasin Bar in downtown Hayward. The flowage has more than two hundred miles of undeveloped shoreline and 140 islands. It's a great place to see wildlife and take a scenic boat ride. Treeland Resort offers Chippewa Queen Tours (715/462-3874) of the Chippewa Flowage.

Another lunker lurks in Hayward. You can stand inside the mouth of the 4.5-story-high fiberglass muskie at the National Fresh Water Fishing Hall of Fame (715/634-4440). The grounds also have other larger-than-life replicas of freshwater game fish, three hundred antique motors, five thousand fishing lures, and two hundred species of mounted fish.

The Hayward-Cable area draws thousands of people each summer to its private resorts lining the lakeshores, many of them on quiet bays. No state parks are in the area, but deep in the 844,000-acre Chequamegon National Forest the U.S. Forest Service operates the Two Lakes Campground (call the Cable Chamber of Commerce, 800/533-7454 or 715/798-3833). The 95-site facility is on lovely Lake Owen and Bass Lake between Cable and Drummond. It has large, wooded campsites, a beach, and a hiking trail.

No state bike trails are in the area either, but getting into the woods may be easier here than anywhere else in the state. More than three hundred miles of mountain biking trails have been cut through the woodlands, including one about thirty miles long on the rolling American Birkebeiner ski trail between Hayward and Cable. For scenic and challenging single-track mountain biking, try the Rock Lake trails east of Cable (next to Forest Ridges golf course) on County M or ask for maps of the CAMBA Mountain Bike Trail System.

The numerous hiking trails include the American Birkebeiner Trail, the North Country Hiking Trail near Drummond, the Black Lake interpretive trail near Clam Lake, the Forest Lodge Nature Trail east of Cable, the Lake Namekagon Interpretive Trail, the Lynch Creek trails east of Cable, the Mukwonago Interpretive Trail near Lost Land Lake, the Pigeon Lake Interpretive Trail near Drummond, the Trego Nature Trail, the Trego Lake Trail, and the Uhrenholdt Memorial Forest trail near Seeley.

Looking for a great view? Take a drive on Highway 77, also known as the Great Divide Scenic Byway. Starting 15 miles east of Hayward and heading to Glidden, the road is part of the National Forest Scenic Byway. It parallels the divide where water flows north to Lake Superior or south toward the Gulf of

Mexico. On the way, you can stop at the Penokee Overlook (15 miles east of Clam Lake on County GG). You might even see some elk, which were reintroduced to the state near Clam Lake in the 1990s. The herd is doing well.

Up for a hike? You can hoof it to the remote 70-foot Morgan Falls and St. Peter's Dome (elevation 1,565 feet) near Grand View. The Falls and Dome are 0.5- and 1.75-mile hikes, respectively, from a parking lot on Fire Road 199 near Grand View.

At Voyager Village Country Club near Danbury, 17 holes wind through the North Woods. The exception is the 505-yard sixth hole. It runs along a cement airstrip, which is out of bounds, costing you stroke, distance, and all your frequent-flyer miles.

The winding, 98-mile long Namekagon River, part of the St. Croix National Scenic Riverway, is popular with anglers, tubers, and canoeists. Float trips can be arranged through outfitters. The National Park Service operates an information center adjacent to the river at Trego (715/635-8346).

For a taste of the 1920s, check out Al Capone's Retreat & Museum of the Roaring '20s (715/945-2746) in Couderay. The 500-acre getaway once was owned by the infamous Chicago gangster during Prohibition. Visitors can see the jail cell and gun tower, along with displays on life in the 1920s, including a re-creation of the 1929 St. Valentine's Day Massacre.

Other attractions include the Sawyer County Historical Museum (715/634-8053) in Hayward; the Cable Natural History Museum (715/798-3890); the Drummond Museum (715/739-6290); and the popular LCO Casino, Lodge and Convention Center (715/634-5643) near Hayward. The Wilderness Walk (715/634-2893) is a 35-acre animal farm and park. See logrolling and other lumberjack demonstrations at the Scheers Lumberjack Shows (715/634-6923).

Near Hayward are two short golf courses, Roynona Creek (par-30; 715/634-5880) and Lakeview Golf and Pizza (par-27; 715/462-3787). The latter is popular with families, partly because of the homemade pizza and setting along Lovejoy Lake. Another good course for beginners is Takodah Hills (715/798-3760) in the Chequamegon National Forest near Cable. It's a regulation-length par-35 but only 2,569 yards with wide fairways. A second nine was under construction in 2000.

## For More Information

Cable: 715/798-3833 or 800/533-7454; www.cable4fun.com

Hayward: 800/724-2992 or 715/634-8662; www.haywardinfo.com or www.haywardlakes.com

Winter: 800/762-7179 or 715/266-2204; www.winterwi.com.

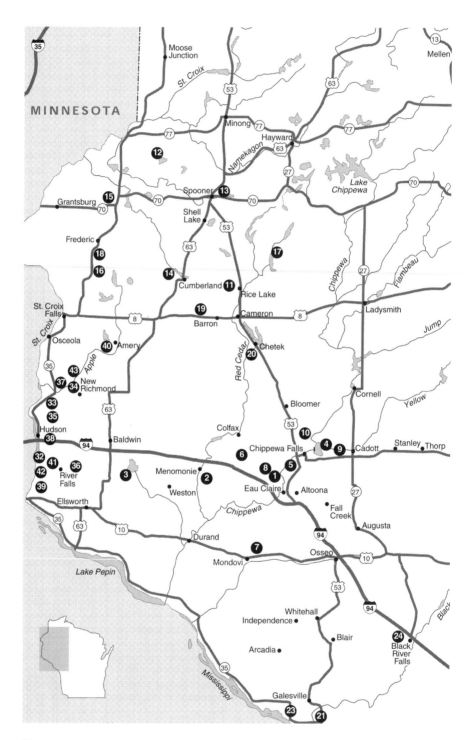

MINNESOTA

Moose
Junction

Mellen

St. Croix

Minong

Hayward

Lake
Chippewa

**12**

**15** Grantsburg

Spooner **13**

Shell
Lake

**17**

Frederic

**18**

**16**

**14**

Cumberland **11**

Rice Lake

St. Croix
Falls

Cameron

Ladysmith

Osceola

Barron **19**

St. Croix

Amery **40**

Chetek **20**

**43**

**37** **34** New
Richmond

Cornell

**33**

Bloomer

**35**

Colfax

Hudson

**38**

Baldwin

Chippewa Falls

Stanley Thorp

**6**

**4** **9** Cadott

**32** **41** **36**

**10**

**42**

River
Falls

**3**

Menomonie

**2**

**8** **5**

**1**

**39**

Ellsworth

Weston

Eau Claire

Altoona

Fall
Creek

Augusta

Durand

**7**

Osseo

Mondovi

Lake Pepin

Whitehall

Independence

Blair

Arcadia

**24**

Black
River
Falls

Galesville

**23**

**21**

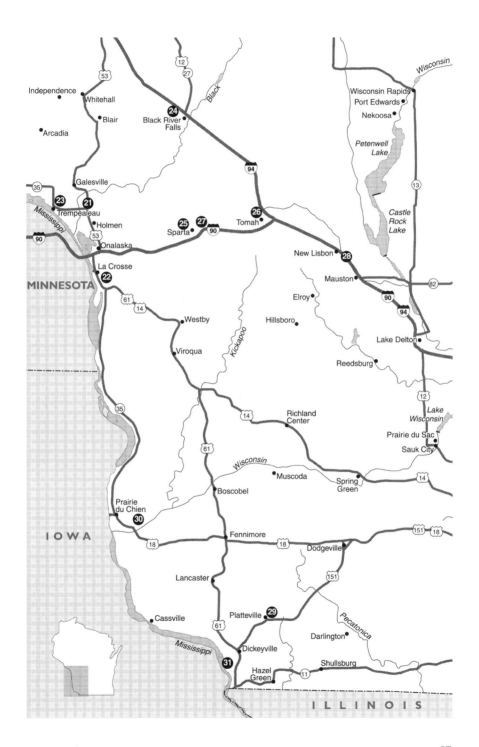

# III

# Great Rivers: Chippewa, St. Croix, and Mississippi

1  Wild Ridge, Eau Claire
2  Chippewa Valley Golf Club, Menomonie
3  Spring Valley Golf Club, Spring Valley
4  Lake Wissota Golf Club, Chippewa Falls
5  Hallie Golf Club, Eau Claire
6  Whitetail Golf Club, Colfax
7  Valley Golf Course, Mondovi
8  Hidden Creek at Mill Run, Eau Claire
9  Whispering Pines Golf Club, Cadott
10  Timber Terrace, Chippewa Falls
11  Turtleback Golf and Country Club, Rice Lake
12  Voyager Village Country Club, Danbury
13  Spooner Golf Club, Spooner
14  Cumberland Golf Club, Cumberland
15  Siren Glen Golf Club, Siren
16  Luck Golf Course, Luck
17  Tagalong Golf Resort, Birchwood
18  Frederic Country Club, Frederic
19  Barron Rolling Oaks, Barron
20  Sioux Creek, Chetek
21  Drugan's Castle Mound, Holmen
22  Forest Hills, La Crosse

# 4

# The Chippewa Valley

In the late 1800s, more white pine was milled in the Chippewa Valley than anywhere in the world. In the 1900s, it was the heart of America's Dairyland. At the turn of the century, it was known for high-technology industry. Since being settled in the early 1800s, the Chippewa Valley region of west-central Wisconsin has changed dramatically, or as one visitors' guide to the area says, it has evolved from "wood chips to cow chips to computer chips."

Residents in this west-central Wisconsin region also take stock in one more type of chip—chip shots. The Chippewa Valley loves its golf, and the golfers have plenty of courses to explore, from must-play 18-hole designs to old-time nine-hole courses, from courses bordering rivers and lakes to those carved from the woods and prairies. You need only consider the words most often used to name the courses—ridge, valley, lake, creek, spring, timber, pine, white tail—to get a feel for how they represent the natural beauty of the area.

The pleasant settings of the Chippewa Valley's courses come from the watershed region of the Chippewa River, the body of water that starts about a hundred miles north near the Chippewa Flowage (also known, appropriately, as the Big Chip) and flows southwest to the Mississippi River. Lakes, streams, and forests are abundant in the lower valley along with ridges, hills, and prairie farmland above the river.

At one time, the Chippewa Valley was almost all white pine trees, or so it seemed to the European immigrants. Logging drove the region's economy in the latter half of the 1800s. Prized white pine, some 100 feet tall, were floated down the Chippewa and Red Cedar rivers to numerous mills in Eau Claire, Chippewa Falls, and Menomonie, the cities that make up the heart of the region. Eau Claire's nickname is the Sawdust City. Menomonie in the 1880s had the world's largest white pine milling operation, Knapp, Stout and Company. In 50 years, the area produced 46 million board feet of lumber.

When the seemingly inexhaustible supply of lumber was depleted at the start of the twentieth century, agriculture—specifically dairy farming—became the number one industry in the Chippewa Valley. In fact, in the 1930s the U.S. Department of Agriculture named Eau Claire the central point of milk production and price supports in the nation, a distinction it held for the rest of the century.

People began selling their farms in the late 1900s, when California replaced Wisconsin as the number one milk-producing state in the nation. Then came high-tech industries, such as Cray Research, Silicon Graphics, W. L. Gore, 3M, and Hutchinson Technology. They made supercomputers, computer disk drives, computer components, and other cutting-edge products. Some people began calling the Chippewa Valley the Silicon Valley of Wisconsin.

The golf courses have changed right along with the region, which is one of the 10 largest metropolitan areas in the state in terms of population. About 185,000 people live in Eau Claire, Chippewa, and Dunn counties. What used to be an area of mostly nine-hole courses in the 1970s now has many modern 18-hole facilities—along with some of the pre–World War II layouts that still are favorites with locals.

Much like the region they represent, the Chippewa Valley's courses feel like middle America—relaxed and playable for all ages (yardages range from 5,800 yards to 7,000), reasonably priced (few courses more than $30), usually not crowded, and usually within sight of a lake, a river, or a woods. Some of the courses in nearby small cities, such as Osseo and Strum, still offer all-day golf specials for the 1970s prices of $10 to $20.

From wood chips to cow chips to computer chips to a great variety of places to play chip shots—no wonder it's nicknamed the Chip Valley.

# Wild Ridge
*Eau Claire*

Throughout the 1970s, 1980s, and early 1990s, the Chippewa Valley matched the golf course construction boom in the country in one sense—quantity—but not in another—quality. Cities like Stevens Point (SentryWorld), Madison (University Ridge), Kohler (Blackwolf Run), Wisconsin Dells (Trappers Turn), and others built so-called destination courses, but Eau Claire was left off the map.

That changed dramatically in 1999 when Wild Ridge opened in Eau Claire. Its greens fees were almost double the next most expensive area course, but suddenly golfers more than an hour's drive away had a reason to consider Eau Claire. Why? Private-course quality fairways and tees, an eclectic design using the best landscape features of a ridge and valley, and a strategic layout that can challenge championship golfers at 7,034 yards and weekend players at 5,830 yards.

Architect Greg Martin of Geneva, Illinois, is proud of his work. "Wild Ridge engages golfers in three ways—visual, strategic, and recreational. I assimilate the golf course into the landscape. I use the surrounding terrain and let the golf hole feed off it," said Martin, who also designed the acclaimed Rich Harvest private

One of the many scenic holes at Wild Ridge.

course in Chicago. "I'm thrilled. [Wild Ridge] feels good. It looks good. It plays well."

The focal point of the course is a ridge top, which also is the site of the clubhouse (and the name for the club's restaurant). The course falls away down the wooded ridge to an open valley. The front nine looks like a Wisconsin prairie (another consideration for the name of the course was Prairie Ridge) with native plants between holes. The back nine plays down and around the backbone of the ridge, a spine-tingling run of holes that easily is the best in the area.

Wild Ridge has bent-grass fairways and tees that wind among 60 sand traps, 60 acres of wetland areas and waist-high grasses (in mid-summer), a waterfall, and five-acre Lake Truax, named after the couple who helped settle the prairie in the mid 1800s. "This golf course just captures your attention. When you hit a shot, whether it's good or bad, you say, 'Wow, this is a pretty neat place,'" former Wild Ridge pro Doug Georgianni says. "What strikes me the most is the way the landscape looks. It's very stimulating, very appealing to the eyes. It has a real sculpted look. It was carved out with a precise hand."

If you play Wild Ridge for beauty and recreation, you won't be disappointed. If you play it for score, its narrow fairways will require patience. Some holes have little room for error. There is scant margin between the fairway and the wild areas (treated as a lateral hazard), which almost always means a lost ball. Says Martin, "I will extract it from you if you play outside your own game. If you get greedy, you'll find trouble."

Holes one and 10 are bookends, lovely par-fours that plummet from the wooded ridge to the lowlands. Let it rip here. Another memorable hole is three, a 657-yard par-five—believed to be one of the longest, if not the longest, in the state—aptly dubbed "Sherman's March" (named for nearby Sherman Creek and the ruthless Civil War general). The 366-yard fourth is so tight that it's named "Needle Pass." The scenic fifth, an uphill par-four, 411 yards, has a waterfall on the left and a place to catch your breath with a wider fairway. The course leaves the prairie briefly for six, a 150-yarder cut from an oak grove; the tee shot is sharply downhill to a small, two-tiered green guarded by trees and sand. Wild Ridge returns to the ridge with nine, which runs up the edge of the woods, a 404-yard, straight par-four that Martin says is a "pure golf hole in the classic sense. You could put it anywhere—Pinehurst, Pine Valley. It's good because it's so simple." The hole is slightly uphill with trees all along the left and bunkers on the right.

Golfers must pass under Kane Road for the final seven holes, which Martin calls "unique, diverse, and challenging." The 12th is all carry—195 yards—uphill and over a ravine. The green is wide and receptive; take plenty of club. A rock-filled stream bed cuts across the fairway on the downhill, 397-yard 13th. The ravine is called Ray Bourne after Jim and Isabel Ray, who gave up their farm to go into the golf business in 1981. Wild Ridge and the adjacent Hidden Creek 18-hole course were run by their sons, Curtis and Randall, until financial problems in late 2000 forced the courses into receivership. New management took over in 2001. Hidden Creek is the old Mill Run Golf Course.

The last five holes require precision shot making. The 15th is a monstrous, 480-yard par-four, but it plays much shorter because it's all downhill. The hole not only is long but probably too narrow (lowland area left, grassy hillside right) to swing away with the driver. Hit the big stick anyway and hope for the best. A five doesn't feel bad on this par-four. The only breather near the end is 16, a 525-yard par-five bending around a hillside and up a pretty valley. Martin's green here blends into the hillside—sloping back to front—to complete one of the most serene holes on the course.

Then things get wild again. The toughest par on the course may be number 17, an unpredictable par-three on the ridge. It's 211 yards into the prevailing west wind—and into a setting sun. The two-level green is guarded by a half-acre bunker. Good luck, and when you hole out check out the view of Truax Prairie all around you.

The back-nine ridge ride has one more thrill—the finishing hole. The 18th goes from ridge top to the bottom in 439 yards. Played in late afternoon with the sun at your back, the rolls on the cascading fairway stand out like waves. The tee shot descends the ridge to a fairway guarded by a fence and tree line on the left and prairie grasses on the right. The second shot must go over a greenside pond to a tiered green, although Martin generously left bailout room left and short of the green for those who prefer to pitch the ball in and one-putt for their par. It's an up and down finish on a wild ridge, on a course that finally made Eau Claire one of Wisconsin's golfing destinations.

*7,034 yards/par-72/73.5 rating/133 slope*
*Architect: Greg Martin*
*Fees: $$*
*Call: 715/834-1766 or 800/241-1766; Web site: www.millrungolf.com*
*Directions: From Interstate 94, take Exit 59 at the North Crossing/Highway*
*124 and go east to County TT (Kane Road). Turn right and the entrances*
*to Hidden Creek and Wild Ridge will be on the left.*

# Chippewa Valley Golf Club
*Menomonie*

The old saying, "The third time's the charm," probably had nothing to do with golf when it was first uttered. However, it aptly describes the evolution of the Chippewa Valley Golf Club in Menomonie. In 1976, the course opened as a nine-holer named Tanglewood. In the 1980s, it underwent several ownership changes, design modifications, and a name change—to Rainbow Ridge. Then, in 1995 the name changed again. Owners Jim and Patty Kloiber were in the midst of making it 18 holes when they sold it to Rick and Gina Budinger, who gave it the current moniker.

The Chippewa Valley Golf Club is by far the best of the three named courses that have been on the 262 acres of hilly woods on the edge of Menomonie. Seven (actually 7.5) of the nine original holes designed by Gordon Emerson remain, but quantity and quality improved with the addition of 11 solid new holes and a commitment to make the course a regional destination for golfers.

The course's three names help tell its story. Chippewa Valley Golf Club features 10 holes that cut through or around thick woods. Hence the first name, Tanglewood. The clubhouse is perched on a rural hillside, and several hilltop tees have views of bucolic Dunn County. Thus, the second moniker, Rainbow Ridge. The third name makes sense as well, because Chippewa Valley Golf Club's 18 holes are on terrain that typify west-central Wisconsin.

Golfers can't nod off at Chippewa Valley Golf Club, even though it's a very relaxing, away-from-the-crowd course. Hole after hole takes players either into, out of, or around woods, past a wetland, up a ridge, or to a valley. Water is a fac-

The 14th at Chippewa Valley.

tor on four holes. Bunkering is moderate, but trees, elevation changes, and contoured greens make the course a challenge. The fairways are rye grass. "It's a nice variety of holes," owner Rick Budinger says. "We have ups, downs, flats, and holes that have a links look."

The challenge begins on one, which isn't the usual warm-up hole. It's a 544-yard par-five with an open tee shot. But the second shot enters the woods and goes down a hill, where a golfer must lay up in order to make a turn and pitch up to the green. "You've got to play conservatively," Rick Budinger says. "It's my favorite hole and the one I hear the most comments on."

The second hole requires a tee shot straight downhill through a chute of trees before doglegging 90 degrees left. You can cut the corner, but at 338 yards it may not be worthwhile. Holes three through seven play through a valley. The par-five seventh, a meadow hole around the wildlife area, plays all of its 600 yards—usually into the prevailing wind—to a large green and past a long waste bunker.

Holes 13 through 16—all of them par-fours—may be the best stretch on the course. Thirteen is 322 yards downhill through a pretty neck of the woods—a birdie hole if you can keep it between the trees and the fairway bunkers. The 14th has a beautiful elevated tee. The 16th runs 356 yards up and over a knoll then down through the woods, the prettiest hole on the course. The finishing hole, 503 yards, can make for an exciting finish. Because it's all downhill—aim for the horse barn off the tee—a good drive makes it reachable in two. However, a pond guards the wide, shallow green. A small layup area makes the second shot the key decision on this hole.

With a quiet, scenic setting and a challenging design, Chippewa Valley Golf Club lives up to its name.

*6,324 yards/par-71/70.3 rating/123 slope*
*Architects: Gordon Emerson (original nine); Jim Kloiber (second nine)*
*Fees: $$*
*Call: 800/494-8987 or 715/235-9808; Web site: www.cvgolf.com*
*Directions: From Interstate 94, exit south on Highway 25. Go 3 miles to 21st*
*Avenue. Turn left and go to County Y (9th Street). Turn right on Y and go*
*0.5 mile to Tanglewood Drive, which leads to the course.*

# Spring Valley Golf Club
*Spring Valley*

S pring Valley is a 45-minute drive west of Eau Claire, and the city looks so small that it couldn't support a nice golf course. But don't be deceived. On a hill above town is the Spring Valley Golf Club, an 18-hole course that's second only to Crystal Cave and Eau Galle Dam—the Midwest's largest earthen dam—as local attractions. Granted, Spring Valley is a sleepy city in a deep valley where the sun goes down early. The Eau Galle River meanders past white church steeples. No golden arches. No four-lane roads. No malls. It seems like Rip Van Winkle should live here.

He doesn't, but Dr. Gordon Emerson does. Emerson was among the top amateur players in the Midwest around 1960, before he settled down and became a dentist. He then took up golf course architecture on the side, designing, remodeling and expanding 27 courses, mostly in western Wisconsin but also several in Minnesota and Colorado. He also bought into the Spring Valley Golf Club and oversaw its growth from nine to 18 holes in 1987. Emerson put extra effort into his hometown course. His design won't be mistaken for a classic American course, but golfers at Spring Valley usually go away feeling they've played a complete round of golf in terms of clubs used and variety of challenges. Your accuracy and course management certainly will be tested, even if the course is on the short side.

Spring Valley is only 6,043 yards, but some holes seem to go on forever. Take eight, nine, and 10, seemingly average par-fours at 386, 369, and 252 yards. All three have tree-lined fairways and significant elevation changes. They are Dr. Emerson's golfing version of a root canal; he planted most of the trees himself around 1970 and extracted them when he built the second nine. The 10th hole can be painful. From a tee perched on a hill, it's possible to drive the green with a 3-wood, but the green is surrounded by trouble. Laying up isn't easy either, because Emerson left a row of pines blocking part of the fairway, in effect making it a dogleg. Look out as well for the two-tiered green.

Like eye teeth, Emerson designed bookend par-fives in the middle of the course. Holes 11 and 12 are straightjacket par-fives through the pines that may require a 3-wood or iron off the tee. Eleven is only 468 yards, easily reachable in two shots, but because the fairway slopes right and the green is elevated those shots must be perfect. Twelve is 518 yards; it doglegs sharply after the tee shot (be careful not to hit through the dogleg). A narrow opening to the green prevents many golfers from trying to get home in two or sometimes even in three.

About half the course is not tree lined, but don't relax. For example, the 16th, 424 yards, turns 90 degrees left and down a steep hill after the tee shot. The green is built into a hillside, meaning any ball short or left will kick yards below. Hopefully not too far below—about 70 feet down the hill near 12 green you can see downtown Spring Valley.

The course in 2000 was owned by Guy and Wendy Leach, who bought it in 1997 and have added an irrigation system and several ponds. Water hazards are on six holes.

*6,043 yards/par-71/70.0 rating/124 slope*
*Architect: Gordon Emerson*
*Fees: $*
*Call: 715/778-5513 or 800/236-0009*
*Directions: Go 2 miles west of Spring Valley on Highway 29 and 0.5 mile*
  *north on Van Buren Road.*


# Lake Wissota Golf Club
*Chippewa Falls*

Here's your chance to play golf near the lake where actor Leonardo DiCaprio fished as a kid. OK, so the fisherman was really a boy named Jack from Chippewa Falls, Wisconsin. Jack was the character played by DiCaprio in the Academy Award–winning movie *Titanic*. The place where Jack supposedly fished, Lake Wissota, is real, all 1,602 acres. On one shore of the big lake is Lake Wissota Golf Club with its southern plantation–style clubhouse. If the *Titanic* were to float by and Jack were to see the lovely setting, surely a port of call and round of golf would be in order.

Lake Wissota Golf Club looks inviting by land or by sea. Previously an old, short, nine-hole course called the Elks Country Club, the course was remodeled, expanded to 18 and reopened in 1997 by Newman Golf. Although it won't be mistaken for a championship test at 6,015 yards, it has the feel of a well-managed resort course with its lakeside setting, friendly holes, and the eye-catching, white clubhouse (reminiscent of the Masters at Augusta National, cupola included).

The lake plays a prominent role on the front nine, where it's usually within view. An inlet crosses the fairways on holes one, two, three, and five, and the lake comes into play down the left side of five, a 350-yard par-four. A pond, however, is the most-discussed feature on the course. The large water hazard divides the fairways on holes seven and 10, which share a tee box. The seventh is a 515-yard par-five down the right side of the pond. The 10th is a 377-yard par-four that goes around the left side.

Because the 377-yard 10th is a boomerang-shaped dogleg from an elevated tee, some long-hitting golfers take dead aim over the water at the green. Most hit a 200-yard layup shot to the corner of the dogleg and take their chances with another scary shot down the shoreline to the green. The 10th hole used to be number one when the course reopened, but golfers complained that it was too tough of a beginning hole. It's the one-handicap hole on the course.

At White Lake Golf Resort in Montello, you may not make a birdie, but you may get lucky enough to see one. Peacocks often can be seen wandering the course.

The back definitely is the port-side nine with more views of rural Chippewa County—including a sand and gravel operation—than of water. At just 2,950 yards, the back nine has several birdie holes, but watch out for the waste area down the left side of the 443-yard 16th—the longest par-four on the course. And don't get greedy on the 306-yard 18th with a pond crossing the fairway 200 yards out and angling toward the green. It's one water hazard that even the crew of the *Titanic* would steer clear of.

*6,015 yards/par-71/69.2 rating/120 slope*
*Architect: Donald Stepanek*
*Fees: $$*
*Call: 715/382-4780 or 888/382-4780*
*Directions: From Highway 53, exit east on County S north of Chippewa Falls.*
   *Go 6 miles and turn left on 97th Street.*

**Other Area Courses**

# Hallie Golf Club
*Near Chippewa Falls*

B etween Eau Claire and Chippewa Falls in the town of Hallie, the Hallie Golf Club is among the oldest and most popular courses in the area. It dates to the Depression, when the 18-holer shrunk to nine because of the slow economy. For 50 years, the old, scenic nine along the Chippewa River and Lake Hallie— featuring short, tight holes—was packed with golfers.

Then new owners in the mid 1980s, the Severson family, designed another nine holes where the old nine used to be, using some of the old routing and mature trees. The new nine also is short, traveling through oak trees and past three ponds. The 551-yard 18th hole has a 150-yard waste bunker that runs up to the deep, narrow green.

After finishing the ninth hole, don't walk the steep hill to 10. Catch a ride on the cable lift car directly below the clubhouse.

*5,787 yards/par-70/67.5 rating/120 slope*
*Fees: $$*
*Call: 715/723-8524*
*Directions: From Highway 53, exit west onto County J. Turn left onto 110th*
*    Street, which takes you to the course.*

# Whitetail Golf Club
*Colfax*

A bout a half-hour drive northwest of Eau Claire, Colfax's claim to fame is that it's halfway between the equator and the North Pole. The dividing line seems to go right through the golf course—the first nine is open with trees coming into play on just the first and ninth holes, while the second nine, added in the 1990s, has trees everywhere.

The most talked-about hole usually is 12, a tree-lined, 517-yard par-five that leaves little room for error. The hole curves sharply through a grove of trees on a hillside, limiting the chances of reaching the green in two and necessitating many layup second shots. The par-three 13th hole, 171 yards uphill, has an unusual obstacle on the green—a large tree that can stand in the way of wayward tee shots and putts.

*6,338 yards/par-71/69.9 rating/117 slope*
*Fees: $*

*Call: 715/962-3888*
*Directions: From Interstate 94, take Highway 29 east and take first left onto*
*Highway 40. Go north about 4 miles and course is on the right.*

## Valley Golf Course
*Mondovi*

For years, golfers in the Eau Claire area and even some in Mondovi ignored the Valley, a 1930s-era nine-hole course that usually was in poor condition and had design quirks, including small, crowned greens. In the late 1990s, new owners ordered seven of the original holes redone and added nine more. The result when it reopened in 1999 was, in effect, a new course with large, receptive greens, modern bunkering, water, and eye-appealing elevation changes.

The best holes are an old one—the 193-yard 13th with a drop of about 100 feet—and a new one—the 490-yard 16th with a plunging tee shot, out of bounds, and lots of sand.

*6,293 yards/par-72/70.4 rating/124 slope*
*Architect: Andy Lindquist*
*Fees: $*
*Call: 715/926-4913*
*Directions: From Interstate 94, take Highway 37 south 15 miles and watch for*
*the course on the left just before entering Mondovi.*

## Hidden Creek at Mill Run
*Eau Claire*

Ever since it opened as nine holes in 1981 and expanded to 18 in 1986, Hidden Creek (formerly just Mill Run) has been one of the most popular courses in the Eau Claire area. A very playable 6,076 yards from the back tees, it's a great place for all ages to make some pars and birdies. The course usually is well maintained and has attractive landscaping around the greens and tees.

Despite being a short course on mostly flat land, Hidden Creek can be deceivingly difficult. Hundreds of trees planted on the once-open course have begun to mature, narrowing many fairways. Several small greens turn short par-fours into tough pars. Water is a factor on nine holes, including the hidden stream, Sherman Creek, which divides the two nines. The main channel of the creek is hidden by a wide band of reedy wetland. Never underestimate the power of the wind at Hidden Creek, which was built on Truax Prairie.

*6,076 yards/par-70/68.7 rating/116 slope*
*Architect: Gordon Emerson*
*Fees: $$*
*Call: 715/834-1766 or 800/241-1766; Web site: www.millrungolf.com*
*Directions: From Interstate 94, take Exit 59 at the North Crossing/Highway 124 and go east to County TT (Kane Road). Turn right and Hidden Creek will be on the left.*

# Whispering Pines Golf Club
*Cadott*

At 6,638 yards, Whispering Pines is one of the longest courses in the Chippewa Valley. It also has the second longest hole—the par-five ninth that is 607 yards, uphill no less. Along with some tough long holes, Whispering Pines has some strategic short ones. The course also has a nice mix of tight and open holes. Mature trees, several ponds, modest bunkering and large greens keep the rural course interesting and challenging.

*6,638 yards/par-72/71.6 rating/122 slope*
*Fees: $*
*Call: 715/289-4653*
*Directions: From Highway 29, turn north on Highway 27 to Cadott. Turn left on County X and go about 1 mile west of town.*

**Best Nine-Hole Course**

# Timber Terrace
*Chippewa Falls*

Although Timber Terrace is not far from downtown Chippewa Falls, it seems miles away from traffic, hidden on a hillside along the Chippewa River.

Try to warm up before you tee off. The first four holes parallel the wooded bank of the river. If you hit through the fairway on three, you could experience your first sawdust trap. It's a small pit filled with century-old sawdust from the lumber mill days along the Chippewa River. Holes five through nine climb a terrace and wind through stately pine trees. Although Timber Terrace is only 2,900 yards and par-35 (with three par-threes), the tight fairways make it a challenge. And the scenery makes it worth a visit.

*2,900 yards/par-35/67.1 rating/118 slope*
*Fees: $*
*Call: 715/726-1500*
*Directions: From Highway 124 in Chippewa Falls, turn onto Court Street. Go 4 blocks to Pumphouse Road. Turn right and go 1.5 miles to the course on the right.*

## More Fun Things to Do

Bring a bicycle or rent one. Eau Claire, Chippewa Falls, and Menomonie all have state bike trails—53 miles of scenic riding along the Chippewa and Red Cedar rivers. The Chippewa River State Trail begins in downtown Eau Claire and goes 23 miles. It connects to the Red Cedar State Trail, which goes 14.5 miles to Menomonie.

The 17-mile Old Abe State Trail is between the cities of Chippewa Falls and Cornell, following near the Chippewa River. In Chippewa Falls, the trail starts only a tee shot away from Lake Wissota Golf Club and a short drive from Lake Wissota State Park (715/399-3111), on big Lake Wissota. The trail finishes in Cornell at quiet Brunet Island State Park (715/239-6888), which is near the river and its backwaters. Both state parks have large beaches and trails.

The Hoffman Hills State Recreation Area (715/232-1242) between Menomonie and Colfax has 9 miles of trails in steep hills, a restored prairie, wetlands, and a 60-foot high observation tower.

Lovely Carson Park is the center for recreation in Eau Claire. The Chippewa Valley Museum (715/834-7871) has exhibits on the Ojibwa culture, farming, and lumbering. The adjacent Paul Bunyan Logging Camp (715/835-6200)—with a statue of Paul and Babe the Blue Ox—recreates life in an 1890s lumber camp. Also near the museum are two circa-1850 structures, the Anderson Log House and Sunnyview School. The park has excellent picnic, hiking, and fishing areas and a large, modern playground. A mini-railroad runs on Sundays and holidays. Have your picture taken with a statue of baseball home run king Henry Aaron outside the historic baseball stadium where he played as a minor leaguer. Or take in an Eau Claire Cavaliers semipro baseball game at Carson Park stadium, which opened in 1937. For ticket information, call 888/523-FUNN.

Southeast of Eau Claire near Augusta is picturesque Dells Mill Historical Landmark and Museum (715/286-2714), a five-story mill that's a working remnant of the days when pioneers had their grain ground into flour. Nearby, try the trails, interpretive center, or Hobbs Observatory at 360-acre Beaver Creek Reserve and Wise Nature Center (715/877-2212) in Fall Creek. If it's hot, check out the beaches at Big Falls, Coon Forks (the area's best beach), and Lake Altoona county parks. A large city pool is on the south side of Eau Claire at Fairfax Park.

Downtown Chippewa Falls, with many restored nineteenth-century buildings, is on the National Register of Historic Places. Take a tour of the Cook-Rutledge Mansion (built in 1873; 715/723-7181), the Museum of Industry and Technology (see some of the world's first and fastest supercomputers engineered by Seymour Cray; 715/720-9206) and Leinenkugel's Brewery (making beer since 1867; 715/723-5557). Irvine Park has excellent picnic areas, a small zoo (free) with bears, deer, bison, and other animals, and 225 acres of natural areas. The city pool is near Irvine Park.

In Menomonie, tour the Mabel Tainter Memorial Theater (715/235-9726), one of the best Victorian theaters in the country, or take in a performance. See the Wilson Place Museum (715/235-2283). At Wakanda Park along Lake Menomin, visit the Russel J. Rassbach Heritage Museum (715/232-8685). In nearby Downsville, stop at the Empire in Pine Lumber Museum (715/664-8452 or 715/235-2833), which is just off the Red Cedar State Trail. Wakanda Park has wooded picnic areas, a nature walk with bison, athletic facilities, and a sparkling city pool.

In Spring Valley, chilly Crystal Cave (800/236-CAVE) is a cool place to escape the summertime heat. If spelunking makes you hungry, visit nearby Cady Cheese Factory (715/772-4218) in Wilson.

Also near Downsville, about eight miles south of Menomonie, is the Caddie Woodlawn Historic Park. In the park is the childhood home of Caroline Augusta, who became the main character from the classic children's book *Caddie Woodlawn*. The book won the 1935 Newberry Award for children's literature.

If you haven't had enough golf, the area has several short courses: Pine Meadow in Eau Claire (par-27, next to the city pool, 715/832-6011), Hickory Hills near Eau Claire (par-63, 18 holes, 715/878-4543), Pinewood in Menomonie (par-29, 715/235-2900) and the Menomonie Country Club (par-30, 715/235-3595).

## For More Information

Chippewa Falls: 800/723-0024; www.chippewachamber.org

Chippewa Valley: www.timbertrails.com

Eau Claire: Chippewa Valley Convention and Visitors Bureau 888/523-3866; www.chippewavalley.net

Menomonie: 800/283-1862; www.menomonie.org.

# 5

# Rice Lake, Spooner, and Cumberland

I f you look long enough at a Wisconsin map, you can see it: The chin where the St. Croix River turns southeast near Prescott. The broad nose straight west of Rice Lake where the St. Croix makes a wide turn east. The eye where the Namekagon River flows south toward the St. Croix. A feather headdress where the peninsula of land between Superior and Ashland arches into Lake Superior.

The northwestern part of Wisconsin is known as Indianhead Country, its jagged border the profile of a rugged, Native American face. It's a fitting name for a part of the state that still is wooded and wild, where people still make their livings near plentiful bodies of water that provide bountiful hunting, fishing, and wild rice harvests. The central part of Indianhead Country is an area chock full of lakes near the cheekbone of the Indianhead. It includes a circle of cities, Rice Lake, Spooner, Siren, Danbury, Luck, Frederic, and Cumberland. It's an area where the farms give way to long stretches of woods and meadows, lakes and wetlands.

Parts of the northwest still are fertile farming regions. In Luck, you can see a historic marker dedicated to one of the state's first creamery cooperatives, the Luck Creamery Company of 1885. But look again and you'll see the signs of the North Woods. Long Lake near Birchwood is the "Walleye Capital of Wisconsin." Birchwood proclaims itself the "Bluegill Capital of Wisconsin." Chetek is famous for its chain of lakes and the annual Fish-O-Rama contest. Cumberland is the "Island City." Rice Lake is known for its Blue Hills region, ancient peaks that once were 20,000 feet high. And all around are those rustic, white arrow signs at rural crossroads pointing one way to the Misty Pines resort and another to the Whispering Oaks resort.

The northwest long has been known for its quiet lakes and family resorts, and it slowly is developing a trail of quality golf courses. Many of the old nine-hole municipal and country courses have been revamped and expanded, although you still can play what may be the only sand greens course left in the state at Yellow Lake, near Danbury. But most visiting golfers flock to the finely groomed and designed Turtleback in Rice Lake, remote and quiet Voyager Village at Danbury, popular and historic Spooner Golf Club, and the challenging new Siren Glen in Siren. Or you can go to Birchwood and play essentially the same nine holes where the reigning U.S. and British Open champions played a match at Tagalong in 1925.

The Indianhead area doesn't have any destination courses designed by Pete Dye or Jack Nicklaus, but it does have well-kept, fun-to-play and near-championship-level courses. Expect moderate greens fees, relaxed clubhouses with scenic views, and lush conditions, usually from May through September, while golfing Wisconsin's north face.

# Turtleback Golf and Country Club
*Rice Lake*

The bent-grass fairways are immaculate and well defined with eye-catching mounding and large, gaping bunkers. The greens are large, undulating, true and fast, set off by grass depressions and sand bunkers. Some holes are reminiscent of Scotland and others of U.S. Open venues. One reminds you of Augusta National. The condition of the shimmering green course—including its bent-grass practice range—looks good enough to hold a pro tournament. One national golf magazine ranked it among the two hundred best public courses in the nation.

With all that it has going for it, some golfers might find it hard to believe that Turtleback Golf and Country Club is in a small city in northwestern Wisconsin and a long drive from any major metropolitan area. The owners and operators of Turtleback don't think that way. In fact, they think that the course's somewhat remote location is all the more reason to make it one of the best-conditioned in Wisconsin.

When superintendent Todd Severud and the owner of the Rice Lake Golf Course got together in the early 1980s and decided to do better than their old nine-hole layout, they considered where they were. "We wanted to have something upscale because of our location," Severud said. So they went to work. In 1985, nine new holes opened, and in 1994 a second nine was built, finally eliminating the quirky old course altogether. Along with a highly acclaimed restaurant and conference center, Turtleback has become the destination facility that Severud and his boss once envisioned.

Although the course then was sold by the local owner to the Wilson Golf Group, Severud remains the superintendent and deserves much of the credit the course receives. Severud not only keeps Turtleback neat and green, but he designed it. For someone who is a schoolteacher nine months of the year and who home-schooled himself on the fine points of golf course architecture, he is more

Number 18 at Turtleback Golf and Country Club.

than pleased with how his design debut turned out. "I just enjoy playing out there, and I hope people enjoy playing it. That's what golf is all about—having fun," says Severud, who followed in the footsteps of his father, Lloyd "Snowball" Severud, a greens keeper by summer and Olympic ski jumping coach by winter.

Severud chose grass mounds and a sprinkling of big sand traps as key features for his course. The mounds are so prominent that the course was named after them. "I liked the style with a lot of mounding and a lot less sand. Grass is a hazard, and the mounds are a hazard," Severud says. On some holes, Severud inverted the mounds to create grass bunkers. The result is a course that is a bit o' Scotland and a bit o' Severud. "There's a Scottish flavor, but there's also trees. It's not a links course."

The mostly open, par-35 front nine is the shortest and easiest, but on mostly level ground it plays all of that. Seven and nine are strategic gems. At 367 yards with a big dogleg right, most golfers try to cut the corner at seven, only to find two large fairway bunkers over the mounds and two more on the sides of the green. Before you tee off, consider that the narrow green is easiest to hit from straight on. At 287 yards, the ninth can be birdied if you play to the right and get to use all the green on the approach. A pond shouldering the left of the green discourages long hitters.

The terrain is more varied and the holes more interesting on the back nine. The 12th hole, for example, is a 398-yard par-four with a big fairway and room to cut the dogleg-left corner. However, rows of tall red pines pinch the opening to the deep, narrow, elevated green. The 13th is a classic par-three—187 yards downhill to a wide green that has a grass bunker on the left, a sand bunker on the right, and a ledge between. More rows of red pines behind the green make the perfect hitting background. "I really enjoy hitting the ball off that tee and watching it fly," Severud says.

Holes 14 through 16 and 18 also are outstanding, with only the par-four 17th somewhat uninteresting, although troubling mounds and 454 yards of fairway are enough. The driving area on the 523-yard 14th is wide open, except for rows of mounds that you don't want to stray into. Hitting off the mounds usually means inventing a shot. Hitting a precise second shot is vital because the fairway slips into a woods about 100 yards from the green. Another word of caution: Even though you may not see a pond, don't miss the 14th green to the left or you'll be surprised by a splash. That pond forms an intimidating hazard on the 175-yard 15th hole; water runs nearly from tee to green. Although the pond is on the right side of the green, the hole plays much like the famed 16th at Augusta National, home of the Masters tournament.

The 16th is the only woods hole at Turtleback, but keep your driver out even though the tree-lined fairway looks unusually tight. The farther you hit it, the wider the fairway gets, finally opening up past the woods at about 230 yards. Turtleback's 18th is such a pretty and strategic hole that you'll want to play it again and again—or watch others play it from the clubhouse. Golfers have two options to reach the green on this 530-yard par-five. After the tee shot, you need to carry a broad pond as the hole makes a righthand turn toward the clubhouse. Complicating matters, you're forced to play left or right around several trees to reach the far shore of the pond. Left usually is best. If you go right, a longer carry over water and then sand is needed to get near the green. "A lot of people try [shooting right of the trees], but they never find their golf ball," Severud says.

In addition to Turtleback, Severud has designed 27 holes in Minnesota and was in charge of the expansion and redesign at Rolling Oaks in nearby Barron, Wisconsin.

*6,604 yards/par-71/72.0 rating/129 slope*
*Architect: Todd Severud*
*Fees: $$*
*Call: 715/234-7641; Web site: www.turtlebackgolf.com*
*Directions: On Highway 53, exit Highway 48 west at Rice Lake, go 0.25 mile*
*    to West Allen Road and go 1 mile to the course.*

# Voyager Village Country Club
*Danbury*

When most golfers head down the two-lane Kilkare Road deep into the woods that leads to Voyager Villager, they usually become skeptical. The winding road goes so deep into the woods—14 miles—they either think they are lost or that if there is a golf course that far from nowhere it can't be very good. Only when they come around a bend in the road and see a smooth, green fairway and a sand trap do their spirits brighten. Within minutes they realize they've found a golfing and recreational oasis in the midst of a northern Wisconsin forest. Finding the course is a refreshing experience, even if you've already been to Voyager Village.

Opened in 1970, Voyager Village golf course near Danbury is the marquee attraction of a large residential development around four lakes that goes by the same name. More than twelve hundred people belong to the association. The 280 golfing members get preferred tee times, but the course always has been open to the public while maintaining the look and feel of a private club. The land has been used as a getaway since about 1940, when the Kilkare resort had a dance hall and a nine-hole sand greens golf course.

Much like the road that leads to the course, the holes at Voyager Village are solitary, winding paths through the woods. And sometimes you don't know if you'll ever make it to the green. "There are only two adjoining fairways, one and 10, and then you go off on a different voyage each nine," says longtime pro Tim Smith, who has made his home at Voyager Village after once teaching at Hazeltine National in Chaska, Minnesota.

Each nine makes a large loop through the forest. Voyager Village once was rated among the top five public courses in Wisconsin after it opened. "It's not an overly long golf course, but it has some very, very challenging holes," Smith says.

The only hole that doesn't fit with the woodland design on the front nine is the sixth, a flat, 505-yard par-five that runs entirely along an airstrip. The good news is that the right bounce off the runway can add 50 yards or more to a tee shot—if it comes back into play. Otherwise, the airstrip is out of bounds. The back nine has several outstanding holes, but the 11th is the most memorable. It's a double dogleg downhill, left through a chute of trees, past a pond, and then right to an elevated green tucked behind more trees. It's a three-shot par-five, although it's just 482 yards. "It's not overly long, but you've got to be precise," Smith says. "They tempt you a lot on this golf course." You can cut one corner with a blind tee shot over a stand of pines, but the best way to play the 11th is a little fairway at a time.

The 12th tee, near a pristine wetland, is one of those places where if anyone is close behind you gladly let them play through and take a moment to enjoy the view. The sidehill, 367-yard par-four runs straight along the wetland. Holes 13 through 16 climb a hillside, work their way back down to the lowlands, and go back up.

Near the main course, Voyager Village also has one of the prettiest par-three courses in the state. Five of the holes play along Birch Island Lake. The par-three course also attracts the inexperienced vacationing golfers, speeding up play on the main course. The association's beaches, beachhouses, swimming pool, restaurant, and other facilities also are open to guests, in some cases for small fees.

*6,638 yards/par-72/71.6 rating/123 slope*
*Architect: William Spear and Associates*
*Fees: $$*
*Call: 715/259-3911*
*Directions: North of Webster on Highway 35 to County A, then 14 miles east*
*    to Kilkare Road.*

# Spooner Golf Club
*Spooner*

The history of most modern golf courses can be found on their scorecards: Architectural companies or course designers are hired, and several years later golf courses appear. Spooner Golf Club may look and play like a modern 18-hole golf course with its fast greens, strategic bunkering, and irrigated bent-grass fairways, but its history is a long one. In 1930, a man named Thomas Vardon designed the first nine holes with sand greens. His design fee: $35. The cost of the 80 acres of farmland: $1,123. The greens fees: 50¢ on weekdays, 75¢ on weekends. Vardon was an accomplished golfer from White Bear Lake, Minnesota, and is believed to be a relative of Harry Vardon, the six-time British Open champion golfer of the early 1900s for whom the Vardon (overlapping) grip and PGA Tour scoring trophy are named.

Thomas Vardon's signature hole—although no one had heard of such a term back then—was his finishing hole, a 396-yard par-four with the fairway doglegging and sloping to the right toward a wetland that runs the length of the fairway and in front of the green. Vardon may have been ahead of his time. The final hole seemed so hard years ago that members didn't play it from the mid 1950s until 1965, according to Barry Benson, whose grandfather, Guy Benson, and other members helped Vardon build the course. Spooner members put in grass greens at a cost of $3,000 in 1951, and in 1983 architect Gordon Emerson designed a second nine when the course purchased a second 80 acres of rolling, wooded farmland.

The 18th hole at the Spooner Golf Club.

After seven decades of change, Spooner Golf Club has become one of the most popular courses in northern Wisconsin. With more than thirty thousand rounds packed in annually during the short northern summer, members have considered adding a third nine holes. The third nine would do well to follow Emerson's lead. "He did a really, really nice job of blending the new nine with the old. You really can't tell the difference," Benson says.

Vardon and Emerson combined for a challenging, straightforward design that members—some from as far away as Duluth, Minnesota—and vacationers love to play over and over. Spooner has big trees, one feature of a typical North Woods course, but the spacing of the trees provides a contrast to a through-the-woods experience. Fast, undulating, and sometimes small greens can make the course play tougher than its 6,416 yards. "It's a golf course where if you miss the greens you have to get creative," pro Bryan Mulry says. "It's a scoreable course, but it can bite you."

The front nine, par-35, with three par-threes seems like the best place to score at just 3,086 yards. However, the par-threes are all mid- or long-iron shots. The best of the bunch is number six, a pretty 184-yard downhill shot. A pond is just off the right edge of the green, and the green slopes severely toward the water.

The tougher back nine features excellent risk-reward holes. On 11, golfers can reach the 296-yard par-four with their tee shot if they can carry a grove of trees. On 13, a bold second shot over a hill can set up an eagle or birdie try—or something worse if you don't know where the pond is. The 17th may be one of the course's toughest pars—222 yards uphill with out of bounds lurking right of the small green. Spooner members still talk about the threesome one day that needed 33 shots to finish the par-three hole.

Vardon's 18th, slightly remodeled when it reopened in 1965, has a double-S-shaped shoreline along the wetland. The contour-mowed fairway contrasts with the blue water and amber reeds, making the hole as scenic as it is tough. At 396 yards, most golfers aren't as in awe of the distance as they are of the fairway, which slants to the right toward the water. Then there's the white-knuckle approach shot downhill over the bog. The smart play is left off the tee, which makes the hole play longer but gives you a better angle (less water to carry) to the green. "The cool thing about it is it's very scenic. It gives you all the room you need on the left. It's the perfect risk-reward shot," Mulry says. The classic 18th hole is considered one of the prettiest and best in northwest Wisconsin. It's been that way for more than 70 years, minus the 10 when the Spooner Golf Club members decided it was too tough for them.

*6,416 yards/par-71/70.9 rating/128 slope*
*Architect: Thomas Vardon (original nine); Gordon Emerson (second nine)*
*Fees: $$*
*Call: 715/635-3580*
*Directions: Highway 53 to County H then east 1 mile.*

# Cumberland Golf Club
*Cumberland*

Surrounded by lakes, Cumberland is known as the Island City. With the water table always plenty high, it's no secret what type of hazard is plentiful at the Cumberland Golf Club. Water is everywhere, or so it seems. Actually, it's only on 10 of the 18 holes, but the hazards seem more prevalent because on four holes you have to hit over or around them twice. In addition, ponds come into play three times on two other holes. No lakes, rivers, or streams. Just pond after pond, 17 in all.

Each nine has five water holes, an equal dose of pain, although the front nine is 200 yards longer but plays easier because it's more open. Thirsty? On the front, drives must carry a pond and stay to the left of another pond as well on the 351-yard third hole. The 151-yard fourth hole has a peninsula green.

The picturesque back nine is double trouble. It not only has water but tree-lined fairways. Some holes look like they have no landing areas. Holes 11 through 15 all have water. Tee shots on the 337-yard 11th hole must stay out of the trees and find a garden spot between two ponds that creep onto the right side of the fairway. The approach shot then must clear another pond. The 373-yard 13th is similar—a dogleg around woods and over a pond to a small landing area. Approaches must carry another pond to the green, but you can't be long or left or there's—no surprise—more water. With the back nine only 3,033 yards long, play conservatively and check the scorecard for the ponds before teeing off. A few of them are hidden behind hills or so small that they are hard to see.

The challenges of Cumberland came together over a number of years. Cumberland opened in 1929 as a five-hole course with sand greens. Four more holes and grass greens were installed before World War II, much to the delight of local cows who grazed there when the course closed during the war. Several owners ran the course until the 1960s, when it was taken over by the city, according to Dick Lau, whose parents owned the course in the 1950s. In 1989, architect Don Herfort built nine new holes and redesigned most of the others. Only three of the early greens remain. One of the early greens now is the number one tee.

*6,271 yards/par-72/70.7 rating/131 slope*
*Architect: Don Herfort*
*Fees: $$*
*Call: 715/822-4333*
*Directions: West of Cumberland off Highway 48.*

# Siren Glen Golf Club
*Siren*

Scheduled to open in 2001, Siren Glen is a championship layout on hilly terrain west of Siren. The 7,035-yard, par-72 course has four sets of tees and bent-grass fairways. Most of the holes play through or around stands of pine and hardwood trees. Four holes cross a marsh. The par-three third hole features a 25-foot-high stone wall in front of the green.

*7,035 yards/par-72*
*Architect: T. L. Haugen*
*Call: 715/349-8000*
*Directions: West of Siren on Highway 70, turn left on Peterson Road then*
  *right on Waldora Road.*

## Other Area Courses

# Luck Golf Course
*Luck*

In a city that likes to have fun with its name (in town and you're in Luck, out of town and you're out of Luck), golfers have been lucky since 1938, when the city opened a park and a nine-hole course on the shore of Big Butternut Lake. Workers with the old Works Progress Administration hauled rock, drove horses, and set dynamite charges while building the course.

When the course was expanded to 18 and remodeled in 1990, residents really got lucky. Their course has matured into one of the best small-town layouts in the area. The pretty older nine winds among mature oak trees not far from the lake. The newer holes cut through stands of oak and pine, some so tight that golfers occasionally think they would have no luck if it weren't for bad luck.

No luck is needed to keep the golf course green. The clay-based soil holds its water well, and nearby Big Butternut Lake (which often is visible but doesn't come into play) makes a great reservoir for the fairways.

*6,122 yards/par-71/70.0 rating/122 slope*
*Architect: Ernest Tardiff (original nine); Gordon Emerson (renovation and*
    *expansion)*
*Fees: $$*
*Call: 715/472-2939*
*Directions: East of Highway 35 on the south shore of Butternut Lake*

# Tagalong Golf Resort
*Birchwood*

For many years in the latter half of the 1900s, reading about the 1920s Scottish history of Tagalong was better than playing the course, which had gone through several owners and fallen into disrepair. Since Tom Kennen and Scott Kennen took over in 1977, the course has been returned to its original glory—and then some.

Tagalong opened along the shore of Red Cedar Lake in 1923 as a playground for millionaire businessman Frank Stout. Stout allegedly named his golf course after a comic strip by the same name that used to appear in the *Chicago Tribune*. He hired a Chicago architect, who is said to have modeled the course after St. Andrew's in Scotland. Scottish grasses and workers were brought to the course, and seven miles of pipes were laid for a fairway watering system. Agronomists from the University of Minnesota in recent years found grass at Tagalong that they had never seen.

The grand opening was held on Aug. 26, 1925, when the reigning U.S. Open and British Open champions, Willie McFarlane and "Long" John Barnes, respectively, squared off in front of 250 spectators. McFarlane shot a 71 to Barnes' 78 and won their match six and four.

Stout, one of the wealthiest men in Chicago at the time, was president of two railroads, including one in Chicago, and a bank and two hotels. "He had some pull back then," Scott Kennen says. Frank Stout's brother, James, started what now is the University of Wisconsin–Stout and was a U.S. senator. Their father, Henry, was a partner in Knapp Stout Co., of Menomonie, once the world's biggest lumber company. Stout died in 1927, and neglect nearly killed his golf course in the 1940s, when it closed and became a cow pasture. In 1962, it was rescued and reopened. The Kennen families took over in 1977 and began updating the facilities. The biggest change was the addition of nine holes, which opened in 1998. More importantly, they preserved the original layout and slowly have returned it to its once grand condition.

At Gateway Golf Course in Land O' Lakes, you literally can hit a ball into another state. The third tee is in Wisconsin, and the fairway is in the Upper Peninsula of Michigan.

The first nine is the old links layout with open fairways, big greens, and deep grass bunkers. The eighth hole, for example, is only 315 yards, but grass pits 12 feet and 15 feet deep on the sides of the green make the second shot a knee-knocker. Red Cedar Lake is behind the green. "We have very little sand. Nobody knows how to play out of deep grass bunkers anymore," Scott Kennen says. The front nine has eight par-fours and one par-three, the 216-yard third hole.

Part of the back nine, designed by Tom Kennen, was built on what used to be a grass airstrip. It then winds around the original stone clubhouse and finishes near the lake. It has a traditional configuration—two par-fives and two par-threes. The 12th hole is a 552-yard par-five. Among the better holes are the 310-yard 14th along a wetland and the 95-yard 17th, a steep downhill pitch to a green guarded by Sucker Creek. If you overclub here into the creek, you know what your friends will call you. "The back nine is target golf. The yardage is short, but it plays a lot longer," Scott Kennen says.

Many of the original Stout-built buildings remain. The old stone clubhouse still is visible as part of the pro shop. A bar and restaurant overlook the lake.

Many buildings still have the original cedar shingle roofs, Kennen says. A new irrigation system has been installed. Frank Stout built the course near his $1.5 million, Adirondack-style summer home on a 14-acre island. In its early years, the course was accessible only by boat. His Red Cedar Lake island home remains, but it has been turned into a 31-room resort called Stout's Lodge on the Island of Happy Days. Guests again are taking a boat to the golf course.

*6,035 yards/par-71/71.6 rating/no slope rating*
*Architect: Alex Pirie (original nine); Tom Kennen (second nine)*
*Fees: $$*
*Call: 715/354-3458 or 800/657-4843*
*Directions: One mile south of Birchwood on South Highway 48 then 2 miles*
*south on Loch Loman Boulevard.*

# Frederic Country Club
*Frederic*

After nearly 50 years as a nine-hole course, the Frederic Country Club expanded to 18 holes in July of 2000. Architect Andy Lindquist built nine new holes and redesigned many of the old ones. The course is on rolling hills and plays through some stands of pine trees and rock outcroppings.

*6,470 yards/par-72/70.6 rating/124 slope*
*Architect: Andy Lindquist*
*Fees: $$*
*Call: 715/327-8250*
*Directions: Highway 35 south of Frederic.*

# Barron Rolling Oaks
*Barron*

An expanded and redesigned Rolling Oaks course is scheduled to open in 2001. Todd Severud, who designed the Turtleback Golf and Country Club at Rice Lake, laid out the new nine holes and remodeled many old holes. The new course will be 6,207 yards, par-71. It will be on wooded, rolling terrain with numerous doglegs. A stream will come into play on four holes and ponds on three others. The course is owned by the city of Barron.

*6,207 yards/par-71*
*Architect: Todd Severud*
*Call: 715/537-3409*
*Directions: On the west side of Barron on Highway 8.*

## Best Nine-Hole Course

# Sioux Creek
*Chetek*

Although quality 18-hole courses have become the norm in northwestern Wisconsin in recent years, a few nine-holers remain from the days when links were built by hand. Among them are quaint Sunset View (par-34) on the shore of Pokegema Lake in Chetek, Pine Crest (par-35) at Dallas, and Yellow Lake (par-34) near Danbury. Yellow Lake is believed to be the last course in the state that still uses sand greens. At Yellow Lake, you can play all day for five dollars, and that includes the chance to grab a carpet attached to a pole and smooth the tiny "greens" after putting out. The sand greens at Yellow Lake are the originals from 1923.

The best nine-hole course, however, is a modern one, Sioux Creek on the banks of the Chetek River near Chetek. At 2,938 yards, it's a good length for golfers who only pull out their clubs on vacation. Yet it's scenic and challenging, especially the 477-yard, par-five fifth hole, with the river on the right and trees on the left.

The river, wetlands, and a pond provide plenty of obstacles on holes four through nine, the heart of Sioux Creek. Water guards the green on the 154-yard seventh hole and the left side of the 475-yard, par-five eighth hole. Golfers can cut the corner and aim for the green on the 283-yard sixth hole—if they aren't nervous about carrying the marsh. In summer and fall, colorful prairie grasses and other wetland vegetation divide some of the holes. Sioux Creek, designed and owned by Lee Johnson, opened in 1993.

*3,027 yards/par-36/68.1 rating/112 slope*
*Architect: Lee Johnson*
*Fees: $*
*Call: 715/924-3139*
*Directions: From the Chetek exit on Highway 53, go west on County I about*
*    1.5 miles.*

## More Fun Things to Do

In Indianhead Country, nature is the big attraction year-round. The natural beauty of the northwest can be enjoyed via boat, bike, hiking trail, or automobile.

Three state bike trails cross the region. The Gandy Dancer starts in St. Croix Falls and goes north 66 miles to Superior; it features a 520-foot-long bridge high over the St. Croix River. The Tuscobia State Trail is 74 miles—the longest in Wisconsin—between Rice Lake and Park Falls. The Wild Rivers State Trail extends 40 miles between Rice Lake and Solon Springs.

Along the St. Croix River on the state's northwestern border is the Governor Knowles State Forest with campsites, 38 miles of hiking trails and a self-guided auto tour. Try a canoe trip on the popular Flambeau River. Or take a hike—on the Blue Hills Segment of the Ice Age Trail in Rusk County.

Ever wonder where the nine hundred lakes in Washburn County alone and the more than fifteen thousand in Wisconsin get all those fish? Take a tour of Governor Tommy G. Thompson State Fish Hatchery (715/635-4147) in Spooner and find out. It's the largest muskie hatchery in the world, producing one hundred thousand a year. It also rears two million walleye a year. At the hatchery, you can learn how fish swim and why they bite on lures, and you can test what you've learned by fishing at a nearby pier.

The Great Northern Railroad in Spooner offers rides in refurbished railway cars from the early twentieth century. While there, check out the Railroad Memories Museum (715/635-2752), which fills 10 rooms in the former Chicago & North Western Railway depot. The largest rodeo in Wisconsin, the Heart of the North Rodeo, is held each summer in Spooner.

Gaming facilities in the area include: St. Croix Casino and Hotel (800/846-8946) in Turtle Lake; the Little Turtle Hertel Express (715/349-5658) in Hertel; and the Hole in the Wall Casino, hotel, and RV park (800/238-8946) at Danbury.

Near Grantsburg is the Crex Meadows Wildlife Area (715/463-2896 or (715/463-2899), a 27,000-acre reserve of wetlands and prairies. On a self-guided auto tour, you can see nesting herons, eagles, osprey, and rare trumpeter swans and sandhill cranes. Crex Meadows also has a flock of twenty-five hundred Canadian geese. Crex Meadows is named after the former Crex Carpet Company, which owned the land in the early 1900s and sold products made from prairie grass. Wildlife viewing areas, picnic areas, and restrooms are provided.

South of Spooner is the Hunt Hill Audubon Sanctuary (715/635-6453), 500 acres of forests, meadows, and glacial lakes along with many varieties of birds, including loons. The reserve has programs for canoeing, camping, hiking and nature study for all ages. The Fish Lake Wildlife Area and Amsterdam Sloughs Wildlife Area, both in Burnett County, also are excellent places to see wildlife.

Between Danbury and Webster is the Forts Folle Avoine Historical Park (715/866-8890). Forts Folle Avoine is at the site of an early 1800s fur trading post on the Yellow River, and it includes guided tours with costumed interpreters, an Ojibwa village, a log cabin museum, a history center, hiking trails, and a visitor center.

You can whittle away spare time at the Museum of Woodcarving in Shell Lake (715/468-7100). It features more than a hundred life-size carvings by a former Spooner schoolteacher, including one of the Last Supper. Another popular attraction is the 32-building Pioneer Village Museum (715/458-2841) near Cameron. Sawyer County and Washburn County also have historical museums.

In addition to the par-three course at Voyager Village, the area has several other short golf courses. Barronett Hills Golf Course (715/468-7184) in Barronett is nine holes, par-31. Fox Run (715/866-7953) in Webster has a par-three course along with a regulation-length nine-hole course. Butternut Hills (715/635-8563) at Sarona is a par-70 but only 5,500 yards long. The Grantsburg Municipal course (715/463-2300) is a par-33.

## For More Information

Birchwood Area Lakes: 800/236-2252; members.aol.com/birchwoodlakes
Burnett County Tourism: 800/788-3164; www.mwd.com/burnett
Rice Lake: 715/234-2126; www.chamber.rice-lake.wi.us
Rusk County: 800/535-RUSK or 715/532-2642; www.ruskco.org
Shell Lake Area: Chamber of Commerce 715/468-4567
Washburn County: Tourism Association 800/367-3306 or 715/635-9696; www.washburncotour@centurytel.net
Wisconsin Indianhead Country, Chetek: 715/924-2970, 800/472-6654 (from Wisconsin only) or 800/826-6966 (from U.S.); www.wisconsinindianhead.org.

# 6

# Coulee Region

Native Americans used to call it the *Messipi* or *Mee-zee-see-bee*, a.k.a., the Big River or Father of Waters. Today we call it the Mississippi River, Big Muddy, or the Muddy Mississippi. Children use its name to count the seconds when they play hide and seek or when they want to impress friends with their spelling skills. Just the mention of it conjures an image of a powerful ribbon of water that cuts the country in half. Starting as a trickle of water at Lake Itasca, Minnesota, it grows to more than a mile wide in places as it flows 2,350 miles to the Gulf of Mexico. The river has 1.2 million square miles of watershed, which includes 33 states and two Canadian provinces. On its way south between Minnesota and Wisconsin, the Mississippi slides past thick green forests that adorn steep bluffs. Just think of the Mississippi and you can see high bridges spanning it, long barges navigating it, and eagles soaring over it.

In the La Crosse area, the residents call it God's Country and the Coulee Region. The Ice Age glaciers rounded off the hills and left thousands of lakes in northern Wisconsin. But they melted before they reached the southwestern corner of the state, where the Mississippi forms Wisconsin's western border. As a result, jagged, rock-faced bluffs and steep valleys—known as coulees—dominate the terrain.

Wisconsin's most dramatic scenery is the setting for some enchanting golf courses. Forest Hills Golf Course, for example, in La Crosse has a stretch of holes on the back nine that play up a green coulee while the front nine plays around the base of majestic Granddad Bluff. Trempealeau Mountain is a flat course, but it's set in a serene valley surrounded by bluffs. The namesake for Drugan's Castle Mound is a sandstone bluff. On several courses, you can see Minnesota while you hit a tee shot in Wisconsin. But bluff to bluff, it's several miles across the river so not even Tiger Woods could drive the Mississippi.

Golf along the river is a great way to relax. With no true destination courses in the region, most of the play comes from local residents out for a quick nine after work or 18 on a weekend morning. The greens fees are low, the people friendly, and the pace of life at times just as lazy as the Mississippi in mid-summer.

The Mississippi River border area has relatively few courses compared to the southeastern Wisconsin metropolitan areas and busy resort areas of the north. Maybe that's part of the Coulee Region's charm—select courses tucked in the hills of small river cities that require you to take long, winding drives (often on the 300-mile Great River Road) and see what's around the next hill or the next bend in the Mississippi. You'll find history in places like Prairie du Chien, Wisconsin's second oldest city, and the rough river spirit still alive in places like La Crosse, where even that most famous of Mississippi River travelers, Mark Twain, once made a port of call while writing—what else?—*Life on the Mississippi.*

# Drugan's Castle Mound
*Holmen*

It's not unusual for golf courses to undergo design changes years after they were built, but often they just are basic alterations to make holes more visually appealing or more playable. Few courses have changed more than Drugan's Castle Mound, a well-kept 18 holes that shoulder a quiet coulee. If you haven't played it since the early 1980s, then you haven't played the real Castle Mound. If you haven't played it, put it on your must-play list.

Castle Mound opened in 1969 when a farm family that owned the land decided to put in a golf course. The result was a nine-hole layout with such low-budget features as tiny greens, back-to-back par-threes, and sandy, unwatered fairways. Three years later it was bought by the Drugan family, and a metamorphosis began. Over the next decade, holes began to change for the better and a restaurant—the original dream of the Drugans—opened. Then, in 1982, a second nine opened.

By the end of the century, Castle Mound bore little resemblance to the course it once was. Only one original green and parts of a few old fairways still are being used. The design flaws are long gone, replaced by well-planned holes that are fun and challenging. Eye-appealing bunkering. Large greens. Contoured fairways. Tight bluegrass fairways. Castle Mound has completed its long trek from one of the least playable courses in the Coulee Region to the best public layout.

Much of the credit for the transformation goes to Mike Drugan, who, with his wife, Mary, took over operation of the course and restaurant from his parents in the 1990s. Mike, among the best amateur golfers in the Coulee Region, hired architect Jim Ciha and developed a 10-year master plan to make the course so good people would travel miles to play it. "We're trying to be like the public's country club. We try to have really nice conditions all the time. Our standard bar is high, and we try to keep raising it," Drugan says.

Although the 18th hole finishes along busy Highway 53, the other 17 holes at Castle Mound offer a country club–like escape into quiet valleys and along shad-

Drugan's Castle Mound.

owy hillsides. The two nines are complementary—each one an out-and-back run starting on the flats, marching up a hill and coming back down. "What's really unique about our course is it doesn't have development around it. Our scenic look represents western Wisconsin, the Coulee Region, very well," Drugan says.

An old barn is the definitive feature on the front nine. It's part of a three-hole corner where the course comes to life. After the first three holes work their way toward the valley, the fourth hole—rated the toughest on the course—is a dandy. It's 503 yards, but few golfers can reach it in two or would even try. The first 400 yards run along a hillside and require two straight shots. Then the hole makes a right turn straight up the hill to a small, slippery green.

The 390-yard sixth hole is easy to remember with one of Wisconsin's most enduring symbols defining the out of bounds on the right. The circa 1900 barn is aesthetically pleasing with its moss-covered blue roof, weathered red siding, and sandstone foundation. Some golfers find it downright beautiful; at about 230 yards from the tee, shots that have been pushed or sliced occasionally ricochet off the barn and back onto the fairway. The barn makes a nice sideboard.

The back nine is about 75 yards shorter than the front but tougher. "The risk-reward is greater on the back," Drugan says. After a flat but solid par-five 10th, the back nine heads toward the hills. The 377-yard 11th passes a pond and a grove of 70-foot-high cottonwood. The 303-yard 12th shoots through a chute of trees to the wide landing area in front of the green. Another birdie chance awaits on the 135-yard 13th, and if you don't get a deuce you'll appreciate this remote hole in a sleepy hollow. Then get ready for a challenge on 14. The 376-yard hole is the most elevated and prettiest on the course, curving left around a forested hillside. The tee is tucked into a grove of mature oak trees; sit quietly for a minute in this secluded spot and listen to the sounds of the forest. The fairway descends then doglegs left at about 230 yards, but oaks stand over both sides of the landing area. More trees, including a grove of red pines on the right, require an accurate approach shot.

The finishing holes head back down to the flats but don't get any easier, finishing at Castle Mound itself. The 18th hole is 396 yards, a sharp dogleg right. Brave golfers try to cut off about 50 yards—setting up a wedge approach—by aiming over the corner of the mound and hoping for a good kick down the cleared hillside.

What exactly is Castle Mound? Mike Drugan doesn't know the origin of the name, although the low, sandstone hill has a fortress-like appearance sitting hundreds of yards from the nearest bluff. Protruding among farm fields, it has been a landmark for decades. A small cave can be seen on the west side of the mound, and legend has it that Jesse James, the 1880s bank robber, once hid his loot there.

A variety of mature trees is one of the scenic pleasures of playing Castle Mound. Another is several acres of wildflowers decorating the margins between holes. Castle Mound is part of the National Audubon Society's cooperative sanctuary system, which encourages environmentally compatible courses.

*6,579 yards/par-72/71.5 rating/126 slope*
*Architect: Jim Ciha*
*Fees: $$*
*Call: 608/526-3225; Web site: www.drugans.com*
*Directions: Six miles north of Holmen on Highway 53.*

# Forest Hills
*La Crosse*

One of the best feelings in golf is to hit a booming drive off an elevated tee and watch it fall toward a fairway far below—the little ball defying gravity because of your power. Similarly, there's pure joy in hitting a powerful shot toward a hillside and watching it attempt to climb a canopy of trees.

At La Crosse's Forest Hills golf course, wedged between Mississippi River bluffs, you can experience those simple thrills time and again as you play a round of golf that's as visually pleasing as it is physically demanding. Golf experts always say to keep your head down when you swing, but at Forest Hills you'll be tempted time and again to peek—heck, even to stare—at the verdant bluffs towering overhead.

Golfers have been enjoying the views for a hundred years. In 1901, the course at the foot of La Crosse's most famous landmark—Granddad Bluff— opened as a country club. For the first five years, it was named Schaghticoke before it became the La Crosse Country Club. It remained a private course for the next 90 years, even though it was on public land. La Crosse residents finally decided, via referendum, that it was time they got to play on what essentially was their land, and the La Crosse Country Club became a public course in 1994. It then was known as The Bluffs. In 1998, the name was changed again to Forest Hills. Locals still call it the Old La Crosse Country Club. Members of the La Crosse Country Club built a new Arthur Hills–designed private course by the same name several miles away near Onalaska. The public golfer easily won on this transaction.

Take the tram to see the view from the tee of the 268-yard par-four ninth hole at Alpine Resort, Egg Harbor.

With its scenery and a layout that has stood the test of time, Forest Hills is one of the must-play courses in the Coulee Region. In fact, it's the only regulation-length golf course in La Crosse, where building space is at a premium between the river and bluffs. The old country club also has history. Sam Snead once played an exhibition there and, as a story goes, tried to hit a shot from Granddad Bluff to the seventh green. Don Iverson grew up playing the course before becoming a successful PGA Tour pro in the 1970s and 1980s. The club held the 1905 and 1910 State Amateur tournaments.

At just more than six thousand yards, Forest Hills probably played long during the days of wood-shafted clubs. Today, it's a good recreational-length course where most golfers can find a few pars and birdies along with a little solitude as the fairways wind up a coulee and around the bluff. "It's the kind of course you want to come back and play. Everybody loves being at the foot of the bluffs," says Dick Cotter, the pro at the course for many years.

Forest Hills is anything but a walk in the woods, however. With sloping fairways, tricky old greens, elevation changes, and mature trees, it plays much tougher than most short courses and much harder than it appears. The front nine is a good example. It's the flatter of the two nines. Five of the six par-fours are 375 yards or less, and no water comes into play. Yet it's deceivingly difficult, with large trees and overhanging branches separating the fairways.

The 15th hole at Forest Hills.

One of Forest Hills' old-course quirks is the railroad tracks. More than 40 trains a day pass through hauling freight—and occasionally passengers—between Chicago and Minneapolis. The rails run parallel to holes eight and nine; the fast-moving boxcars rumble only 30 feet from the ninth tee. The tracks also are out of bounds on both holes. On holes one and 18, golfers occasionally have to wait for the boxcars to pass and resist the temptation to hit over them. Course manager Dave Holtze, part of Holtze and Associates that runs the course, says trains have the right of way. Engineers who see golfers hit toward the trains have called the pro shop on their cell phones, resulting in warnings for the offenders, Holtze says. Golfers whose balls land on the tracks don't have to play off them, however—it's a free drop. And golfers are warned not to race their power carts over the crossings on one and 18.

The back nine is the most scenic and challenging, pushing straight up Miller Coulee between Granddad and its neighboring bluff and then running back down the valley. Holes 13 and 14 are new since 1980, and several others have new greens.

Holes 11 through 17 are an unforgiving stretch requiring well-placed tee shots. The 11th is just 301 yards on a plateau between trees and a steep hillside. Tee shots must pass a row of wide, old maple trees on the left to reach the corner of the dogleg. The 508-yard 12th is straight but not straightforward. Overhanging coulee trees and out of bounds line the entire left side of the fairway, which slants to the right. The key shot here is the second one—a sidehill lie with Hixon Forest lurking on the left.

The 14th and 15th are only 342 and 326 yards and both downhill. Easy birdies? The 14th will yield some with a landing area that widens at about 250 yards, almost forcing golfers to hit driver and reach the opening. The downhill-all-the-way 15th, with a tiny opening to a green guarded by sand and a pond, encourages layup shots. Take a minute to enjoy the view of the Mississippi River valley from this alpine tee. The hills on the horizon are in Minnesota.

Par-threes don't come any tougher than the 192-yard 16th: From an elevated tee, shots must carry a deep, grassy ravine to reach an elevated green. Par-fours don't get much prettier than 17. Tee shots fly toward a tree-lined fairway in the valley—yet another great view of the bluffs from this tee, if you take time to look up—and approach shots are uphill to a green guarded by sand traps.

An old course, Forest Hills can be trying. The bumpy, sloping fairways can give golfers some unusual lies, but they are a reminder the course was built long before machines came along to smooth out the soil. Forest Hills is on only about 80 acres of land, half the amount used for today's 18-hole courses. When in doubt, play for putts and the grain of the grass to break away from the bluffs, or west toward the valley. Forest Hills plays 6,063 yards from the blue tees, but blue tees are set out only for tournaments, Holtze says. White tees are 5,788 yards.

"Golf is a beautiful walk in the fresh air, and we've got nice scenery as you're walking," Dave Holtze says. "It doesn't matter what time of year, it's gorgeous."

Forest Hills is easy to find. When you get to La Crosse, look east for a rock-faced bluff with a U.S. flag swaying from its summit. No, it's not one of Forest Hills' flagsticks, but the course is right below (although the clubhouse is a few blocks north on Losey Boulevard.). And no matter what your swing guru says, always remember to look up after your shots at Forest Hills.

*6,063 yards/par-71/69.3 rating/123 slope*
*Fees: $*
*Call: 608/779-4653; Web site: www.forest-hills.net*
*Directions: Located at the intersection of Highway 16, Losey Boulevard and*
*La Crosse Street.*

# Trempealeau Mountain Golf Club
## *Trempealeau*

For a course named after a mountain, Trempealeau Mountain Golf Club is surprisingly flat. No mountain, no hills, not even a short climb that will raise your heartbeat. Nary a tree, either. In short, outside of a few long walks between tees this is one course where you can skip the power cart.

Trempealeau Mountain is named after a famous Mississippi River island bluff of the same name. But the bluff is somewhere on the horizon from the golf course, not even noticeable among the pretty ridge of Mississippi River hills that surround the course. Don't be deceived, however. The word *Trempealeau* means "mountain soaking in water," which is true of the island bluff. With water on nine holes, architect Edward M. Riley soaked nearly half his course in water. Riley also took advantage of a wide, flat piece of farm land, moved a little dirt, and shaped a course that is fair and challenging for a reasonable greens fee. Trempealeau Mountain is his first course. "The average golfer really enjoys the course," pro Bill Pearse says. "The course plays extremely well for scratch golfers, yet a 35-handicapper still enjoys it because you don't get beat up from tee to green."

Pearse warns that the severity of the wind blowing through the valley can turn what appears to be a docile course into a monster. And then there are the water hazards, tough greens, and mounding. "The course wasn't designed to be the hardest, yet very few players break par here. It's a deceptive course," Pearse says. Much like its name.

A consortium of four private owners at Trempealeau Mountain takes pride in true greens, close-cropped, hybrid bluegrass fairways, and bent-grass tees that set up square to the fairways. The course also has a 150-yard long, bent-grass practice tee.

Opened in 1997, Trempealeau Mountain still is maturing and will play much differently when strategically planted trees take root. Golfers now can spray the ball off the tee and hit a recovery shot. But keep playing wildly, and your score is sure to rise on a course that has severe, strategically shaped greens. Many of the greens can be testy, adding another element of difficulty to a course that looks easy. "You could put a ball at 150 yards from the green and still have to play well to shoot par. The greens demand a well-placed shot. You can have a shot eight feet away and not have an easy putt, which is typical of modern courses, like Pete Dye's," says Pearse, a native of La Crosse.

The front nine at Trempealeau Mountain has an out-and-back routing. Several holes often play short with the wind and several long against it. The back nine has several championship holes and water on the last seven holes. The best holes are 12 through 17, a demanding stretch that will wreck your first impression of the course. The 12th is only 388 yards, but a pond stretches about 300 yards down the right side. The hole is even tougher than it looks because of two aspects: one, the tee shot must be hit diagonally across the pond toward a fairway bunker, narrowing the fairway; two, the pond plays wider than it looks because anything close to it kicks down a cut bank to the water, again making the fairway narrower than it looks.

The 12th hole sounds the alarm for a set of holes than can leave you scrambling. It also makes you realize that this is a looks-can-be-deceiving course. Water hazards on all the other holes are deceptive, too, either because the sloping banks increase their size or because they aren't always visible. A good example is 13, a 412-yard par-four slightly downhill over a knoll. It's possible to drive into the water, which crosses the fairway, but you can't see the water from the tee. The 184-yard 16th hole has a hump in the middle of the green, an unconventional putting obstacle. You might think you've found Trempealeau Mountain. Be careful on 17, a 405-yard par-four that's slightly uphill; keep the drive left because a push or slice will wind up in the water, even though you can't see it. Remember, looks can be deceiving at Trempealeau Mountain.

*6,485 yards/par-71/70.1 rating/120 slope*
*Architect: Edward M. Riley*
*Fees: $*
*Call: 608/534-7417*
*Directions: On Highway 35, go 1.5 miles north of Trempealeau on the Great*
    *River Road.*

# Skyline Golf Course
*Black River Falls*

The name chosen for Skyline Golf Course is a good indication of what type of golf awaits in Black River Falls, a Jackson County city known for the river that runs through it and for the nearby state forest around it. The Black River (which flows southeast 60 miles into the Mississippi at La Crosse) isn't a factor at Skyline, but the hilly terrain around the river's watershed is. Of the 18 holes at Skyline, only four are flat, and two of those are par-threes. All other holes either ascend, descend, or play along sidehills on land at the city's edge. It's a good power cart course, but it's also a good course if you value variety, shot making, and scenery in a round of golf. "Skyline has the most fantastic views in Jackson County, one of the highest points in the county. It's very picturesque," says Chris Foraker, the former Skyline pro.

Skyline opened as a nine-hole course in 1957, but in 1990 a second nine opened in a wooded valley. Three new holes also were added on the front nine, and a new clubhouse was built on the hill that overlooks many of the holes. The result is a fun-to-play course that is only a few hundred yards short of a championship test. And don't let the hills turn you away. Only a couple of holes have significant elevation changes. The rest of the ups and downs are manageable, unless they're of your own making.

The first five holes and the ninth hole were part of the original course. Their small, oval greens give them away and also make them tough pars. Two of the three new holes, six and seven, are short par-fours that can be birdied, but their newer greens have more roll and are easily three-putted if you land above the hole.

Whereas the front nine is hilly and mostly open, the back nine descends into a wooded valley that is defined by a stream. The stream comes into play only on two holes, but many of the other holes slope toward its wooded valley. The 498-yard 10th hole is a great place to go for the green in two because it's a downhill approach. The same strategy may work on the other par-five, the 475-yard 16th. The green on the 16th, like the 10th, sits in a depression near the stream, giving golfers extra kick downhill on their attempt to reach the green in two.

More conservative play may be needed on holes 12 through 14, three par-fours that act like a gauntlet through the trees. "Twelve through 14 are awfully nice holes that will test any level of player," Foraker says. For example, the 12th is just 355 yards, but after a tee shot through a chute of trees, the green sits well below the fairway just in front of the creek. Don't overclub.

Fittingly, Skyline finishes uphill. The 380-yard, par-four 18th has a two-level green, and then it's an uphill walk again from the green to one last destination—the 19th hole.

*6,371 yards/par-72/70.6 rating/123 slope*
*Architect: Gilmore Graves (redesign and second nine)*
*Fees: $$*
*Call: 715/284-2613; Web site: www.skyline.com;*
*Directions: Highway 54 west to North Eighth Street. North to Golf Road, then*
*    left.*

# The Monastery

*Sparta*

While Pete Dye was busy building golf courses at Kohler, not the least of which were courses at Whistling Straits, he made a few side trips to a monastery in central Wisconsin. No, he didn't go there to confess for making golfers pay like the devil for hitting bad shots. He was working on plans for a new course for the Our Lady of Spring Bank Cistercian Abbey near Sparta. Dye, a devout Catholic, agreed to waive his designing fee as a favor to the church and the five monks who own most of the land.

Father Bernard McCoy, the head of the project, said that construction could begin in 2001, providing fund-raising goes according to plan. The $16 million development will include a 50-room hotel, resort, and conference center, a golf training center, and gourmet restaurant.

If Dye's preliminary design is followed, the course would be more than 7,400 yards. The varied terrain includes bluffs, valleys and meadows. "The course will not be religious in nature, but there will be a monastic ambiance that will go with the course," McCoy says.

## Other Area Courses

# Hiawatha Golf Club
*Tomah*

It's only a few miles off Interstate 94, but quiet Hiawatha Golf Club feels much farther away. The course was built on farmland in 1959, and 40 years later not much around rural Monroe County has changed. Gently rolling hills, farms, meadows, and mature trees make Hiawatha a place for a relaxing round of golf. The course, however, has changed. The old nine-hole layout became 18 holes in 1994, and three of the old holes were remodeled as well. The result is a pleasant but challenging rural course, which has a reputation for some of the best greens in the area.

Hiawatha has numerous doglegs. With large trees guarding the fairways and greens on several holes, patience, and good course management are needed to play well. Several holes also have blind tee shots over hills; wooden viewing towers were built on the fourth and 15th tees to help golfers see if all is clear. "There aren't a lot of straight-away holes where you can pound it out here," says Dan Wagner, the pro.

Hiawatha's hills offer several great views from the tee boxes. On the third and seventh holes, you'll feel like you can hit it into the next county because you can see for miles. A country cemetery is visible from the 14th tee, which may be apropos for some golfers after playing the 544-yard, uphill 13th hole. Part of Hiawatha's remodeled clubhouse dates to the original 1920s farm on which the course was built.

*6,469 yards/par-72/70.5 rating/122 slope*
*Architect: Gilmore Graves (redesign)*
*Fees: $*
*Call: 608/372-5589*
*Directions: Take Highway 12 north from Tomah to Highway 21; turn west and*
*    go about 1 mile.*

# Sparta Municipal Golf Course
*Sparta*

S parta Municipal Golf Course never will be mistaken for an exclusive country club, but it is known as one of the most popular courses in the region. With eleven hundred members and 250 privately owned golf carts, it's always busy. The front nine is next to a busy city recreational complex. And a cemetery is in the middle of the back nine. At 6,537 yards, Sparta also is a solid test of golf with several tight holes and large sand traps.

The front nine is pure municipal golf. Golfers can hear shouts from the nearby athletic fields and city pool and watch people fish in Perch Lake, a storybook scene. One hole plays near railroad tracks—the 584-yard seventh, the toughest hole on the front—and another hole is below a silver highway bridge.

The front nine opened in 1918 as six holes and quickly expanded to nine, but it still has six of the original holes. The much quieter back nine, away from the recreational complex, opened in 1983. Holes 10 through 13 play near skinny pine trees along the La Crosse River, although it doesn't come into play.

The state cemetery is part of the reason the back nine is so quiet. About three hundred children who once were wards of the state are buried in the Wisconsin Child Center Cemetery. The graves date to the early 1900s. Signs in the golf course parking lot tell visitors to the cemetery that they first must stop at the clubhouse. Course manager Roger Johnson says only one other course in the country is built around a cemetery.

*6,537 yards/par-72/70.8 rating/127 slope*
*Architect: Art Johnson (back nine)*
*Fees: $*
*Call: 608/269-3022*
*Directions: Two blocks off Highway 21 on Montgomery Street.*

# Castle Rock Golf Course
*Mauston*

I f you're in the area, especially on a Friday, don't pass up a chance to visit Castle Rock for fish fry and golf. A few miles from Castle Rock Lake and Petenwell Lake, the course has great scenery as it winds through woods, past ponds, and over a trout stream. The rolling fairways sit amidst river bluffs near the Wisconsin Dells. About 250 people come to the course every Friday night for the club's popular fish fry, and many take in a round of golf first. With woods on most every hole, it's also a treat to play in the fall.

With water on 15 holes, Castle Rock may seem like a golfing version of a Dells water park. The water hazards are mostly ponds on the front nine and the stream on the back nine. The first nine opened in 1980 and the second nine in 1990.

*6,160 yards/par-72/70.1 rating/126 slope*
*Fees: $$*
*Call: 800/851-4853 or 608/847-4658; Web site: www.castlerockgolfcourse.com*
*Directions: Two miles north of Mauston on Highway 58, 0.25 mile west on*
    *Welch Prairie Road.*

# Platteville Golf and Country Club
*Platteville*

The southwestern corner of Wisconsin is known for its rugged hills, many of which harbored lead ore and attracted miners in the 1830s and 1840s. To really appreciate the rugged terrain, try the Platteville Golf and Country Club. Opened in 1921 as nine holes and expanded to 18 in 1987, Platteville has the charm of an old course, the conditioning of a private course, and enchanting scenery of a coulee course. The greens—even some of the new ones—are small and have severe slopes. The typical hole seems to descend precipitously from the tee to the fairway then climb again to the green. The greens have mounded edges and angle steeply toward the fairway, requiring golfers to stay below the hole on approach shots.

At 6,066 yards, Platteville requires more precision than power. "The greens are the special part of the course, and some people might not use the term *special*. They're severe," pro Peter Reif says. The greens "protect the integrity of the course." Old trees frame most of the fairways on the front nine, which is a par-37 with three par-fives. The par-34 back nine has slightly less severe greens, but the newer holes still complement the old ones, minus the mature trees. The course is closed to the public on Wednesdays, Thursdays, and Friday mornings.

*6,066 yards/par-71/68.3 rating/122 slope*
*Fees: $$*
*Call: 608/348-3551*
*Directions: From Highway 151 in Platteville, go north on Highway 80 about 1*
    *mile.*

# Prairie du Chien Country Club
*Prairie du Chien*

Nestled in the bluffs between the Wisconsin and Mississippi Rivers, the Prairie du Chien Country Club is a modern 18-hole course with excellent scenery. Although the rivers aren't visible, at least four holes, seven, eight, 15, and 16, have beautiful views of the hills from elevated tees. From the clubhouse, golfers can see Wyalusing State Park, where the two great rivers meet.

Only two of the original nine holes—designed in 1958 by George Vitense of Madison—remain. But architect Gilmore Graves did such a nice job of blending the old with the new in 1995 that golfers are surprised the course is mostly new. "The nice thing about it is we've incorporated the old course with some of the greens and some of the angles of the fairways. Most people are amazed when they think we've only been open a few years," pro Scott Kennedy says.

Forests surround the course but don't come into play often. Selected large trees remain to frame the fairways and penalize wayward shots. Major elevation changes on holes provide most of the drama. The 16th hole is just 303 yards, but Kennedy calls it the signature hole. Some players try to drive the green over a ravine while others lay up with an iron.

*6,240 yards/par-71/68.8 rating/119 slope*
*Architect: Gilmore Graves*
*Fees: $*
*Call: 608/326-6707; Web site: www.pdcgolf.com*
*Directions: East on Highway 18, 4 miles from Prairie du Chien. Course is at the intersection of Highways 18, 35, and 60.*

**Best Nine-Hole Course**

# Birchwood Golf and Development
*Kieler*

It's as far southwest as you can go in Wisconsin and still play golf. Birchwood Golf and Development near Kieler is just 2 miles north of Dubuque, Iowa. The 3,291-yard, par-36 course is on a bluff overlooking the Mississippi River. Two par-three holes have spectacular views high above the river, making them two of the few places in Wisconsin you can watch a river barge and play golf at the same time. They are the 142-yard third hole and the 130-yard sixth hole. When it opened in

1988, most holes were cut from the forest, and most have some elevation change. The combination of tight fairways and uneven lies makes it a challenging round.

*3,291 yards/par-36*
*Fees: $*
*Call: 608/748-4743*
*Directions: Two miles north of Dubuque off Highway 151/61 on Eagle Point*
    *Road. Exit on Badger Road.*

## More Fun Things to Do

In his book *Life on the Mississippi,* Mark Twain called La Crosse "a choice town" more than a hundred years ago when it was just a city of twelve thousand people. Today it's a city of more than fifty thousand, and the still-bustling downtown along the riverfront is known for its specialty shops, award-winning restaurants, nightlife, festivals, and historic buildings. Nearly one hundred buildings downtown are part of the historic district. Some of those same buildings caused Twain to write that La Crosse has "blocks of buildings, which are stately enough, and also architecturally fine enough to command respect in any city."

Also downtown is popular Riverside Park, a perfect place to relax and watch paddle-wheelers, steamboats, barges, and pleasure craft ply the river. Or you can board a boat for your own cruise, such as the steamboat Julia Belle Swain (800/815-1005). The park, home to the annual Riverfest during Fourth of July week, was designed by John Nolen, who also designed Central Park in New York City and had a hand in laying out Madison. In the park is the Riverside Museum (free; 608/782-2366), where you can learn about the War Eagle, a riverboat that sank in 1870. Directly across the river from Riverside is Pettibone Park; the land once was partly owned by the famous western showman, William Frederick Cody or Buffalo Bill.

Other attractions include the La Crosse Doll Museum (608/785-0020), the Gertrude Salzer Gordon Children's Museum (608/784-2652), and the Museum of Modern Technology (608/785-2340). Myrick Park, 0.5 mile from Forest Hills Golf Course and next to the University of Wisconsin–La Crosse, has a free zoo (608/789-7190) along with a concession stand and amusement rides for toddlers. Near the zoo is Kids Coulee, a multilevel playground built to resemble a fort. Not far from Myrick Park is the La Crosse Skate Park.

Near Forest Hills, take the steep drive to 600-foot-high Granddad Bluff overlooking the city and the Mississippi River valley. The city-run swimming pools next to the Forest Hills clubhouse are open to the public. About 7.5 miles of hiking trails also are nearby in the 720-acre Hixon Forest. The Hixon Forest Nature Center (608/784-0303) has exhibits and programs.

The pace of life always seems to slow down near the Mississippi River, but that isn't for a lack of things to do and see. A good place to start is at one of the numerous state parks along the Mississippi and its tributaries.

Merrick State Park (608/687-4936) at Fountain City is on the backwaters of the Mississippi River, offering excellent fishing and bird watching. Perrot State Park (608/534-6409) in Trempealeau is at the confluence of the Trempealeau and Mississippi Rivers, featuring views from 500-foot bluffs. Nearby is the Trempealeau National Wildlife Refuge (608/539-2311) operated by the U.S. Fish and Wildlife Service.

At Wyalusing State Park (608/996-2261) near Prairie du Chien, you can take in ridgetop views above the convergence of the Wisconsin and Mississippi Rivers.

Across the river are Pike's Peak State Park (319/873-2341) in McGregor, Iowa, and Effigy Mounds National Monument (319/873-3491) in Harpers Ferry, Iowa.

At Cassville in the far southwest, Nelson Dewey State Park (608/725-5374) has blufftop views of the river. Stonefield Village (608/725-5210) is a re-created nineteenth-century Wisconsin farm community on the estate of Dewey, Wisconsin's first governor. Attractions include Dewey's home and the Museum of Agricultural History. Riverside Park in Cassville has a playground and picnic facilities, and the Cassville Car Ferry can give you and your vehicle a lift across the Mississippi.

Near Tomah, Mill Bluff State Park (608/427-6692) has unusual rock formations while Wildcat Mountain State Park (608/337-4775) is on a ridge above the Kickapoo River Valley.

The Black River State Forest (715/284-4103) near Black River Falls has 67,000 acres of land for hiking and backpacking. Nearby is Majestic Pines Bingo and Casino (800/657-4621) in Black River Falls.

Goose Island Campground (608/788-7018) near La Crosse is a popular county park on the Mississippi River backwaters.

Fort McCoy (608/388-2407), near Sparta, opened in 1909 and still is a bustling U.S. Army Reserve training area for 120,000 soldiers each year. Visitors can tour the 62,000-acre facility, camp and fish on the grounds, or see the Commemorative Area, which has five buildings depicting the life of a soldier during World War II. Military equipment also is on display.

A visit to the Tomah area isn't complete without checking out cranberry country. The area is known for its rectangular cranberry bogs, which turn bright red in the fall when the tart berries are harvested. Wisconsin is the nation's number one producer of cranberries. Visit the Cranberry Expo museum (608/378-4878) in Warrens, south of Tomah, and in the fall don't miss the big Cranberry Fest in Warrens, which draws a hundred thousand people. Some of the bogs offer harvest tours in the fall.

Scenic southwest Wisconsin looks great on wheels. The two-lane Great River Road, Highway 35, hugs the banks of the Mississippi and passes sleepy villages south of La Crosse. Keep your eyes peeled for 400-foot-long barges heading to St. Paul or St. Louis or the Gulf of Mexico carrying grain, petroleum products, coal, or sugar.

Hop on a bicycle and try the Great River State Trail (24 miles, Onalaska to Marshland), the La Crosse River State Trail (22 miles, La Crosse to Sparta), the Elroy-Sparta State Trail (32 miles, Elroy to Sparta) or the Hillsboro State Trail (4 miles, Union Center to Hillsboro).

The Sparta-Elroy Trail, featuring three tunnels that, combined, are about a mile long, opened in 1972. It was the nation's first trail built on an old railroad bed. Antique bikes and unusual bikes are on display at the Deke Slayton Memorial Space and Bike Museum (608/269-0033) in Sparta, which bills itself as the Bicycling Capital of America.

Tour Villa Louis (608/326-2721), Prairie du Chien's 1870 Victorian mansion near the riverfront. The grounds include the site of a battle from the War of 1812 and the ruins of Fort Crawford at Prairie du Chien Museum.

Platteville is home each summer to the Chicago Bears training camp and the Wisconsin Shakespeare Festival.

Other area attractions include canoeing on the popular Kickapoo River; Kickapoo Indian Caverns in Wauzeka; the Mining Museum–Rollo Jamison Museum (608/348-3301) in Platteville; Norskedalen Nature and Heritage Center (608/452-3424) in Coon Valley; Dickeyville Grotto (religious and patriotic shrine; 608/568-3119) in Dickeyville; Tomah Area Historical Society Museum (608/372-5771); the Harris G. Allen Telecommunications Museum (608/374-5000) in Tomah; the 1850s Hixon House (608/782-1980) in La Crosse; and the Hamlin Garland Homestead (608/786-1675), the West Salem home of the Pulitzer Prize–winning author.

Short golf courses include Hillview (par-27; 608/788-2072) and Walsh Golf Center (par-32; 608/781-0838) in La Crosse. Walsh Golf Center also has a mini-golf.

## For More Information

Black River Falls: Chamber of Commerce 715/284-4658 or 800/404-4008

Cassville: Department of Tourism 608/725-5855; www.cassville.org

La Crosse: Convention and Visitors Bureau, 608/782-1980 or 800/658-9424; www.explorelacrosse.com

Mauston: Chamber of Commerce 608/847-4124; www.mauston.com

Ontario: www.windingrivers.com/Pages/ontario.html

Platteville: Chamber of Commerce 608/348-8888; www.platteville.com

Prairie du Chien: Chamber of Commerce 608/326-8555; www.prairieduchien.org

Sparta: Sparta Chamber of Commerce and Tourism 608/269-4123 or 800/354-BIKE

Tomah: Chamber of Commerce 608/372-2166 or 800/94-TOMAH; www.tomah wisconsin.com

Trempealeau County: Chamber of Commerce 608/323-7076 or 800/927-5339; www.win.bright.net/~tctours

Vernon County: Viroqua Chamber 608/637-2575; www.viroqua-wisconsin.com

# 7

# St. Croix River Valley

When French explorer Daniel Greysolon Duluth was looking for a route from Lake Superior to the Mississippi River in 1680, he and his French voyageur companions paddled down what is now the Bois Brule River before they stumbled upon a magnificent waterway. The headwater was a lake, now known as the St. Croix Flowage, in northwestern Wisconsin near Gordon. Out of it came a river that flowed southwest through steep, forested hills, all the way to their Shangri-la, the Mississippi.

Today, that region is known as the St. Croix National Scenic Riverway. The boundary between Wisconsin and Minnesota always has been revered for its natural beauty. Locals like to refer to it as the "Rhine Valley of America"; settlers called it "Little New England." Numerous downhill ski hills dot the region, and in the summer thousands of sailboats, cruisers, and fishing boats are docked at 12 marinas.

In recent years, the lower part of the river—52 miles from St. Croix Falls to Prescott—has been rediscovered. St. Croix County has become one of the fastest-growing regions in Wisconsin and a far-flung suburb of the sprawling Twin Cities. Duluth built one of the first fur trading posts in Wisconsin. Latter day entrepreneurs are building golf courses. St. Croix County and parts of Pierce and Polk counties have become great golf destinations.

Even Duluth (for whom the city of Duluth, Minnesota, was named) would be proud of how the region's natural beauty has been incorporated into the valley's golf courses. Taking advantage of water and woods, ridges and hills, a cluster of 18-hole courses offers golfers great natural views and even greater challenges. The St. Croix Valley Golf Trail includes 14 courses and 243 holes of golf. One measure of the tremendous golf course development: Half the courses are new since 1990.

Part of the attraction of golf in the St. Croix valley is the pace—slow. Most of the cities, like New Richmond, River Falls, Somerset, and Prescott, are small. Even the hub of the region, Hudson, only has eight thousand people. Most of the roads leading to the courses are winding two-laners that go through farms and over and around hills. That's changing in some parts, but it's mostly laid-back, country golf with a championship feel—especially on the weekdays. The people are small-town friendly, even if the bunkers and water hazards aren't.

The jewel of St. Croix Valley golf is Troy Burne Golf Club near Hudson, a course that PGA Tour star Tom Lehman helped design and that someday hopes to hold professional events. It's a great place to kick off your golfing visit to Wisconsin's west-central border region. But don't stop there. Like Daniel Greysolon Duluth, keep discovering what the St. Croix Valley has to offer until you run out of river.

# Troy Burne Golf Club
*Hudson*

In 1996, PGA Tour pro Tom Lehman won the British Open at Royal Lytham in England. It was the first major and the biggest win of Lehman's career. The experience must have made an impression on Lehman because that fall he brought links-style golf to western Wisconsin. In late 1996, Lehman and architects Michael Hurdzan and Dana Fry of Cleveland, Ohio, began designing Troy Burne Golf Club near Hudson. The result was a bit o' the British game in Wisconsin—amber prairie grasses framing an otherwise open landscape, 121 sand bunkers, and a stacked sod wall guarding a pot bunker, a feature common on the old-country courses. The only thing missing is an ocean.

"Our goal in building Troy Burne was to blend this region's natural beauty and characteristics into our design with as little disruption to the natural habitat as possible," said Lehman, who grew up in Austin, Minnesota, attended the University of Minnesota, and played some amateur tournaments in western Wisconsin. "I expect it to be one of the best courses around, private or public, in the Midwest or anywhere else."

At Troy Burne, Lehman was thinking major all the way. It opened in May of 1999, and its first event was a match between Lehman and fellow touring pro Steve Stricker, from Wisconsin. The owners of Troy Burne, Glenn Rehbein Companies of Minneapolis, also had big ideas when they conceived the course. It looks, feels and plays like a championship test of golf. In fact, Troy Burne was patterned after Shinnecock Hills, site of the 1995 U.S. Open.

More than a million cubic yards of dirt were moved to turn a flat farm field into a rolling acreage featuring bent-grass fairways and eight holes with water hazards. The par-71 course is 7,003 yards from the Lehman tees, or the back tees, and has a slope rating of 140, putting it among the top 10 in Wisconsin. With multiple tee boxes—most of them elevated—and generous landing areas, the strategic layout is a good test for tour pros. For the rest of us, it's a place where we can try to get a few pars on a true pro-style layout. "It's such a dynamic design," Troy Burne pro Craig Waryan says. "It rewards great shots,

Troy Burne's number 17.

but it doesn't brutalize poor shots. It's a very fair golf course, and that's a hard balance to hit."

Golfers might even run into Lehman, who occasionally drops in, takes out a cart, and signs autographs while checking on one of his first Tom Lehman Signature courses. Another one of his courses opened in 2000; the Greystone Golf Club is in Sauk Centre, Minnesota, which is best known as the hometown of the late novelist Sinclair Lewis.

The front and back nines circle a rambling, one-story clubhouse, which offers great views of the countryside and a Lehman Room featuring some of the famed golfer's memorabilia, including a signed Royal Lytham scorecard. A Scottish-themed housing development borders the course but doesn't ruin the views of the 420-acre complex, which includes a large practice and teaching facility.

Troy Burne has several distinctive holes on the front side. It opens with a lovely 600-yard par-five that doglegs around a cluster of trees. Those are the only trees that come into play on the front nine. The 450-yard, par-four second hole tests your nerves early with a pond running the left side of the fairway to the front and left of the green. The sixth hole looks a meager 355 yards, but it tests you with 11 bunkers and a small, devilish green that kicks off short shots. High mounding on the 222-yard, par-three eighth creates the effect of playing in a hollow.

The front nine gets you in the mood. But the course really takes off on holes 10 through 15, the start of "one of the best nines I've ever seen," says Bill Linneman, who rated the course for the Wisconsin State Golf Association. Water is a factor on seven holes on the inward nine. A series of man-made ponds connected by a creek—*burne* is the the Scottish name for "creek"—helped give the Troy Township course its name. The boulder-strewn burne isn't ancient, like the one that cuts in front of the first green at St. Andrews in Scotland; instead it was created by a California company named Living Waters.

The 10th is a 420-yard downhill par-four bordered by sand the length of the hole—that's right, a sand trap more than four football fields long—and water half of the way, all on the left side. The 11th is a pretty, 176-yard downhill par-three framed by the bubbling burne on the right and tall pine trees behind the green. A deep but narrow green makes for a tough target.

Decision time arrives at the 483-yard, par-five 12th hole. If you need a birdie, this is your place to make up ground. A pond shapes the left side of the wide fairway but isn't a big threat on the tee shot. The second shot is the key one. With the water running up to the green and behind it, golfers must decide whether to thread a long-iron or wood between the water and a bunker to reach the green in two. The safe option is to play right to a wide layup area.

The 14th is the best par-four at Troy Burne—464 yards with water left and sand right on the drive. The falling burne—a waterfall left of the elevated green—churns up errant approach shots. Then comes 15, only 144 yards but menacing with a 7-foot-high sod bunker wall guarding the wide, shallow green. Glenn's Bunker—named after owner Glenn Rehbein—is one pothole that makes even Lehman nervous. "Do yourself a favor and don't leave it short on the tee shot," Lehman advises golfers. Glenn's pit is every bit as menacing as the one near the infamous Road Hole at St. Andrew's in Scotland.

The final three holes will test your game mentally and physically. The 16th, 617 yards, is a three-shot hole like five, with more water and sand about 400 yards down the left side. Don't be short and right on your approach shot—two more pot bunkers await. The 17th is picturesque—445 yards all downhill sweeping to the right around Ruemmele's Pond. The best tee shot is down the left side to take the water out of play and open up the depth of the green, but bunkers on the left can ruin any well-made plans.

The finishing hole simply is a brute—470 yards straightaway atop a windswept ridge with fairway bunkers pinching the fairway and deep bunkers around the green. It's the demanding type of par-four often seen at the end of a major golf tournament, something Lehman knows a little about.

Troy Burne's amphitheater-style mounding around the greens and between many fairways smartly separates the holes. Those mounds also would make perfect vantage points for spectators. Club officials have spoken with the PGA and Ladies' PGA tours and the United States Golf Association (USGA) about future events, and down the road they're talking about a second 18 holes. It would give golfers a chance to double their pleasure at one of the best courses in Wisconsin.

*7,003 yards/par-71/74.8 rating/140 slope*
*Architects: Michael Hurdzan and Dana Fry, with Tom Lehman*
*Fees: $$$ (includes cart)*
*Call: 715/381-9800 or 877/888-8633; Web site: www.troyburne.com*
*Directions: From Interstate 94 in Hudson, take Exit 2 at Carmichael Road*
    *(County F). Drive south on F for 5 miles. Troy Burne is on the right.*

# St. Croix National
*Somerset*

If one course in the valley deserves the St. Croix name, it's this one. St. Croix National, with dramatic shots up, down, and around the forested hills, truly represents the topography of the region. The course is several miles from the river, but St. Croix National is nestled into the steep hills that make the valley a sightseer's delight. In fact, the course is built on land that for years was a downhill ski area. Unless you're in top aerobic condition, this is one course where you'll happily hop on a cart; think of it as your chairlift to some inspiring views.

In 1995, JP Golf Management of the Twin Cities bought the land that had been Snowcrest downhill ski area until it went out of business in 1983. St. Croix National emerged from architect Joel Goldstrand's plans in 1997. Goldstrand has designed more than 60 courses in the North Woods parts of Minnesota and Wisconsin. This is the land of fabled Paul Bunyan, the larger-than-life logger, and course director Frank Postic likes to say St. Croix National is "bigger than life."

It sure feels that way. Be prepared to hit some of the most dramatic shots of your golfing life, starting with the first shot, a par-four where the fairway is about 100 feet below the tee box. The course then climbs about 200 feet from the first fairway to the third tee. And then it goes back down. And up. And down. The front nine is on the old ski hill land while the more gentle back nine is on land that was used for cross-country ski trails. The variety of holes—no two holes even come close to resembling each other—make it a course you'll remember long after the round. "Some of the holes are absolutely stunning," says Postic.

For example: the first hole, with its plummeting tee shot; the seventh, a 152-yard floater straight down what looks like an old ski run; the 428-yard eighth, a beauty that runs sharply downhill then uphill; the 426-yard ninth, a down-the-chute tee shot and back-up-the-ridge approach to a green perched on the hillside. St. Croix National is a thrill ride, one that will test your nerves and your imagination.

With 60 bunkers, five ponds, seven doglegs, some semiblind shots up and over hills, and elevation changes that test your club selection, St. Croix National can be tricky. Playing cautiously is advised. You even need to be careful driving the cart—signs on the hairpin cart paths remind golfers not to lock their brakes as they descend.

While the course flattens some on the back nine, 10 through 18 still are imaginative and fun to play. There's a double-dogleg par-five, a par-four cut by a deep ravine, and a par-three guarded by a pond. The ravine hole, 14, with a landing area that's hard to judge, is one of only a few holes on the difficult terrain that seems unfair. On the back nine, enjoy the view of the peaceful white country church. It's a great reminder that city life is miles and miles away. The 18th is 560 yards, a downhill, sidehill, uphill, sharp dogleg that sums up the challenges offered at St. Croix National.

*6,909 yards/par-72/73.9 rating/138 slope*
*Architect: Joel Goldstrand*
*Fees: $$$ (includes cart)*
*Call: 715/247-4200, (612) 888-5988; Web site: www.saintcroixnational.com*
*Directions: From Highway 35 north of Hudson, turn right on County V, go 4.5*
*miles; the course is on the right near the intersection of V and Highway*
*35/64.*

# New Richmond Golf Club
*New Richmond*

When it opened, it may have been one of the worst golf courses in Wisconsin. Now it's among the best. In 1929, the New Richmond Golf Club had sand greens and, believe it or not, cement tees. Yes, cement tees on which golfers mixed sand and water to mold a hitting prop. "When they first built the course, the people had little idea of what it was supposed to look like. They thought they had to literally build the tees," says Tom Doar, a longtime member familiar with the history of the club.

The course took a step toward respectability in the 1940s when well-known Twin Cities pro Willie Kidd designed nine new holes and decided that grass greens—and tees—would be a good idea. In 1984, the course finally came of age when nine holes were added and others redesigned by Don Herfort. Now it's a fine and modernized 18-hole test of golf with a mature look and feel. In addition, a nine-hole New Richmond Links course (featured later in this chapter) was added in 1998 to alleviate playing pressure on the original course. The prairie-style Links course has a separate clubhouse.

More than thirty thousand golfers a year from western Wisconsin and the Twin Cities line up at the first tee of the respected original New Richmond course. With a 136-slope rating and a lovely routing past rivers and through woodlands and a reputation for smooth greens, it's worth getting off the Inter-state to find. "It's one of the best kept secrets in the state," says Bill Linneman of the Wisconsin State Golf Association, which has held state amateur qualifying at the course.

In addition to tight bluegrass tees and fairways, golfers like New Richmond because it's a straightforward but tough test of golf. No blind shots. No layup holes. Just one solid hole after another that make golfers use most clubs in their bag. "Good bunkering. Water. Good short and long holes and great par-threes. It's a gem," Linneman says. Or as course manager Gary Johnson says, "It's a golf course that makes you think."

Think fast: Water is on holes four, five, six, and seven. On the 372-yard fourth hole, the Willow River cuts a path 20 yards wide in front of the green, which is framed by pine trees and bunkers. The same river runs the length of the 409-yard fifth, maybe the tightest driving hole on the course, and cuts through the 194-yard seventh too.

The back nine doesn't start until 13, or so it seems. That's when you make the turn past the clubhouse—a reminder that this course's routing has changed dramatically over the years. Thirteen through 18 are the newest holes, wonder-fully carved out of a pine forest that Tom Doar and others planted in the 1960s with foresight that the land would be needed someday for the golf course. The trees were cheap back then—1¢ apiece for seedlings—but now the big trees can cost golfers dearly.

The final six holes include three fine par-fours. The 13th is flat, doglegging to the right 367 yards around the pines. Fourteen is 426 yards but doesn't play as long because it's downhill, and it has a pleasant view of the countryside. One of the toughest pars on the back can be 15, only 352 yards but doglegging left through a neck of trees. Keep the driver in your bag here.

The days of sand and cement have passed by at New Richmond, but they're not completely gone. If you look hard enough you still can find one of the ill-advised cement tees hidden behind the eighth green.

*6,713 yards/par-72/72.5 rating/136 slope*
*Architects: Willie Kidd; Don Herfort (redesign)*

*Fees: $$*
*Call: 715/246-6724*
*Directions: From Highway 64, go 1 mile west of New Richmond. Turn right on*
*    County K. Go 0.25 mile and turn right to the 18-hole course or turn left to*
*    the nine-hole Links course.*

# White Eagle Golf Club
*North Hudson*

E ven before it opened in August of 2000, early reviewers were saying that White Eagle would become one of the best courses in west-central Wisconsin and the Twin Cities metro area. If you get the chance to stand on any one of its elevated tees or fairways that roll past forests and 20 wetland areas, it would be hard to disagree.

White Eagle will challenge you and grab you with its beauty from the first tee, where you hit toward a marsh, to the last green, where you finish beside a waterfall. Set on 240 acres of hills and valleys—part of which was a third-generation farm dating to 1887—White Eagle features scenic rises and drops in elevation.

Architect Garrett Gill of River Falls designed a course that plays nearly 7,200 yards from the back tees but considerably different from the other four tee blocks. He did some earth-moving but left alone large tracts of the existing topography. The terrain ranges from flat to spectacular. "White Eagle has all the attributes to make it a championship course," Gill says. "Parts of the course are slow and melodic while other parts are fast and hard. The game will be intense at times and relaxing at others."

Gill and White Eagle owners Dan Schaaf and Bill Block built a course that's a little bit of everything. Foremost, it's demanding but fair. The fairway landing areas are wide, and the doglegs have deep corners where you can hit driver all day. Because the terrain can be trouble enough, they built big, gently sloping greens. However, six of the elevated greens aren't visible from the fairway. They also built a course that will be a walk in the woods or past a wetland on every hole. The 42 home sites being built around the course won't ruin the natural setting because the lots will be three acres and often hidden behind trees.

The first four holes are flat—holes one and two require carries over wetlands—before the course drops 70 feet from tee to green on the 225-yard third hole. The 410-yard sixth hole drops about 100 feet off the tee then rises 60 feet to the green. Top holes on the rolling back nine include the wooded, 185-yard 13th, sharply downhill past a pothole pond; the 543-yard 16th through a ravine and up a hill; and the par-four 17th through a wetland.

White Eagle plays through oak, aspen, maple, birch, pine, and other varieties of trees, which make for a beautiful round of golf anytime but especially in the fall. The course is between Hudson, Wisconsin, and Stillwater, Minnesota.

*7,178 yards/par-72*
*Architect: Garrett Gill*
*Fees: $$$ (including cart)*
*Call: 715/549-4653 or 888/465-3004; Web site: www.whiteeaglegolf.net*
*Directions: From Interstate 94 in Hudson, take Exit 1 at Highway 35 north. Go 5 miles to County V, turn right. Drive 2 miles and White Eagle is on the right.*

# River Falls Golf Club
*River Falls*

Built in 1929 and expanded to 18 holes in the 1960s, the River Falls Golf Club has stood the test of time. It's still considered one of the best old courses in the western part of the state. It has rolling hills, wooded terrain, and a reputation for being in excellent shape. At almost 6,600 yards and requiring some precision shot making on tight holes, the course is playable for heavy hitters and weekenders. Water comes into play on two holes. The 17th hole, 175 yards over a wide ravine, is part of a trio of strong finishing holes.

*6,596 yards/par-72/72.0 rating/126 slope*
*Architect: Gordon Emerson (second nine)*
*Fees: $$*
*Call: 715/425-7253*
*Directions: From Interstate 94 east of Hudson, take Exit 3. Drive south on Highway 35 for 9 miles. Turn left on County M. The course is 0.5 mile on the right.*

# Bristol Ridge
*Somerset*

Opened in 1994, Bristol Ridge may be one of the best values in the St. Croix valley. It offers a championship test of golf without the high prices of most upscale courses. Yet Bristol Ridge plays like an upscale course with its large greens, smart bunkering, and risk-reward holes. Water comes into play on eight holes, and six holes wind up, over, and around a heavily wooded ridge.

The signature hole may be five, a skinny, 537-yard par-five through the trees with a severely sloping fairway that leaves little room for error. Most golfers play it safe so they have a clear shot up a hill to the green. It's a conversation-piece hole, one that will leave you talking about it or talking to yourself. The par-threes at Bristol Ridge also generate some discussion. Three of them have water hazards.

6,582 yards/par-72/72.1 rating/128 slope
Architect: Kevin Clunis
Fees: $$
Call: 715/247-3673 or 888/872-5596
Directions: From Highway 64, go 1 mile east of Somerset, turn north on County
    C and go 2 miles. Bristol Ridge is on the left.

# Hudson Golf Club
Hudson

This mature, well-conditioned, 18-hole course in this growing city offers great scenery, with many elevation changes and tree-lined holes. Because of roadwork on Interstate 94, several holes were redesigned and a new clubhouse was built in 1999. The course, which opened in 1956, is semiprivate. Fridays are the only day when the public can play all day. The course is open to nonmembers at selected times other days of the week. Be sure to call first to see if the course is available when you want to play.

6,435 yards/par-71/71.0 rating/129 slope
Fees: $$
Call: 715/386-3390.
Directions: From Interstate 94 in Hudson, take Exit 2 at Carmichael Road.
    Turn left and drive 0.5 mile and the clubhouse is on the left.

# Clifton Highlands
Prescott

The Highlands long has been popular with local and Twin Cities golfers because it's usually in good shape, has reasonable greens fees, and has challenging but fair holes. Also, in the quiet Pierce County countryside, it's miles away from the fast-paced Twin Cities and close to scenic Prescott, where the St. Croix and Mississippi Rivers meet.

The front nine has water on five holes. The key to the back nine is a series of holes—14 through 18—that circle the base of a wooded hill. The 14th is only 296 yards, but with a birch tree guarding the elevated green it can be a tough par. The 18th is a strong finishing hole, 544 yards with a dogleg at the end that requires a well-placed second shot.

Clifton Highlands opened in 1974. A scenic par-three course built on the back-nine hill is scheduled to open in June 2001.

*6,632 yards/par-72/71.8 rating/127 slope*
*Architect: Gordon Emerson*
*Fees: $$*
*Call: 715/262-5141 or 800/657-6845; Web site: www.pressenter.com/-clifland*
*Directions: From Interstate 94 in Hudson, take Exit 2. Turn right on County F*
*and drive south 13 miles. Clifton Highlands is on the left at County MM, 3*
*miles north of Prescott.*

## Other Area Courses

# Amery Golf Club
*Amery*

The Amery Golf Club opened in 1922, but it was expanded and reopened with 14 new holes in 1990. The course has some very tight and some not-so-tight holes, making for a pleasant experience. Befitting Amery's nickname, "City of Lakes," water comes into play on nine holes. The best of the water holes is 10, a fine downhill par-four with a landing area restricted by two water hazards. The green is on the banks of South Twin Lake.

*6,286 yards/par-72/69.4 rating/122 slope*
*Fees: $$*
*Call: 715/268-7213*
*Directions: On Highway 46 in Amery, turn west on County F and go 0.5 mile.*
*Course is on the left.*

# Kilkarney Hills
*River Falls*

Opened in 1994, the 18-hole layout features mature trees, rolling hills and water on six holes. After a somewhat open front nine, the back is tighter with mature hardwoods on holes 14 through 17, including water on 15, 16 and 17.

*6,434 yards/par-72/71.1 rating/121 slope*
*Fees: $$*
*Call: 715/425-8501 or 800/466-7999; Web site: www.kilkarneyhills.com*
*Directions: From Interstate 94 in Hudson, take Exit 3 and go 5 miles south on*
    *Highway 35. Turn right onto Radio Road and course is 1 mile on the left.*

# Clifton Hollow
*Prescott*

Clifton Hollow, opened in 1974, has a 6,444-yard 18-hole course and a par-three course in a parklike setting. The 18-hole course has challenging par-fives. The seventh hole is a double-dogleg, and the ninth hole is 637 yards. The course finishes with a 450-yard par-five that has a pond guarding the left side of the green. Four holes have water hazards.

*6,444 yards/par-71/70.6 rating/121 slope*
*Architect: Gordon Emerson*
*Fees: $$*
*Call: 715/425-9781 or 800/487-8879*
*Directions: From Interstate 94 in Hudson, take Exit 2 at Carmichael Road and*
    *go south on County F for 9 miles. Turn right on 820th Avenue and the*
    *course is 1 mile on the right.*

**Best Nine-Hole Course**

# New Richmond Links
*New Richmond*

Designed by Minnesota architect Joel Goldstrand and opened in 1998, this gem can be played backward or forward—they call it the South or West course, depending on the day. It's a reversible course with 10 greens and 18 tees. For example, the first fairway also is the 18th fairway. The first green also is the 17th green. It sounds confusing, but Goldstrand did such a fine job with the routing that you're not even aware another course exists right before your eyes.

Unfortunately, the course isn't reversed on the same day (a logistical nightmare with golfers going both ways), but if you plan it right, you might be able to play both courses within a two- or three-day period. The course was shaped out of gentle farmland and is a pleasant walk. The holes are nicely framed by wildflowers, prairie grasses, and a dairy farm.

*3,395, 3,332 yards/par-36, 36/rating 36.3, 35.9/slope 125, 124*
*Fees: $*
*Call: 715/243-8028*
*Directions: Go 1 mile west of New Richmond on Highway 64, turn right on*
*County K and go 0.25 mile to the clubhouse on the left.*

## More Fun Things to Do

Numerous recreational possibilities and small-town charms and many bed and breakfasts await in the valley, which includes the Minnesota side of the river and cities such as Stillwater and Afton.

Quaint downtown Hudson has antiques shops and cafes. While in town, tour the historic Octagon House, built in 1855, or the nearby Bass Lake Cheese Factory (715/247-5586). The city was founded in 1840 by two fur traders and later was named Hudson by the first mayor, who said the area reminded him of the Hudson River valley in New York.

Stillwater, the birthplace of Minnesota, has enough antiques shops, eateries, and gift shops in its preserved nineteenth-century downtown to easily fill a day. There are candy shops, used book stores, a trolley tour, a dinner train (the Minnesota Zephyr; 800/992-6100), and a historic lift bridge over the St. Croix, one of only two lift bridges left in Minnesota.

A short distance west of Hudson are dozens of big-city attractions in Minneapolis–St. Paul, including two nearby outlet malls just off Interstate 94 in Woodbury, Minnesota. Farther away is the huge Mall of America in Bloomington, Minnesota.

An excursion train begins at a 1916 depot in Osceola at the Osceola & St. Croix River Valley Railway (800/711-2591). Osceola also has the 25-foot Cascade Falls.

Take in a performance at the Northern Lakes Center for the Arts (715/268-6811) in Amery, a city ranked among the hundred best small arts towns in the nation, or at the Phipps Center for the Arts (715/386-8409) in Hudson. The New Richmond Heritage Center (715/246-3276) is in an 1884 farmhouse along with a granary, barn, one-room schoolhouse, and agriculture pavilion.

If the weather's good, there's motorboating, sailboating, fishing, hot-air balloon riding, or strolling along the St. Croix River. Boat rentals are available. Hudson and Stillwater have riverfront parks and walkways. Dinner cruises and river excursions are available on the St. Croix. The lazy Apple River in Somerset proclaims itself the tubing capital of the world, drawing thousands of tourists each summer who ride inner tubes down the shallow river. At St. Croix Falls and Taylors Falls, Minnesota, take an excursion boat ride to the falls or cool off on an alpine slide, go-cart or at a water park.

Or just take a drive. Follow the St. Croix River south to Prescott, where it empties into the Mississippi. The Great River Road on the Wisconsin side of the Mississippi begins at Prescott and goes south.

If you prefer pedaling, explore the Gandy Dancer bike trail, which begins in St. Croix Falls and goes 47 miles north to Danbury.

If you prefer slot machines or games of chance, turn east at St. Croix Falls on Highway 8 and head for St. Croix Casino and Hotel (800/846-8946) in Turtle Lake.

Six state parks are in the valley. Three are in Minnesota: Wild River (651/583-2125), Afton (651/436-5391), and William O'Brien (651/433-0500). Here are the ones in Wisconsin:

- Interstate State Park, St. Croix Falls: The oldest state park (1900) features a deep gorge, the "Dalles of the St. Croix," with breathtaking views from rock walls up to 200 feet above the river. The park is the terminus of the 1,000-mile state Ice Age Trail across Wisconsin and has an excellent interpretive center and trails. 715/483-3747.
- Kinnickinnic State Park, River Falls: It's at the confluence of the Kinnickinnic—a top-notch trout stream—and the St. Croix rivers. 715/425-1129.
- Willow River State Park, Hudson: Great views of Willow Falls and Willow River Gorge along with a nature center, a lake and a trout stream. 715/386-5931.

## For More Information

Hudson: Chamber of Commerce 715/386-8411 or 800/657-6775; www.hudsonwi.org

Osceola: Chamber of Commerce 715/555-3300 or 800/947-0581; www.OsceolaChamber.org

Prescott: Chamber of Commerce 715/262-3284; www.prescottwi.com

River Falls: Chamber of Commerce 715/ 425-2533; www.rfchamber.com

Somerset: Chamber of Commerce 715/247-3366

St. Croix Falls: Chamber of Commerce 715/483-3580; St. Croix National Scenic Riverway Visitors Center, 715/483-3284

St. Croix Valley tourism: www.uwrf.edu/scvrta

Stillwater, Minnesota: Chamber of Commerce 715/483-3580; www.ilovestillwater.com

Taylors Falls, Minnesota: Chamber of Commerce 651/257-3550; www.wildmountain.com

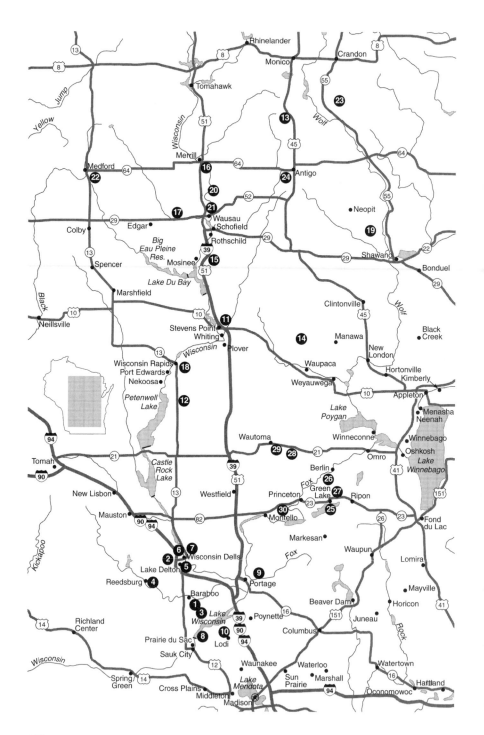

# IV

# Central Sands
# and the
# Wisconsin River

# 8

# The Wisconsin Dells
# and the Baraboo Range

Until a few years ago, the mention of golf in the Dells could get you directed to some of the fantasy "goofy golf" venues in this Midwest tourist Mecca where a pirate ship poses as a hazard. No more. Golf in the area around Wisconsin Dells and the rocky Baraboo Range has come of age. Most tourists flock to the area for the kitsch of the Dells (yes, there are fudge shops and a Ripley's museum), the water slides, and the amusement rides. Putt-putt golf, too, is one of the attractions. But now a bevy of real 18-hole courses have been built, re-created, remodeled, or rediscovered—making this a bona fide golf destination.

But long before golf and water slides, the Dells was one of the state's biggest tourist draws because of stunning natural sites such as the Dells of the Wisconsin River and Devil's Lake. The nineteenth-century photography of H. H. Bennett, who captured the beauty of the Dells in black-and-white shots still viewed in awe today, helped make it a famous place and a getaway for rich Chicagoans. A new H. H. Bennett Studio and History Center in the Dells honors the man who made these timeless shots.

In 1931, old Kilbourn City, the river community at the head of the Dells, became Wisconsin Dells to better attract tourists. In the 1950s, promoter Tommy Bartlett made water ski shows a "must" Dells experience. "Duck Boat" rides achieved similar status.

But all of those Dells attractions wouldn't be there without Mother Nature's handiwork. Native American legend has it that a huge snake created the towering, craggy, red-rock formations along the state's namesake waterway. Today's geologists say the formations were caused by rushing water from melting glaciers; the surging force eroded Cambrian sandstone.

Nearby, some of this glacial water got blocked by the Baraboo Range, forming Devil's Lake. The spring-fed lake, with no visible outlet, is surrounded by three steep, rocky bluffs and is part of a popular state park with many rustic Civilian Conservation Corps buildings from the 1930s. Devil's Lake is a favorite place for divers, anglers, rock climbers, sail-boarders, and other lovers of the great Wisconsin outdoors.

The Baraboo Range is also a unique Midwestern habitat harboring many birds and other creatures in its Appalachian-like environment. Conservancy and state park holdings are helping to preserve some of the best of nature in the best tradition of Aldo Leopold, who molded modern conservation thinking in 1935–1948 from a converted chicken coop on his Wisconsin River land downstream from the Dells.

Time slows in some parts of the Wisconsin River Valley, where eagles swoop for fish (good viewing at the Sauk City dam), where motorists still cross the river on a ferry (running from Merrimac since 1844), and where vintners craft fine wine in traditional ways (try Wollersheim Winery, on the hillside spot that was the site of grape-fermenting in the mid 1840s by Hungarian Agoston Haraszthy, who helped found the California wine industry).

Before then, white settlers clashed with Native Americans in one of the deadliest battles of the 1832 Black Hawk War (the Battle of Wisconsin Heights) and set up Fort Winnebago in 1828 to guard the important link between the Fox and Wisconsin Rivers (where Portage stands today). Before encroachment by European settlers, Native Americans lived off the bountiful resources of the area and left landmarks like the thousand-year-old, 150-foot Man Mound Effigy east of Baraboo; it's the largest human effigy in North America, but its exact purpose still is unknown. These effigies are part of a wild and wonderful place that still holds many secrets unknown to millions of tourists who come only to ride the water slides or try for birdies.

# Baraboo Country Club

*Baraboo*

Close by is the noisy honky-tonk of the Dells business district and the nostalgic shouts of circuses past at the Circus World Museum in Baraboo. But here, amid the bluffs, a walking round at Baraboo Country Club can be quiet enough to hear the cries of a hawk overhead—all the more to show respect for those who have come before us.

Several Native American Indian mounds lie on this picturesque course close to the 12th tee and begin the club's own "amen corner." If you finish this stretch with your round intact, say a little prayer of thanks to the golf gods. Number 12, a 412-yard par-four that doglegs slightly right, mandates a tee shot over a creek and the mounds. The second shot is a long one to an elevated green protected by two traps and high prairie grass. Number 13, a 202-yard par-three, is a hemmed-in hole with that same creek at the tee box. Two traps await you greenside.

Number 14 doesn't look too bad, according to the numbers: 531 yards from the back tees and only 489 from the white tees. But this double-dogleg left has enough trouble for several holes. The creek (There again! It comes into play on seven of the final nine holes.) crosses in front of the tee and runs along the left side before coming back into play in front of the big hill that's topped by the green. The second shot must find a small landing area at the base of the hill. One fairway trap and two traps at the corner, plus a severely sloping green, complete the hole from hell. This is how the card says to play it. Hit a 200-yard tee shot to the right of the fairway trap at the first dogleg. Then hit a 180-yard shot to the base of the hill in front of the creek, where the hole turns left again. Finally, hit your approach up the hill.

That's the start of a good finishing stretch. Take a breather. Fifteen is a relatively easy par-four of 341 yards. Sixteen is a tricky 163-yard par-three with trouble on the right. Seventeen is a 90-degree dogleg right measuring 398 yards; this par-four requires about a 230-yard tee shot from an elevated tee 60 feet down to the corner, and the next uphill shot has to fly the creek to get to the green, which has a sand trap on the left. Eighteen is another short par-five—only 471 yards from the back. But you have to hit a blind tee shot and avoid a creek that winds across the landing area. The creek is as close as 191 yards and as far away as 282 yards. From there, the hole doglegs right uphill to a green flanked by sand traps.

This course began with nine holes designed by Lawrence Packard and opened in 1962. Nine more, designed by Art Johnson, were added in 1989. The holes, over hilly, often wooded terrain, mix well and provide a great variety despite the short par-fives (only one over 500 yards from the blue tees).

The front has a few very good holes, too. After a series of par-four warm-up holes comes number four, a 386-yard par-four that doglegs right then sharply uphill to a severely sloping green. Then enjoy the view from the tee of five, a 175-yard par-three that plays downhill to a green protected by a large bunker on the left and big drop-offs on the other sides. Number nine, a 426-yard par-four, features a creek along the entire right side and an oval green with big trap on the left side.

The course is close to Devil's Lake State Park, giving families with competing interests the option of splitting up for the day. The course has a restaurant, lounge, and driving range.

*6,592 yards/par-72/71.4 rating/124 slope*
*Architects: E. Lawrence Packard and Art Johnson*
*Fees: $$*
*Call: 800/657-4981; Web site: www.baraboocountryclub.com*
*Directions: From Madison, take Highway 12 north. Go east on Highway 159*
   *then north on Highway 123.*

# Christmas Mountain Village
*Wisconsin Dells*

This is a golf course on the way up. For years after its 1980 opening, the Art Johnson–designed 18-hole course, amid pretty pine-studded hills and vacation homes north of the central Dells district, was shunned by many golfers because of poor maintenance.

Lately, Christmas Mountain is a surprise gift just waiting to be unwrapped. A new nine-hole addition, opened early in 2000 on the design of Atlanta's D. J. DeVictor, has been joined to nine of the original layout to form the Oaks course. It measures 6,731 yards from the back tees, and it's a good, tough course. The remaining nine holes, measuring 3,087 yards from the back tees, are dubbed the "Pines."

No matter which course you play, there's no shortage of trees—oaks or pines. You may be tempted to pay a forester to sneak onto the course and thin out some of these trees after a round at the new Christmas Mountain. But even if you did that, there'd still be lots of trouble—water, sand and many uneven lies. Play the Oaks course and see.

The Johnson-designed front Oaks nine has well-placed water hazards on five holes, including a stretch of four straight (three through six). One of the most intimidating water hazards—at least from the tee—is on four, a 396-yard par-four dogleg left with a lake along the left side and a big stand of pines along the right side. At the end is a tiny green. But six, a 422-yard slight dogleg left that goes up and then down, is probably the front nine's toughest hole because of trees on both sides, a little pond situated right in front of the green, and a sloping putting surface. Nine isn't too far back in difficulty. The 398-yard par-four dogleg left, which used to be a par-five, has water along the left side from the landing area on.

But it's the new back nine that really sparkles at Christmas Mountain, one of about 40 Bluegreen timeshare resorts. The new nine flows nicely over and around steep-sided hills used by skiers in the winter. Ten, a 523-yard par-five, offers a grand view of the Wisconsin countryside from elevated tee boxes. Big trees on the left down the hill prevent all but the biggest hitters from cutting the corner, and a group of sumacs further down the fairway on the right makes you calculate the second shot. It's followed up by a 514-yard uphill par-five that bends to the left around a huge trap. Woods on the second half of the hole increase the difficulty. Then it's farther up the hill to the pretty par-three 12 hole, which measures 208 yards from elevated tees. You feel all alone on this hole, surrounded entirely by trees.

More woods and tricky tee shots come into play until 16, a great 385-yard par-four that could be a tad unfair for high-handicappers. The tee shot is easy enough on this dogleg right—a wide fairway and equally wide rough contain all but the most errant drives. But don't hit your driver here; a drive of more than 250 yards likely would land you in a thick wetland. Rather go for position—left of the big tree on the right side. From there, you have no choice but to go up and over the wetland to a big two-tiered green. It's all carry, so use an extra club. For good measure, a sand trap guards the green at the left front.

Seventeen is a 193-yard, par-three gimmick hole—unneeded really. The green is in the shape of Wisconsin, the sand trap represents the Upper Peninsula, and the water is supposed to be Lakes Superior and Michigan. But from the slightly elevated tee, none of that is really apparent. You're left to wonder why the trap is so far out of play. What can be clearly seen, however, is the giant flag-pole behind the green, which gives you a good indication of the wind direction. (The green on 12, by the way, is shaped like Illinois.)

Number 18 is a solid finishing hole, a 364-yard par-four dramatically uphill with the fairway sloping off to the right and then over an embankment. The shallow, ele-vated green is surrounded by trees, providing a nice backdrop to the hole and a per-fect finish to Christmas Mountain's present to the Wisconsin golf community.

*6,731/par-71/72.7 rating/131 slope*
*Architect: Art Johnson (original 18); D.J. DeVictor (third nine)*
*Fees: $$$*
*Call: 608/254-3971 or 608/253-1000*
*Directions: Off Interstate 90/94, take Exit 87. Turn left on County H. Located*
    *4 miles west.*

# Devil's Head Lodge

*Merrimac*

If you've laughed off Wisconsin's ski hills as puny, just try walking a course like Devil's Head. You'll have new-found respect for the Baraboo Range. This may not be the Rockies—or even the Appalachians—but these hills are some of the closest things to mountains in Wisconsin. The rock-strewn terrain makes for good skiing in the winter and good golf the rest of the year. At this resort, there's also a network of mountain biking trails, tennis and indoor and outdoor pools.

Nature made the Baraboo Range in a day or so, according to biblical legend. Devil's Head was made in a single year, 1971. Willis Stoick, a Michigan developer who also had a hand in developing Alpine Valley near East Troy, was practically a one-man building crew. "He was the boss, and he drove the grader and the earth movers," recalled Art Johnson, who designed the golf course to a par-73.

129

"The golf course was an important part of the resort to him," Johnson said. "The area was beautiful. We were able to conserve the natural amenities. We used the rolling topography and existing woods." That's evident on the front nine— from the nifty tree-saturated second hole (a 372-yard par-four) to the breathtaking contrast between the elevated tee and fairway on the par-five fourth hole, much tougher than its 479 yards would indicate. Now, add some water—or a lot of it, in the cases of five and six. Five is a 400-yard par-four that sweeps right around woods and water, and six, a 386-yard par-four, bends in horseshoe shape around the same pond to an elevated green.

But it's the back nine that really captures the feel of this uncharacteristically rugged Midwest landscape. Check out the ski slopes to the left of the 10th fairway. Holes 11 through 15 are situated around and atop the highest part of the course, providing some of the best reasons to play Devil's Head. Eleven is a par-five with a 90-degree dogleg right after the drive. This uphill 519-yard hole has woods along the entire left side and a trio of big bunkers in front of the sloping green. The short final approach is steep, to a small green. Twelve is an uphill par-three of 201 yards to a shallow green over a deep sand trap.

The nine-hole New Richmond Links course is a lot like the weather in Wisconsin— wait a while and it will change. The course can be played forward or backward.

Numbers 13 and 14 are holes where you don't want progress in your golf game to hit a stone wall. An old, three-foot-high stone wall provides a unique hazard as it crosses both fairways and serves as a reminder that even a bad day on the golf course beats trying to farm this land. "The farmer really put a lot of backbreaking work into it, so we left it there," Johnson said. The good news is you get a free drop if the ball is within 10 yards of the wall. Even with a drop, pay attention to the signs that warn: "Beware of ricochet."

Thirteen is intimidating enough—even without The Wall. It's 449 yards from the tips. Hit downhill to the left and let the fairway carry the ball in front of the wall, about 270 yards from the tee. Then rip one to the elevated, sloping green. The uphill 515-yard par-five 14th comes back the other way. Here, the wall is close to the tee. Drive over it while avoiding trees right and left; after the drive the rest of the dogleg left opens up a bit. Fifteen is a devilishly difficult par-four of 416 yards that bends sharply right. Hit left of the marker flag atop the ridge to the far corner for the best look at the green. A shot to the right will get you in trouble with trees and remnants of the rock wall.

After the 541-yard, open par-five 16th, and the 199-yard uphill par-three 17th comes one of the state's toughest finishing holes. It measures 448-yards from the back, elevated tees. The premium drive is far down the left side. No matter where the drive, the approach must fly a large pond to a sloping green backed by a bunker and a hill.

Whew! You've just experienced alpine golf, Wisconsin style. Johnson will get a chance to improve upon his work. He has designed a new nine, the Glacier, built on the eastern bluffs of Devil's Head and providing views of Lake Wisconsin and the Wisconsin River.

*6,725 yards/par-73/71.6 rating/127 slope*
*Architect: Art Johnson*
*Fees: $$$*
*Call: 800/338-4579; Web site: www.devils-head.com*
*Directions: From Interstate 90/94, exit at Highway 78 and go south 8 miles to*
    *County DL. Turn right on DL and go to Bluff Road and the resort*
    *entrance.*

## Reedsburg Country Club
*Reedsburg*

This course, a 1924 creation updated by the old Nugent-Lohmann-Killian team, still has that out-of-the-way feel. And that's because Reedsburg Country Club still is a little out of the way for the average tourist. So just keep this our little secret, okay?

Reedsburg is a honey of a course and difficult, despite what appears to be a relatively short measurement of 6,302 yards from the back tees. This course calls for keen game management, not brawn. And if you yip with a putter in your hands, watch out. These are some of the trickiest and fastest greens around. Ample water and stands of trees complete the picture.

The course's attributes come into view on a neat stretch of holes on the front nine. Number three measures only 340 yards, but it requires utmost precision; drive with a fairway wood or long-iron to the right-center of the fairway but before the creek to give yourself an open approach. Drive left, and trees block your view. Number four, a 516-yard par-five, has tall pines on both sides and two stand traps at the green. Five is another tricky and relatively short par-four at 332 yards; again a long-iron or fairway wood off the tee is the best bet to land it in premium position on this dogleg left lined by trees. And six is a pretty par-three of 199 yards with two big traps right and two pot bunkers left. Another good water hole is 11, a 525-yard par-five dogleg right; a good drive sets up a decision: lay up or go for the green in two and risk dumping it in a creek. We say lay up and hit the short approach to this green protected by a creek in the front and two traps.

The best of Reedsburg comes together on a hole the locals call "Alligator Alley." A gator is about the only thing missing from this hole, a 391-yard par-four dogleg left from the tips. The long driver must beware because the hole narrows in the middle where trees and thick brush follow a creek. Hit a strategic shot with a long-iron or fairway wood to the bend so you can get a line on the big green, which is surrounded by three sizable traps at the top of a slight rise.

That signature hole begins a fine stretch of finishing holes. Fifteen is a 170-yard par-three over and pond and then a serpentine creek to a big green surrounded by three traps. Sixteen is a 539-yard par-five. A pond lies in front of the tee boxes, and a big tree and two fairway traps pinch the landing area at the corner of the dogleg left. Hit the second shot to the right of the big trap in the left rough. Then you should have a decent approach to the shallow green.

Number 17 is a 421-yard par-four beauty. You drive from an elevated tee downhill to the left center of the fairway, trying to avoid tree trouble on both sides. From there it's uphill to a hard-to-hold green surrounded by big, leafy trees. Eighteen, at 336 yards, is something of a letdown—until you get to the green. A big trap lies on each side of this green, which slopes steeply from back to front. It's not fun to four-putt before clubhouse spectators.

*6,302 yards/par-72/70.8 rating/130 slope*
*Architects: Dick Nugent, Bob Lohmann, and Ken Killian*
*Fees: $$$ (includes mandatory cart)*
*Call: 608/524-6000*
*Directions: Eleven miles west of Highway 12 on Highway 33 just east of*
*    Reedsburg.*

# Trappers Turn
*Wisconsin Dells*

This is the course that began a new era in Dells-area golf. Credit owner Robert Francis's vision and money for making possible a 27-hole complex that has set the standard by which all other area courses are judged. That development has been good for the golf consumer.

It all started in 1991, when the design team of North (Andy North, two-time U.S. Open champion, television commentator, and Senior Tour golfer from Madison) and Packard (Roger, son of Lawrence Packard and a fine architect in his own right) crafted an 18-hole beauty on a big parcel just off the Interstate.

Despite its location, the land and course had a distinctive "up-north" feel, featuring pines and canyons and waterways that provided a wonderfully varied golf experience. The original 18, though measuring a bit on the short side for major courses at 6,360 yards, got good reviews. And Trappers Turn kept improving.

First, course managers tinkered with the initial layout, making a very good course even better. Among the trouble spots smoothed were the picturesque 16 "canyon hole," a sharply downhill par-three where the green suffered because of a climate not suited to growing short grass. Some shade trees were cut, and big fans were brought in to help bring airflow to the green, which is wedged between rock formations. Several new greens, including one on 18, plus a few new tees and other dirt-moving added yardage and made the revamped 6,733-yard course one of the best in the state.

In spring 2000, course managers added another North-Packard nine called the Arbor course. The par-36 course measures 3,405 yards and begins on a ridge overlooking Rocky Arbor State Park. The new course carries on the themes of the first, featuring towering pines, sandstone walls, water hazards, pot bunkers, and dramatic elevation changes. A few wrinkles set it apart—the 195 par-three seven hole has a peninsula green with water short, long and right, and the 524-yard par-five eighth hole has twisty "church pew" traps. There are also some good, straightforward holes, like the 425-yard par-four dogleg right ninth hole that travels downhill to Mystic Lake, a 17-acre man-made body of water.

When you're finished playing the ninth hole at Hallie Golf Club near Eau Claire, don't walk the hill to the clubhouse. Take the cable car and enjoy the view of Lake Hallie and the Chippewa River.

The new nine complements the 3,400-yard Lake nine, centered around Mystic Lake. The opening hole is tough: the 435-yard par-four is a dogleg left with water along the right side. And the 504-yard par-five ninth hole doglegs right around Mystic Lake; complicating the approach is a stream in front of the green. Big hitters beware.

The Canyon nine measures 3,333 yards and includes the "canyon hole," a 158-yard par-three with the green down in the rocks. It's not as tough as you think because caroms often carry to the bottom, where the green lies. The two best holes begin and finish this nine. Ten, a 413-yard par-four, begins from an elevated tee and bends left around a forested hillside. A creek presents problems in several spots, winding in front of the tees, along the left then back across the fairway in front of the green.

Number 18, a 549-yard par-five, is one of the most handsome finishing holes around. Extensively reworked, 18 is now a very fair and very tough test of golf. The first shot, from a hilltop tee, has to negotiate a big pine in the middle and a bunker to the right. The landing area dips after that, bringing into play a stream that runs diagonally from the right to the left down to Mystic Lake.

Four sets of tees on all the holes provide a way to accommodate several skill levels within a foursome. And the top-notch learning facility is a good place to work out the kinks before or after a round. But unless you're a die-hard competitor, talk over the highlights of your round from a seat in the well-appointed clubhouse, where you can appreciate good food and drink and a nice view. Locker rooms are available inside, too.

The longest 18 is a combination of the Arbor nine and the Lake nine.

*6,831 yards/par-72/73.3 rating/133 slope*
*Architects: Andy North and Roger Packard*
*Fees: $$$ (includes mandatory cart)*
*Call: 800/221-TURN; Web site: www.trappersturn.com*
*Directions: Take Exit 85 off Interstate 90/94. Go east on Highway 12/16. Then take a left to the course, about 1.5 miles from the interstate exit.*

# Wilderness Resort
*Wisconsin Dells*

The owners of this place in the heart of the Dells heard the calls of "fore" at Trappers Turn and were motivated to transform the old Dell View course into a layout where the new Dells meets the old Dells head-on. The resort features water parks—one 95,000-square-foot water park outside and two inside water parks totaling 90,000 square feet. For a while, six "practice" holes were preserved from the 1920s vintage course, but those are being transformed as well into Little Links, a six-hole executive par-three course for beginners and families. Every round comes with a set of clubs to use. A new fine-dining restaurant also was added as part of the latest $8.5 million expansion and face-lift, enhancing the resort's 281 rooms and 28 villas.

The new Wilderness Woods course combines the best of both worlds in the Dells. Some of the holes are a bit tricked-up, and sometimes you might think golf is playing second fiddle to water slides. But, hey, you're in the Dells—where people have never been shy about "improving" on Nature. No windmills are present on the course, but sometimes you think this is a fantasy putt-putt course where you get to use your real clubs. Six is a 172-yard par-three that starts on a cliff with a splendid view of Lake Delton; it then drops about 40 feet to an island

A picturesque hole at the Wilderness Resort.

green surrounded by a moat. The course's signature hole and the back nine's most spectacular par-three is 12, measuring 240 yards from the elevated back tees down to the green, which is flanked by woods in the back and a big rock retaining wall and manmade ponds to the right and left.

Water, trees, and dramatic elevation changes are everywhere on this course, which puts a premium on placing the ball in usually tight landing areas. This is the kind of course where you might score better without using your woods at all. Don't fight it; have fun. The new 18th is one of the best holes. It's a 514-yard par-five dogleg right along the road with trouble lurking down the fairway. A gorge cuts across the dogleg, within driving distance for the big hitters. The approach shot is to a green protected by two ponds and framed in the background by water slides. Now that's Dells golf with a view.

*6,629 yards/par-72/73.1 rating/131 slope*
*Architect: Art Johnson*
*Fees: $$$ (includes mandatory cart)*
*Call: 608/253-4653; Web site: www.golfwildernesswoods.com*
*Directions: Use Exit 92 off Interstate 90/94 and go 2 miles east on Highway 12.*

## Other Area Courses

# Coldwater Canyon Golf Course
*Wisconsin Dells*

This golf property for years was the site of a charming 2,444-yard par-33 course that opened in 1923. The old course played a lot tougher than the yardage because of trees, dramatic elevation changes and small greens. The long-standing record on that nine: a six-under 27, shot by Hugh Byington in 1939. Another nine—with a Scottish links theme—was added in 1999.

*5,666 yards/par-70/66.5 rating/113 slope*
*Fees: $$*
*Call: 608/254-8489; Web site: www.golfcoldwater.com*
*Directions: Two miles north of Wisconsin Dells on River Road, next to Chula Vista Resort.*

# Lake Wisconsin Country Club
*Prairie du Sac*

This short course, well maintained and in a pretty spot, is always fun. Some par-fives are reachable in two, and some par-fours are reachable in one. But that doesn't mean you should try. For example, resist the temptation to go for broke on the heavily wooded 282-yard six hole on the plateau above the lake. Most fairways are tight and undulating; sloping greens demand steady hands on the putter. Try to play here in the shoulder seasons, before Memorial Day and after Labor Day, when you can linger a bit along the dammed-up part of the Wisconsin. The blue tees on the 169-yard par-three 12 hole just might be out on the island tee box, providing the perfect spot for reflection.

*5,860 yards/par-70/68.2 rating/116 slope*
*Fees: $$*
*Call: 608/643-2405*
*Directions: One mile north of Highway 60 on Golf Road.*

# Portage Country Club
*Portage*

This course goes up and down hilly, wooded terrain next to pretty Swan Lake, close to a big bend in the Wisconsin River. The only hole set along the big lake, the 242-yard par-three third hole, is worth the price of admission and worth bragging about if you get par. The course dates from 1906, when it was a five-hole layout associated with the Portage Yacht Club. In 1942, the course went to 18 holes, many of them doglegs to toughen up a relatively short course.

*6,356 yards/par-72/70.4 rating/127 slope*
*Fees: $$*
*Call: 608/742-5121*
*Directions: Five miles east of Portage on Highway 33.*

**Best Nine-Hole Course**

# Lakeland Hills Country Club
*Lodi*

This course is set high above Lodi, just across the Dane County border in Columbia County. The hillside setting provides great views (Lake Wisconsin and the Baraboo bluffs), tough sidehill lies, and turf that drains fast. Next time it rains hard, keep your tee time at Lakeland Hills.

"Nine-hole gem" is a hackneyed phrase in the golf-writing business. But Lakeland Hills fits the bill. It maintains a character matching the small town of Lodi. Lakeland Hills, established in 1962, measures only 2,899 yards and plays to a par-35. But it's one of those courses where local knowledge goes a long way. Hitting shorter, well-targeted shots to the few level spots will get you further than longer shots with no zip code.

Number one is a 272-yard hole, going slightly downhill. But out-of-bounds is to the left, the fairway slopes dramatically off to the right, and the green has more rolls than a bakery. Two and four are both par-fours measuring under 370 yards. But they dogleg sharply to the right, and big pines are at the corners to snare your ball and block your second shot.

Perhaps the toughest hole is the 373-yard seven hole, laid out across a steep right-to-left slope. Hit a drive over the hill and hope you're far enough for a level lie. Even with a good lie the shallow green is hard to hit. Nearby you'll see an old brown church steeple without the church. Theories abound about how it got there; nevertheless, it's now a course landmark.

Eight is a mere 293-yard par-four. But it's very tight, with a steep hillside to the left and trees near the driving area. The regulars tee off with a long-iron. No matter where you put your tee shot, you'll likely have a blind second shot over a ridge. And the course ends with a tricky 128-yard par-three lined by towering oaks on both sides. Now go around again. You may have played it once already. But the locals say the back nine is always tougher at Lakeland Hills.

*2,899 yards/par-35/34.1 rating/122 slope*
*Fees: $$*
*Call: 608/592-3757*
*Directions: Located on the west side of Lodi. Follow the signs from the downtown.*

## More Fun Things to Do

Some groups of golfers and nongolfers, no doubt, will want to sample gambling at the Dells. The local tribe in charge is the Ho-Chunk Nation, which operates one of Wisconsin's biggest and most profitable casinos in Lake Delton. 800/746-2486.

Fine Wisconsin wine? That is not an oxymoron. Go to the Wollersheim Winery in Prairie du Sac along the Wisconsin River. A pleasant venue for tasting the fruit of the vine. Go to www.wollersheim.com or call 800/VIP-WINE.

Train buffs will whistle with joy during visits to the Mid-Continent Railway Museum in Freedom (go to www.mcrwy.com or call 608/522-4261) and Riverside & Great Northern Railway (608/254-6367). Train rides available at both locations.

Some Dells family attractions are outlined below, because that's probably why you're in the area. But let's concentrate on the natural attractions first. State parks and trails abound.

- Devil's Lake State Park, Baraboo. Bluffs of 500 feet tower above a glittering 360-acre lake. Camping and many trails, including a segment of the Ice Age Trail. 608/356-8301.
- Mirror Lake State Park, Baraboo. Except for the hum of the interstate, you'd think you were in far northern Wisconsin. Camping, swimming, and trails. 608/254-2333. A Frank Lloyd Wright–designed cottage also is available to rent, but it fills up quickly. 608/254-6551.
- Rocky Arbor State Park, Baraboo. Just 1.5 miles from the heart of the Dells. Features camping and nice trails among pine-studded sandstone bluffs. 608/254-8001.
- The 400 State Trail, a 22-mile bike or hiking trail between Reedsburg and Elroy featuring rock outcroppings along the Baraboo River. Connects to the Elroy-Sparta, Hillsboro, and Omaha trails. 608/337-4775.

Nature-lovers of all ages will marvel at the work done at the International Crane Foundation, which preserves endangered cranes. Fifteen crane species displayed. 608/356-9462.

Kids of all ages will enjoy the Dells amusements, too. On a very hot and humid Wisconsin day, what's better than sliding down a chute into a pool of cold water? It could be better than sweating over your golf game. The Dells water parks—indoors and out—are proliferating at such a rate we can't list them all here. Call Dells tourism central at 800/22-DELLS or visit the Web site (www.wisdells.com).

For a different water experience, board one of the Ducks for river tours aboard amphibious World War II landing crafts. Available at two venues: Original Wisconsin Ducks (go to www.wisdells.com/ducks or call 608/254-8751) and Dells Duck Tours (go to ducksrfun@dells.net.com or call 608/254-6080).

A visit to the Dells wouldn't be complete without seeing the Tommy Bartlett Thrill Show. The late promoter helped put the Dells on the map with his show featuring professional water-skiers and daredevils. Go to www.tommybart lett.com or call 608/254-2525. If you've never taken your kid to the circus, go to Baraboo's Circus World Museum. You'll marvel at the world's largest collection of antique circus wagons and other memorabilia, and the kids will love the circus performances (608/356-8341).

## For More Information

Baraboo: 800/227-2266; www.baraboo.com/chamber
Portage: 800/474-2525
Reedsburg: 800/844-3507; www.reedsburg.com
Sauk-Prairie Area: 800/68-EAGLE; www.saukprairie.com
Wisconsin Dells: 800/22-DELLS; www.wisdells.com
Dells and Lake Delton: 800/94-DELLS; www.dells-delton.com

# 9

# Stevens Point, Wisconsin Rapids, Wausau, and Antigo

The Wisconsin River has been called one of the hardest-working rivers in the country. Every ounce of water, it seems, is put to some kind of use. Many dams, paper mills, power plants and other concerns use the river as an industrial resource—in stark contrast to the lower, free-flowing part of the river below Prairie du Sac that's become a state recreation area. But the upper Wisconsin River region is a great recreational playland, too, and the miles of scenic, rolling and sometimes hilly countryside on either side of the great river provide a perfect landscape for golf. While the river works, why not play?

You can do a lot of exploring and pleasant sightseeing on your way between golf courses in this region, served by Highways 51 and 29 and a network of county roads that takes you to some of the most pleasantly out-of-the-way places in Wisconsin. Here are a few of them:

- Poniatowski, the exact center of the northern half of the western hemisphere at 45 degrees north, 90 degrees west. See the marker and register your visit in the historic Gesicki Tavern.
- Timm's Hill, between Medford (the original home of Tombstone Pizza) and Prentice. It's Wisconsin's highest point at 1,952 feet. Go to the top for a great view.
- Colby, home of the famous cheese.
- Neillsville, site of Wisconsin's Vietnam Veterans' Memorial Park. A dove-shaped effigy mound honors the war's prisoners of war (POWs) and soldiers missing in action (MIAs). Thousands of motorists pass another war memorial, to Wisconsin's Korean War vets, while driving Highway 51 south of Plover.
- Iola, a Norwegian settlement and old mill town that has come back from a 1999 fire that gutted a half-dozen century-old buildings on Main Street. In 1994, *Wisconsin Trails* magazine named it "Wisconsin's Best Norman Rockwell Small Town."
- Rural, a mid-nineteenth-century Yankee settlement on the Crystal River. Seemingly frozen in time, this community lives up to its name.

- The Dells of the Eau Claire River, south of Highway 52 between Antigo and Wausau. This 190-acre park preserves rare plants and geology. While the Wisconsin Dells is often hidden by the glare of amusements, this dells is still much like it was centuries ago.

Explore and golf. Along the way you'll see cows, barns, and silos. Marathon County, around Wausau, has the most dairy cows of any county in the state—64,000 at last count. You'll see acres of shaded ginseng fields. Marathon County also is the world's largest producer of the medicinal plant so prized in the Far East. In Marathon City, Chinese letters on store fronts remind you that ginseng is bound for a faraway market.

And you'll see pounds and pounds of potatoes growing in the Antigo silt loam. The official state soil, named for the city that serves as the Langlade County seat, is left over from the great glacial melt-off. The glaciers melted and left rich "potato flats" to the south and west of the ridge that marks the ice sheet's terminal moraine, its final advance. That great melt-off also provided the network of streams and rivers that provide a lot of the good scenery—and many of the water hazards—you'll encounter when golfing in central Wisconsin.

# SentryWorld
*Stevens Point*

The invitation to the June 13, 1982, inaugural of this course came from John W. Joanis, the president of Sentry Insurance Co. He called the opening "an important day for Sentry Insurance and an important day for me."

It also was an important day for Wisconsin golf, because the opening of Sentry-World paved the way for a rush of big-time courses by name designers. Over the next 20 years, Wisconsin golf would be transformed by Joanis' quest to put Stevens Point and Sentry on the map. And over that time, the Robert Trent Jones Jr.-designed SentryWorld would remain one of the state's top courses (it was ranked fourth in the state by *Golf Digest* in 2000). It's a fitting tribute to Joanis, a man who had a penchant for doing things in a big way. It's said he wanted "instant tradition" with this golf course. He got it. Jones, the designer, once called this course "very possibly my Mona Lisa." And SentryWorld is a course that can be held up as a work of art. Could Leonardo da Vinci have painted a prettier picture than the one the golfer sees at the Flower Hole?

Sixteen, a 173-yard par-three that starts a great finishing stretch at Sentry-World, is worth the price of admission. The shot is to a green surrounded by flower beds full of forty-five thousand individual annuals. A shot into the flowers

The signature 16th at SentryWorld.

is treated like a shot into a water hazard. But even without the flowers, this is a very good golf hole. The large, slightly elevated green is also protected by three artistically shaped traps. And the heart-shaped putting surface slopes significantly from back to front. The Flower Hole was Joanis's idea. But Jones crafted it with his artistic touch. "When a course is properly done, there's a completeness to the theme. SentryWorld is the flower theme—low-lying, relatively flat course, lakes, flowers, and rocks," Jones said at the time. "I let the land reveal its secrets to me and then design to the land."

The Flower Hole is the opener in a trio of fine finishing holes that combine beautiful landscaping and terrific golf. Seventeen is a testy, tree-lined downhill dogleg right—a 412-yard par-four that tempts the big driver into trouble. Hit a good drive, and the second shot still gets your knees shaking a bit. The approach must negotiate a narrow opening formed by a pond on the right and trees on the left. A trap sits at the back for good measure.

The 18th, a brawny, 448-yard par, is uphill all the way and leaves you gasping— at your big score and for your breath. The dogleg left starts out of a chute of trees over a streamlet. The hole becomes progressively more open, but then sand takes the place of trees. Nine traps, four at the green, populate this hole. This kind of daring design was very uncommon at the time for Wisconsin. Thus was Joanis's quest for "instant tradition." It didn't come cheap. A globe-trotting,

14-handicapper who died in 1985, Joanis spent an estimated $10 million in corporate funds to transform 270 acres of swamp and woodland into a golf course and sports complex enjoyed by company employees and visitors. So what if some state insurance regulators saw it as endangering the company's financial health?

"He had an ego the size of King Kong," Lee Sherman Dreyfus once said of Joanis, his long-time friend. Dreyfus, a former governor, worked briefly for Sentry after leaving the governor's mansion in 1982. "It's the kind of course God would have created had He had the money," Dreyfus joked. "It was his baby," recalled former course superintendent Bill Roberts. "John Joanis wanted the best golf course he could get. The only thing he couldn't get was 50 years of tradition."

SentryWorld opened amid much hoopla in the summer of 1982. "This course was built to make a profit, and it will be operated to make a profit," Joanis crowed to the press at the opening. Joanis also sought to bring a major pro tournament to the course. That has yet to happen, in part because Stevens Point, while centrally located, is a big drive from the big population centers of Milwaukee, Green Bay, and Madison. Joanis probably didn't help things when he laid down his own rules. "But I would be careful about bringing in an event," Joanis said. "The course must stay as it was built. If anybody touches that course, I'll break his head."

That didn't apply to Joanis, of course. He reversed the numbering of the holes after the course opened, presumably to better showcase the Flower Hole to television audiences. Alas, the major tournament has yet to arrive. Consider it the pros' loss and your gain. Fortunately, Jones designed the course to give high-handicappers a break—at least on distance. The course ranges from 6,951 yards to 5,197 yards. No matter what the yardage, you'll have the experience of playing in a well-kept arboretum where deer, geese, and other wildlife abound. Flowers mix with a forest of birch, pine, and hardwoods, and granite boulders blasted free during construction. An extraordinary number of sprinkler heads (some four thousand in all) help keep everything green and growing.

There's also plenty of water in hazard form. Thirty-five acres of open water became part of Jones' design, and the main lake and a connecting stream come into play on five holes—three, four, five, 12, and 13. Augmenting the water hazards are some 80 sand traps. Water and sand come into prominent play on two of the back nine holes. Twelve, a 223-yard par-three, mandates a tee shot over part of the big lake. It's all carry. Two traps also guard the green on this pretty hole. The 13th hole, a 395-yard par-four, follows the inside of the lake's curving shoreline. This big dogleg right would seem to favor a big tee shot over two sprawling traps at the corner. But with the narrow fairway framed by trees and water on the left, and sand and trees on the right, the best shot is a smart one of about 200 yards to the elbow of the dogleg. From there, it's a full shot to a green protected by water on the left front and sand in the back.

On the front nine, the 507-yard fifth hole is another great sand and water hole. Here, a narrow band of fairway horseshoes from right to left around water and a small island. Traps and trees lie along the outside perimeter of the horseshoe, requiring three good shots to get to the two-tiered green. More subtle, but just as tough, is the 502-yard par-five ninth hole. A stream cuts diagonally across the driving area, requiring most golfers to lay up with an iron. Then it's another iron to the tree-lined dogleg. From there, it's a touchy short-iron over the same stream to a smallish, trapped green. Take your par gladly here.

And so it goes all around the course. Seldom, if ever, is there a shot that you don't have to think about. That didn't come about by accident. Jones, who became friends with Joanis, credits the insurance executive for many of the ideas that went into SentryWorld. "John is co-author," Jones once said. "We did it with the soles of our feet." So, slip into your Footjoys, and follow their footsteps on this great central Wisconsin course.

*6,951 yards/par-72/74.5 rating/144 slope*
*Architect: Robert Trent Jones II*
*Fees: $$$*
*Call: 715/345-1600*
*Directions: Take Exit 161 off of Interstate 39; located at 601 North Michigan*
   *Avenue east of Business Highway 51.*


# Lake Arrowhead

*Nekoosa*

For years, Lake Arrowhead was the best Wisconsin course most seldom played. That's changing with the addition of a new top-flight course and the development of this pinelands as a weekend retreat for city-dwellers in Madison and beyond. But before Memorial Day and after Labor Day, you can still hear the whistle of golf balls among the whispering pines in relative quiet. It's a bit like the sandhills region around Pinehurst, North Carolina, but without the tradition that comes with a resort founded in the early 1900s. In fact, there's a Pinehurst Drive in the development.

The history of Lake Arrowhead, named for a nearby 300-acre lake, dates back only to the 1970s. A golf course was always planned for the development, but money problems kept the initial developer, N. E. Isaacson, from following

Going for the green at Lake Arrowhead. Photo courtesy of Gary Knowles.

through. Under new ownership, the course was built—one nine at a time—for a relative bargain of less than $1 million, according to former course superintendent Jeff Parks. Clearing of the land began in the fall of 1979, and Parks came on board the following spring. The design by one-time partners Ken Killian and Dick Nugent required relatively little major landscaping (the sandy soil provided easy drainage), and the first nine opened for play in 1982. Course managers liked what they saw and gave Parks the go-ahead for the second nine. "The front nine was a learning experience. Once the seeding took place, it was my baby," Parks said. "They gave me a free hand on the back." The second nine opened in 1985, but for years after, the home sites along the course sold slowly. And oftentimes a camper parked in the pines marked the spot of a future home.

But as golfers discovered the lush fairways, large undulating greens, sculptured bunkers, natural sandy areas, and tall pines, the lots got bought up by retirees and commuters from Wisconsin Rapids and Nekoosa. The development has matured, with new and spacious houses—vacation and primary homes—erected along the smooth, curving roads. The handsome clubhouse—complete with pro shop, pool, locker rooms, and restaurant—now is a bustling place. Property owners have access to two swimming pools, a beach on Lake Arrowhead, tennis courts and discounted greens fees.

The development added a new course in August of 1998. Killian did this job on his own, and the new course was dubbed the Lakes. It has a separate clubhouse about three miles from the original clubhouse. Venture past the new clubhouse going west, and you get the feeling you're in the middle of nowhere, far from the beaten path. You are. Luckily, though, great golf is close at hand.

## *Pines Course*

The feeling of seclusion remains, despite the home building that has taken place over the 130 wooded acres where this course is situated. Tee off on the fifth hole, and you'll get that secluded feeling. The fairway of the 388-yard par-four doglegs slightly to the right and then to the left. At the first bend, on the right, there's a trap that runs for more than 70 yards along the driving area—making it one of the toughest driving holes on the course. At the second bend, on the left, lies a big, sandy waste area. Just ahead is a narrow opening to the 36-yard-long green, bounded on both sides by some of the course's fifty-plus sand areas.

Water hazards complement sand and trees several times on the Pines course, when three man-made ponds come into play. The smallest pond comes into play on the pretty 140-yard par-three fourth hole, featuring a tricky downhill tee shot over water to a narrow green backed up by two sand traps and trees.

Numbers nine and 10 use the second pond very well—maybe too well. Nine, a 516-yard par-five, is perhaps the course's premier hole. It runs slightly downhill at the beginning, then sweeps right to left for 516 yards around the water to a big green, framed on the left by water and a little beach and on the right by two traps. You risk a lot by trying to reach this green in two shots. Ten, a 381-yard par-four, uses the opposite shoreline. Water is to the left on the drive. Further up the fairway, three sand traps are spread along the right side. The green has more sand on its right and left. Then it's into the pines and oaks, until 13 (a 358-yard par-four) and 14 (a 195-yard par-three). These are two good holes located in a burned-over area. An out-of-control campfire burned over the area in the spring of 1980, when the holes were being designed. What remains is a recovering forest amid meadow grasses.

Fifteen is a tree-lined 413-yard par-four that leans at the end to the left, where a huge bunker lurks. Numbers 16 and 17 use the third pond; 16 (a 521-yard par-five) has water on the right side from 170 yards on in, and 17 (a 162-yard par-three) has water along the entire right-hand side. You're best to shoot to the middle of the green on both approaches, no matter where the flag is planted. Eighteen is a strong finishing hole of 460 yards. This par-four has a 55-yard bunker on the outside corner of the dogleg left. Get past that, and it's a long-iron or fairway wood to a two-tiered green protected by three substantial bunkers.

*6,624 yards/par-72/72.1 rating/132 slope*
*Architects: Ken Killian and Dick Nugent*
*Fees: $$*
*Call: 715/325-2929; Web site: www.lakearrowheadgolf.com*
*Directions: Located 13 miles south of Wisconsin Rapids on Highway 13; 35*
*    miles north of Wisconsin Dells.*

## *Lakes Course*

This course is aptly named. Eight little lakes lie throughout the oak and pine forest, making for nice fairways, nice home sites and one of the toughest courses in the state. Water is first encountered on the second hole, a straightaway par-four of 399 yards. The lake lies on the left and complicates approach shots from 100 yards in. More water is on three, a 174-yard par-three that intimidates golfers with a tee shot over a wide pond. For good measure on this signature hole, Killian added a water-fall, which tumbles over rocks to the right and behind the large green.

Big sandy waste areas, tight fairways, and woods are the other trademarks of this course. You get the first taste of that on the 524-yard, par-five fourth hole, which begins with a drive over a big waste area in front of the tees. More sand is along the first part of the fairway to the left. The right side is lined with trees. And another big trap stretches along the entire front of the green. Seven also seems to have as much sand as grass. This 197-yard downhill par-three demands the golfer launch one over a big waste area to a back-to-front sloping green guarded by four traps along the front.

After these two holes, water looks pretty good. If that's your mindset, look forward to 12 and 18, which have two ponds each. The 12th hole is a 537-yard par-five that ends at a green with a "beach bunker" lapped by pond water. The 18th is a double-dogleg 448-yard par-four that demands everything you've got. One pond lies to the right of the driving area. The other one lies to the left from about 130 yards in to the deep, two-tiered green. The best approach may be to the mounded bailout area to the right of the green. A bogey may be a very good score if you're playing into the wind.

*7,105 yards/par-72/74.8 rating/140 slope*
*Architect: Ken Killian*
*Fees: $$$*
*Call: 715/325-2929; Web site: www.lakearrowheadgolf.com*
*Directions: Located 13 miles south of Wisconsin Rapids on Highway 13, 35*
    *miles north of Wisconsin Dells.*

## Other Area Courses

Here are nine courses in central Wisconsin—several just a step below the caliber of the courses at SentryWorld and Lake Arrowhead—offering some of the best bargains in the state.

# Antigo–Bass Lake Country Club
*Deerbrook*

For years this course, built in two stages, was truly a hidden gem. Now it's a polished one. Located north of Antigo on the fringes of the great Wisconsin North Woods, this course offered good and affordable golf amid splendid scenery. Earl Porter designed the back nine in the 1920s. Roger Packard designed the front nine in the 1960s. And Jerry Matthews, the Michigan designer, in 2000 meshed the two designs while lengthening the course, building a fourth set of tees, reshaping old bunkers, building new sand traps, adding strategic mounding, building new greens on 15 and 16, and adding new or enlarged water hazards on holes one, three, nine, and 16.

Depending on how it all turns out, the new Antigo–Bass Lake CC could move into this region's top tier. The course would remain a par-71, but it would grow from 6,166 yards to 6,340 yards. Stop and see for yourself. The drive to the course alone is worth the trip.

*6,340 yards/par-71*
*Architects: Earl Porter (back nine), Roger Packard (front nine), Jerry*
    *Matthews (redesign)*
*Fees: $$*
*Call: 715/623-6196*
*Directions: Take Highway 45 for 16 miles north of Antigo, go 4 miles west on*
    *County B.*

# Glacier Wood Golf Club
*Iola*

This is a course that has been nurtured with community pride. In 1966, Iola built itself a nine-hole track called Iola Community Golf Course. In May 1999, three years after the start of a $350,000 fund-raising drive helped by a big donation from national hobby magazine publisher Krause Publications, nine holes were added and Glacier Wood was born.

The course, now a par-71, has four new holes on the front nine (five through eight) and six new holes on the back nine (11 through 16). The last great glacier certainly left evidence it was here. Massive boulders, found during construction, often line edges of fairways. Boy, talk about funny bounces.

The most talked-about hole usually is the new 12th hole, a 180-yard par-three that plays over a wetland to a green guarded by a big bunker on the right. Trees surround the hole, which also features a wooden bridge that crosses a trail where ox once hauled lumber. The wetland featured on this hole also comes to play on the pretty—and pretty tough!—par-five 15th hole, which horseshoes left to right 535 yards around the swamp.

*6,531 yards/par-71/71.6 rating/130 slope*
*Fees: $$*
*Call: 715/445-3831*
*Directions: Take Highway 161 east from Stevens Point to Iola, go right on*
*Highway 49 for a very short distance, then left on Water Street.*

# Indianhead Golf Club
*Mosinee*

Don't be thrown off by the entrance to Indianhead. Off Interstate 39, past the Central Wisconsin Airport, then through the industrial park. But this is a choice piece of land offering great views on the high point and a feeling of isolation on the wooded holes.

Indianhead offers easy access and good golf. The course started in 1970 with a front nine designed by Max Norris. Bob Lohmann later did a major redesign, taking the course to 18 holes and a whole new level of golf. From atop the hill, where the clubhouse sits, you can see Granite Peak at Rib Mountain State Park and the smokestacks of Wisconsin River paper mills. The front nine is open, running over old farm fields and past pods of brush and little ponds. Part of an old silo still stands between the practice range and the eighth tee. The back nine is

149

## AUTHORS' FAVORITES: CLUBHOUSES

Plum Lake, Sayner. A pretty lake and an old, comfortable log lodge club-house.

Tagalong, Birchwood. Quiet, historic and relaxing.

Trout Lake, Arbor Vitae. Every porch should be like this one.

Forest Hills, La Crosse. Country club atmosphere below a grand bluff.

Lakewoods Forest Ridges, Cable. Ask for a window seat overlooking Lake Namekagon.

St. Germain Whitetail Inn, St. Germain. This is some log cabin! Check out the antler chandeliers.

Eagle Springs Golf Resort, Eagle. Yes, that's a tree growing through the roof of the clubhouse.

Washington County Golf Course, Hartford. You're almost as close to heaven as you would be on Holy Hill to the south.

Whistling Straits, north of Kohler. Nothing beats having a refreshment before the roaring fire in the Irish manor—except the golf.

almost entirely wooded, except for 18, a 383-yard par-four that goes straight uphill to the small green by the clubhouse.

*6,530 yards/par-72/71.3 rating/129 slope*
*Architects: Max Norris; Bob Lohmann (redesign)*
*Fees: $$*
*Call: 715/693-6066*
*Directions: Exit Interstate 39, go east on Highway 153, turn left across from the airport and go through the industrial park.*

# Merrill Golf Club
*Merrill*

Mulligan's Supper Club gets top billing at the entrance, but don't let that deter you from playing Merrill Golf Club. This is a pleasant course on a plateau above the Wisconsin River and Riverside Park, where there's a boat launch, picnic area, and playground. Unfortunately, you don't get any river views on the course. But it's still a pretty track.

This well-maintained course, dating back to 1926 on a Tom Vardon design, was updated in 1992. Eleven new holes—mostly on the back nine—were added. Four, a downhill 468-yard par-five with an approach over water, and five, a neat 405-yard par-four dogleg right with water, trees, and an uphill approach, are the new holes on the front nine. They mix surprisingly well with the old holes, such as the roller-coaster eight, a 423-yard par-four to a small green protected by sand. The trees along the right side of this hole mark the steep hillside down to the Wisconsin River. But you'd have to be a pretty wild hitter to get one in that water hazard.

*6,456 yards/par-72/70.8 rating/121 slope*
*Fees: $*
*Call: 715/536-2529*
*Directions: South of downtown across the bridge. Go to the top of the rise, then 3 blocks east of County K on O'Day.*

# Pine Valley
*Marathon*

This course is far from *the* Pine Valley, the exclusive and ultratough course in the pinelands of New Jersey. But this Pine Valley, in ginseng and cow country west of Wausau, is worth a visit if you're in the area. Golf probably doesn't rate as the number one recreational pursuit in these parts—the local bowling center sign proclaimed it's "never too early to sign up" for leagues. Maybe that means it's easier to get a tee time at this course, opened in 1969. The front nine is a lot shorter than the back—2,893 yards at par-35 compared to 3,273 yards at par-36. But the front nine has more trees and more chances to drop the golf ball into water. Creek water crosses six holes on the front nine and parallels another.

The back nine is more open and features a 588-yard par-five, 14. To make things even more difficult, the fairway slopes from left to right and there's out-of-bounds left. Eighteen is a short but tricky hole. The 298-yard par-four doglegs 90 degrees to the right. The uphill approach is to a small green situated in a grove of trees.

*6,166 yards/par-71/69 rating/118 slope*
*Architect: Larry Lohr*
*Fees: $*
*Call: 715/443-2848*
*Directions: Go west from Wausau on Highway 29 for 6 miles. North of highway.*

# The Ridges
*Wisconsin Rapids*

If you're making a trip to play the courses at SentryWorld and Lake Arrowhead, this course is the perfect stopping-off point when driving between the two featured course sites.

The Ridges' back nine would give a claustrophobic fits. You find out what's in store on 10, where you tee off of a ledge by the clubhouse. The fairway is 80 feet below, with Buena Vista Creek meandering along the right-hand side. It's 201 yards to the preferred landing spot at the dogleg of the 334-yard par-four right-to-left hole. Trees—white birch, green willows, and towering pines—stand where water doesn't. Water also comes into play on heavily wooded holes to follow—12 (a 291-yard straight-away par-four), 13 (a 507-yard par-five that veers right), and 14 (a 361-yard par-four that doglegs at a right angle around a pond).

The relatively flat and open front nine came first in 1963. It has been toughened up since 1996 with new sand traps and water hazards. Trees are present but not nearly as many as on the back nine. While on the short side, the Ridges is a tough little course. A comfortable bar-restaurant, overlooking number 10 and the forest below, offers a nice place to reflect on the round and see how others fare at the start of the back nine.

*6,289 yards/par-72/71.3 rating/129 slope*
*Architect: John Murgatroyd*
*Fees: $$*
*Call: 715/424-3201*
*Directions: About 1.5 miles east of Highway 13 on Griffith Avenue on the*
*     south side of Wisconsin Rapids, just past the entrance to Nepco Lake*
*     County Park.*

# Pine Hills Golf Course and Casino
*Gresham*

Don't be fooled by the name. The new casino-hotel complex is definitely an important part of this resort run by the Stockbridge-Munsee Band of the Mohicans (715/793-4270). But it doesn't overshadow the golf course, a fun 18-hole track built in the late 1990s on the site of a 1960s vintage course. The tribe became the first Wisconsin tribe to own and operate a golf course. The reason? Tourism.

The resort course goes up and down and twists and turns around wooded terrain above Big Lake. You can see this beautiful lake in the fall from the green on two, a 375-yard par-four. Mostly though, you see beautiful stands of pines, maples, oaks, and birch—a mixture due to the course's location at the fringe of the great North Woods. This fairly short course has several blind shots and features more bells than most new courses. But it's a fun ride. The front nine uses several of the holes from the old course, and it's more open. The back nine is much different—cut through the forest with a feeling of seclusion on each hole. Eighteen, all uphill, ends at a three-tiered green. The 350-yard par-four plays like 450 yards. Don't bet on par.

*6,141 yards/par-72*
*Architect: Robert Graves*
*Fees: $*
*Call: 715/787-3778*
*Directions: From Highway 29, take County U to County A to Gresham, then take County G north to Big Lake Road, and follow that around the lake.*

# Trapp River Golf Course
*Wausau*

The address says Wausau, but this course is closer to Brokaw, site of a significant paper mill on the Wisconsin River. After passing the paper mill, you go up a big rise on County WW above the river valley and enter rolling, wooded countryside. That's where you'll find the Trapp River and the course named for it. The course, opened in 1968, is fairly open with few traps. But it has nice stands of pines and aspens—and the Trapp River, of course. The river comes into play on the opening holes of each nine. Golfers hit over the river on the drive at the 341-yard par-four first hole. The 10th hole, a 416-yard par-four, is a slight dogleg right that goes down to the river and then uphill to the green.

*6,335 yards/par-72/69.3 rating/116 slope*
*Fees: $*
*Call: 715/675-3044*
*Directions: On Interstate 39 about 5 miles north of Wausau, turn east on County WW and go for 8 miles.*

### Best Nine-Hole Courses

This part of the state could be the last, best place to experience the solid nine-hole course that aspires to be nothing more. These nine-hole courses are established, well-run courses where a two-hour Sunday afternoon walking round survives, despite the march of progress.

# American Legion Golf Course
*Wausau*

This is an oldie but a goodie. This course, opened in 1928, is in a hilly section northeast of town. It has no par-fives, and only plays to a par-34, but it has some very tough holes. One of the best is five, a 138-yard par-three over water to a severely elevated green. Two of the seven par-fours measure over 400 yards. A pleasant patio awaits after the round, and the Sylvan Hill Park occupies the ridge above the course.

*2,821 yards/par-34/18-hole rating of 65/101 slope*
*Fees: $$*
*Call: 715/675-3663*
*Directions: Take the Bridge Street exit off of Interstate 39, go to North 6th Street, then to Golf Club Road.*

# Black River Golf Club
*Medford*

This course, opened in 1992, is a lovely track just south of the town made famous by Tombstone Pizza. Woods and the Black River come into play. The par-35 course is well-bunkered with water hazards on four holes and challenging greens. A new clubhouse is planned for 2001.

*3,043 yards/par-35/18-hole rating of 70/119 slope*
*Architect: Art Johnson*
*Fees: $$*
*Call: 715/748-5520*
*Directions: On the south side of Medford. Turn east on County O, and the course is about 1 mile on the right.*

# Maplewood Golf Course
*Pickerel*

In winter, the combination post office, restaurant, and bar is a pit stop for snowmobilers. The rest of the year, it's the clubhouse for a golf course that will only get better with age. Big Twin Lake, several glacial pothole wetlands, and a bevy of new trees are the markers on this newer, well-conditioned layout. Water comes into play on seven of the nine holes. Number nine looks easy at 281 yards, but two ponds pinch the fairway near the green.

*3,113 yards/par-36/18-hole rating of 68.6/109 slope*
*Fees: $$*
*Call: 715/484-4653*
*Directions: Located 10 miles south of the Mole Lake Casino on Highway 55.*

# Riverview Golf Course
*Antigo*

Located amid the "potato flats" west of Antigo, this course is surprisingly hilly, wooded, and full of water hazards, thanks to the Eau Claire River. The east and west branches of the river junction on the course before flowing downstream through the Dells of the Eau Claire. One of the prettiest par-threes in these parts is eight, which requires an all-carry tee shot of 152 yards over the river and embankment to a green flanked by big trees.

*3,131 yards/par-36/18-hole rating of 69.8/119 slope*
*Fees: $$*
*Call: 715/623-2663*
*Directions: Four miles west of Antigo, just south of Highway 64.*

## More Fun Things to Do
Exploring the great outdoors could be a full-time pastime in these parts. There's good trout fishing throughout the region—the Prairie River, for example, near Merrill has easy access. If you're in the mood to bushwhack, try fishing in the many, remote spring ponds, where brook trout thrive. The area's many lakes provide good fishing for bass, walleyes, panfish, and other warm-water species.

The Wolf River—loved by trout fishers and whitewater rafters alike—is only about a half-hour east of Antigo. For more placid waters, try canoeing the Plover River near Stevens Point. It's also a trout stream.

Many hiking and biking trails are available. For mountain biking, try the Nicolet National Forest (call the Lakewood Ranger Station at 715/276-6333). If road biking is your desire, just take off on the area's many lightly traveled country roads. Hike the Ice Age Trail or the trails in several of the fine county parks.

Rather take a stroll? Walk through downtown Iola, see the historic buildings (the old mill dates to 1860), and get an ice cream treat at Briq's Soft Serve—"Home of the 1 Pound Cone."

Or how about a blast from the past? Take in a drive-in movie at Wausau's Sky-Vue theater. Fewer than 10 drive-in theaters in Wisconsin still show movies on the really big screen. A devoted drive-in movie buff has information at his Web site: www.execpc.com/~andyhil/index.htm.

In Stevens Point, stroll the University of Wisconsin–Stevens Point grounds, the downtown historic district, or the trails at the Schmeeckle Reserve. The 220-acre reserve also is home to the Wisconsin Conservation Hall of Fame (call 715/346-4992). Beer-lovers must visit the Stevens Point Brewery for a "Point," the local brew. Tour and tasting information at www.pointbeer.com or 800/369-4911.

In nearby Wisconsin Rapids, find all about the papermaking industry, which dates back to the 1830s. The former Consolidated Papers complex occupies a giant slice of the downtown along the river. Consolidated in 2000 was bought up by a Finnish papermaking giant, Stora Enso Oyj. Call 715/422-3789 for tour information.

Wausau promotes several cultural and historical attractions: the Center for Visual Arts, exhibiting art work of local and regional artists, 715/842-4545; the Leigh Yawkey Woodson Art Museum, art of the natural world, 715/845-7010; the Grand Theater, a restored 1927 vaudeville house, 715/842-0988; and the Marathon County Historical Museum, located in the well-maintained Victorian home of lumber baron Cyrus Yawkey, 715/848-6143.

Take the mystery out of the ginseng industry. Tour an operating ginseng farm. Contact Hsu's Ginseng Enterprises in Wausau at 715/675-2325.

Explore the Mead Wildlife Area, a 27,653-acre preserve used primarily for waterfowl and deer hunting and wildlife viewing. Start at the new visitors center being built near Mosinee. McMillan Marsh, a 6,500-acre preserve on Marsh-field's north side, is a short drive away.

Other state nature properties:

- Council Grounds State Park, Merrill (715/536-8773). Located at the site of an annual Ojibwa gathering spot. Later, lumberjacks sorted floating logs and sent them to sawmills along the Wisconsin from here. A physical fitness trail is located at the site. But it's now mostly a gathering spot for water enthusiasts who like to raft or canoe or fish the Wisconsin River.

- Roche-A-Cri State Park, Friendship (608/339-6881). This is one of those out-of-the-way spots that's worth a detour if you're golfing at Lake Arrowhead. The highlight is a 300-foot-high rock outcropping that provides a fantastic view of the countryside. Other outcroppings abound in this part of central Wisconsin, once washed over by the great glacial melt-off that formed the Wisconsin River. Other sandstone features are Ship Rock, Castle Rock, Mill Bluff, and Friendship Mound.

- Rib Mountain State Park just outside Wausau, best known for its ski facility (now called Granite Peak), has 860 acres and features a 60-foot observation tower and trails. The main attraction, however, is Granite Peak, a billion-year-old giant rock that is one of the oldest geologic formations on Earth. The park number is 715/842-2522. Next door is a 32-par nine-hole golf course that measures only 1,887 yards. In the shadow of Granite Peak yet on relatively flat land with ponds and trees, this course is a nice place for a family golf outing.

In Merrill, founded in 1847 at the junction of the Prairie and Wisconsin rivers, families can choose any of nine green spaces in this self-proclaimed "city of parks" for an outing. Merrill is north of Wausau along Highway 51.

Just south of Stevens Point, also just off Highway 51, is the Rainbow Falls Family Fun Park, a water park close to shopping and the Korean War memorial. Call 800/321-2228 for information on the water park.

In Marshfield, take the kids to Wisconsin's fourth-largest zoo. The 60-acre Wildwood Park and Zoo, established in 1924, features snow monkeys, grizzly bears, buffalo, and other animals. 800/422-4541.

All throughout the region, you can find hiking trails, camping spots, and good angling and boating opportunities. The national Ice Age Trail runs on the ridge north of Antigo close to Antigo-Bass Lake Country Club and Veterans Memorial Park, a county-owned park featuring cold, clear Jack Lake, campsites, a volleyball court, and a playground.

# For More Information

Antigo: 888/526-4523
Marshfield: 800/422-4541
Merrill: 715/536-9474
Stevens Point: 800/236-4636
Wausau: 888/948-4748; www.wausaucvb.org
Wisconsin Rapids: 800/554-4484; www.wisconsinrapidsarea.com

# 10

# Green Lake

The pastoral lake country of east-central Wisconsin is often by-passed by tourists on their way up north. They don't know what they're missing. On the east side of Highway 51 (now Interstate 39), the historic road through the state's "central sands" heartland, great golf can be found amid small towns, antique shops, pleasant glacial lakes, clean, cold trout streams, an abundant bird habitat, remote-feeling natural areas, and interesting historical sites.

The best golf is along Green Lake, a wonderful surprise to new visitors who see this glittering gem suddenly appear amidst the corn rows and cow pastures. Native Americans found this area to their liking long before golf came along. The Ho-Chunk long made the area around Green Lake (the state's deepest lake at 237 feet) the site of a thriving village. The name of the lake came from the Ho-Chunk word *Day-cho-lah,* meaning "green waters."

Green Lake and its 27 miles of shoreline then drew white settlers. The first was Anson Dart, who settled south of the lake in 1838. Seven years later, he built a dam and mill at the lake's outlet on the northeast side. The site became Dartford. Later, it became Green Lake. Dartford Millpond and Dartford Bay, part of the waterway that becomes the Puchyan River and eventually flows into the Fox River, are reminders of Anson's work.

By the 1860s, the area became a resort center with people from New Orleans and St. Louis spending their summers at places like Oakwood, the area's first summer hotel built by David Greenway in 1867. The Green Lake Yacht Club followed in 1884, and Tuscumbia Country Club, one of the oldest golf courses in the state, followed in 1896. Green Lake now claims to be the oldest resort community west of Niagara Falls.

But the biggest and most lasting boost to the local tourism economy came with the development of what's now known as Lawsonia. Lawsonia, built in the late 1880s by Mr. and Mrs. Victor Lawson of Chicago, has been managed by the American Baptist Assembly (ABA) since 1943 as a "place of renewal." From the beginning, golf was a part of this extraordinary place. It now boasts two fine golf courses, the Green Lake Conference Center, and an impressive list of celebrity visitors over the years (Hepburn and Tracy among them).

Just north, along the bucolic banks of the upper Fox River, lies Berlin. Today this community, noted for its elegant Victorian-styled homes, is the "fur and leather capital," where several businesses produce gloves, boots, and other products. More than three centuries ago, a tribe of fire-worshipping Native Americans called the Mascoutin lived near here. That's how the fine Mascoutin Golf Club south of Berlin got its name.

A little west, around Montello, famed naturalist John Muir spent his teen-age years before going West and helping to launch a national conservation movement that has become today's Sierra Club. "Oh, that glorious Wisconsin wilderness! Everything new and pure in the very prime of spring when Nature's pulses were beating highest and mysteriously keeping time with our own! Young hearts, young leaves, flowers, animals, the winds and the streams and the sparkling lake, all wildly gladly rejoicing together!" Muir, a native of Scotland, wrote in a 1913 work. You, too, can get that joyous feeling by spending quality time in the many natural areas throughout the region. Or better yet, make a birdie on some of the local courses.

In Montello, you'll find a waterfall in the city center, site of the Montello Granite Quarry. The quarry has produced red granite that has been used for monuments worldwide—Grant's Tomb in New York included. In Oxford, a little west, lies the Summerton Bog, home to rare plants and animals. Around Richford, a little north of Montello, trout fishers and canoeists long have treasured quiet times on the spring-fed Mecan River.

Those with weekend homes in these parts of central Wisconsin have found you don't have to be up north to get away from it all. Golf isn't the only reason to explore the area, but it's a great reason to start.

# Lawsonia
## Green Lake

It's hard to pick between the two golf courses at Lawsonia, so do yourself a favor and play both. But first, appreciate a little history about this special place. If you choose to play on Sunday, you might also offer thanks to the current management—which has waived the rule (in effect until the 1960s) that closed the golf courses on the day of worship.

Credit Victor and Jessie Lawson for most of the rest. Victor founded the Chicago Daily News and cofounded The Associated Press. Jessie Strong Bradley was the daughter of William Henry Bradley, a clerk of the United States courts. Lawsonia began back in 1887, when Jessie Lawson and a few chums took a pleasure cruise on the western end of Green Lake. A storm forced them to shore, and they sought shelter on a secluded spot shaded by a single cottonseed tree. They later named it Lone Tree Point. Jessie talked her husband into buying the first 10 acres. The deed signed in December 1888 was the start of the 1,100-acre Lone Tree Farm.

While Victor concentrated on becoming a publishing tycoon, his wife devoted her time to religion, charity work, and the building of an elaborate estate. No expense was spared in building white-enameled brick barns, hand-laid stone fencing, Italian-tiled boathouses, formal gardens, stone bridges, and a little nine-hole course (now gone) for the amusement of guests. An estimated $8 million was spent on this showcase, which includes the largest barn in Wisconsin (once a white-tiled shelter for prized Jerseys and now a giant maintenance building) and seven water towers. The largest tower, the Judson Tower, is named in honor of Baptist missionaries, and its observation platform rises almost 200 feet above the lake. Mrs. Lawson liked to take tea and entertain friends in a lounge she had built at the top of the tower. You can climb the 121 steps on your own and see the view for yourself.

Mrs. Lawson died in 1914, Mr. Lawson died in 1925, and then the H. O. Stone Co. of Chicago bought the estate. The new owners invested another $3 million, developing exclusive homes and one of the best golf courses in the land—today's "Links Course."

But the 1929 stock market crash sent this and other great ideas into the deep rough. The company completed the Lawsonia Country Club Hotel and casino (now the Roger Williams Inn) on the site of the old Lawson House and operated it as a resort for two years. But the development went bust, leaving the mortgage-holding bank to operate it for about 10 years. The Depression, and then World War II gas rationing, finally closed the resort for two years in the early 1940s, and the U.S. government once considered buying it as the site for the Air Force Academy. Instead the men in blue went West, and the government leased the giant barn along the front nine to house about four hundred fifty German POWs. Things got so bad that in 1944, the front nine of the Links Course served as a cow pasture.

The seeds of Lawsonia's comeback were sown in 1943, when the Northern Baptist Convention bought the property for a mere $300,000. The purchase occurred at the urging of Luther Wesley Smith, a top Baptist official, and with the help of James L. Kraft of Kraft Foods. The first conference, for Baptist youth, was held in 1944. The religious group, later renamed the American Baptist Assembly, has been improving the old Lawson estate ever since. Now it hosts about thirty-five thousand guests who come to play the golf courses and use the other facilities. It's all part of what the ABA sees as a place "for a closer walk with God." Come to Lawsonia and see if a divine caddie can help your score.

## Links Course

This is the course that draws the real golf buffs to the Golf Courses of Lawsonia, as the facility is now officially called. And in recognition of that, Lawsonia recently has committed to bringing back some of the old course's hidden features. Fairways have been widened, and more than one hundred fifty trees have been removed to enhance the links nature of the course. Some old bunkers will be restored, and some new bunkers will be added along with an improved practice area.

Bill Ellis, a well-traveled former public relations executive now living in Stevens Point, calls the Links course "one of the finest golf courses in the United States ... It's really unique in this country." Ellis grew up in Ripon and was part of the work crew that did the grunt work of bringing back Lawsonia after World War II. He worried in later years that the course was being "Americanized," but now he's "glad they're trying to bring it back." He appreciates the Scottish flavor of the course and complementary stone bridges and building.

Even before that work, the Links was almost always a pleasure to play thanks to fine maintenance and a splendid, solid design by William Langford and partner Theodore Moreau. The team traveled to Scotland to sketch and photograph holes at famous courses to use as models. An Illinois architect, Langford had a childhood bout with polio, took up golf for rehabilitation, and went on to be a member of three National Collegiate Athletic Association (NCAA) championship teams at Yale. Langford and Moreau designed more than two hundred fifty other courses, including several country club courses in Wisconsin (the Ozaukee Country Club among them).

The Links course lies mostly atop a windswept plateau above Green Lake and features steep bunkers and rolling greens. There are more than 90 bunkers, often surrounded by deep rough. And the fairways, while in good shape and fairly open, rarely provide a level stance. About $250,000 was spent to build it. It opened in 1930 and later hosted the Little Lawsonia Open, which attracted names such as Ben Hogan, Sam Snead, and Byron Nelson. Nelson shot a 69 here in 1939, then a course record. Johnnie Stevens and Ron Gilkey held the Links record of 65, as of August 2000.

Langford's team used old Model T Ford trucks to haul around dirt, and local legend has it an old boxcar was used to provide the base for the memorable seventh hole. Even if it's only legend, shooting to the seventh green is sometimes like trying to land an iron shot on the top of a moving boxcar. The tee ball on this 161-yard par-three is an all-or-nothing shot. Miss the green, and the shot falls down the steep sides of this dramatically elevated green.

Hole after hole at the Links will test your game like that. Two of the toughest are on the back nine. Ten is a 239-yard par-three that often plays into the wind. Trees surround the green, which also is guarded by a long, narrow and deep bunker on each side. Thirteen is a 568-yard par-five that requires three good shots to get to the green. The hole doglegs slightly left, but cutting the dogleg is dangerous because of three traps and trees to the left. A pond is left of the elevated green, but only the most errant shot will bring that water into play. If you miss on this hole, miss right.

But it's the par-fours (four over 400 yards) that typify the enduring test of the Links. The 443-yard 16th hole has five big traps and an S-shaped fairway that pulls you into the traps on the right side of the green. This hole could be a round-breaker, so don't gamble. Save the gambling for 18, a finishing hole where you could make up a stroke to win the match. This 503-yard par-five is reachable in two, especially if you're lucky to be downwind that day. But the green tilts steeply from back to front and has a hump down the middle of it, kicking approach shots off line. A tough pin placement could make it hard to get it close enough for birdie or par.

*6,764 yards/par-72/72.8 rating/130 slope*
*Architects: William Langford and Theodore Moreau*
*Fees: $$$$*

## Woodlands Course

Though it doesn't have the history or the traditional feel of the Links course, the Woodlands is a gem unto itself (rated 10th best in the state by *Golf Digest* in 2000). This course, first opened as a nine-holer in 1983, was designed by Joe Lee and Rocky Roquemore. Their second nine opened in 1991. Roquemore's Atlanta firm also helped create three courses at Disney World in Orlando and Cog Hill's Dubs Dread in suburban Chicago. But its first Wisconsin course provides a stunning contrast to Links.

Trees are spread out along the Links, mostly for background; trees are everywhere at the Woodlands—maples, pines, aspens, elms, and walnut—and they come into play frequently. Water comes into play on only two Links holes; the Woodlands course provides great views of Green Lake and brings water into play on four holes. Elevation changes are usually subtle on the Links; they're dramatic on the Woodlands. This new classic has one thing in common with the Links—plenty of sand, about 80 traps in all. But here, it's target golf most of the way.

You get a full taste of the Woodlands early on. The second and third holes are prime examples of both the beauty and terror that characterize this layout. Two, a par-four of 341 yards from the back tees, works its way around the left side of an abandoned rock quarry. It's a little more than 215 yards to the quarry from the tee, so the best approach is to hit short, then play a shot of about 125 yards to the green. A more dangerous route is to aim for the extension of the fairway off to the right of the quarry, which leaves a shorter approach with a better angle. Some brave souls might also try to blast a tee shot down the left side and hope for

Number 16 on the Woodlands course at Lawsonia. Photo by Paul Hundley.

a favorable bounce close to the green, but trees along the left and a big tree on the left front of the green make that a risky approach. Unsure of your approach? Look to the Judson Tower for inspiration.

Number three is a 168-yard photo opportunity. The green lies some 60 feet below the tee, making for a muscle-tensing tee shot. The lake lies even farther down the cliff. Trees stand close to the left of the green, which is guarded by two large sand traps at the front and another in the back. To the right is a steep drop-off to the lake. So pretty. And so easy to make a triple bogey.

Sixteen is another memorable par-three with water. Here, a big, inland pond laps along much of the left side of the green and landing area. Trees line the right side. And the swirling wind complicates the club choice. From the elevated tees 189 yards away, the green looks awfully small. But this green is deep, 45 yards. So hit an extra club if you like to avoid the trouble in front of the green. Good luck.

But the toughest holes might be the two par-fours that precede it. Fourteen is a 438-yard par-four that doglegs slightly right. This tree-lined fairway slopes left and then dips sharply in front of the green. A fairway trap left catches many drives and one at the left front of the green seems to snare those who avoided the first. Fifteen is a 418-yard par-four that doglegs sharply right up a hill. Trees line this fairway, too, and block approaches on drives to the right. Take your medicine, and aim to the far left corner of the dogleg for the long but open approach to this deep green. If you come through numbers 14 through 16 without losing too many strokes, you've got a chance for a good round.

But don't breathe too easily. Seventeen, a 376-yard par-four dogleg left, and 18, a 524-yard sweeping par-five, seem to get tighter—in part because of the many sand traps. Each has six sand traps with relatively small elevated greens. The 18th green, for good measure, has an elevated two-tiered putting surface with plenty of pine trees standing by. The Woodlands has become an instant classic and perfect complement to the history-laden Lawsonia.

*6,618 yards/par-72/71.5 rating/129 slope*
*Architects: Joe Lee and Rocky Roquemore*
*Fees: $$$$*
*Call: 800/529-4453 or 920/294-3320; Web site: www.lawsonia.com*
*Directions: Entrance is 2 miles west of Green Lake on Highway 23.*

# Mascoutin Golf Club
*Berlin*

The Packards, Lawrence and son Roger, collaborated on a neat design amid the hills south of Berlin on the upper Fox River. The Packards produced a course at Mascoutin that's devoid of gimmicks but strong because of the variety of holes. Their 18-hole course, changing every year because of an aggressive tree-planting program, opened in 1975. Rick Jacobson created a more modern, dramatic nine-hole course, which was added in 1999. But it maintains a strong link to the old 18, in part because Jacobson worked for Packard during his early days in the business.

The three nines now are named Red (the old front nine), White (the old back nine), and Blue (the new Jacobson nine). The 27-hole combination is not to be missed, especially if you're putting together a week-long stay in the Green Lake area, just to the south of Berlin. It offers one of the best values in Wisconsin golf—27 holes and a cart for $80 in the year 2000.

The Mascoutin golf story began in the early part of the twentieth century. The original nine-hole course, built in the 1930s, was located within Berlin's city limits. But the club moved when club members Dr. and Mrs. L. J. Seward donated 220 acres for a new course south of town. Then it was up to the Packards. They had plenty to work with—century-old trees, gentle hills, and ample water. The duo added lots of sand—some 65 traps, mostly big sand pits that flank the large, sloping greens.

## *The Red and White Nines*

The 18 holes designed by the Packards flow smoothly without shocking the golfer. Yet they demand constant attention. The Red third hole is a long, difficult par-four of 465 yards. Four Red is a short par-three of 158 yards, with a green that's almost completely surrounded by sand. The fifth hole on the Red course is a 346-yard par-four that doglegs left to a sloping, well-trapped green. The 562-yard par-five sixth hole on the Red course offers a blind tee shot to the crest of a ridge, followed by a second shot down a natural gully; the third shot is uphill to another well-contoured green.

The White nine (the old Packard back nine) opens with a sharp dogleg right of 406 yards. The dogleg is guarded by a cluster of sand traps, forcing you to aim left and adding length to the hole. The fourth and fifth White holes, side by side, play radically different. Four plays downhill to a green that's only 355 yards away, while five stretches uphill for 403 yards. Once you putt out on the five green, take in the wonderful view north toward Berlin and the Fox River.

There are no easy routes back to the clubhouse from here. The finishing holes on the Packards' White nine will test your entire game. Each of the four finishing holes has a water hazard. Six, a 412-yard par-four, has a narrow landing area off the elevated tee, with out-of-bounds on the left and a pond on the right. The approach shot, which can require anything from an 8-iron to a 2-iron, depending on the wind, is to an elevated green. The seventh hole is a long par-five of 549 yards, with a double turn to the left. The challenge comes on the second shot, where mature trees loom on the left and a pond lurks on the right. The hazards on both sides come into play quickly, and even a mid-iron lay-up shot requires accuracy. The green also proves to be a tough target because of two sand traps at the front. The eighth hole measures 180 yards, and your tee shot must clear a pond and hold a green with a hard back-to-front slope.

That leaves the White nine's 382-yard par-four finishing hole, which will decide many a match. The fairway slopes left toward the woods, and a row of old oak trees prevents an easy bailout to the right. For the best angle to the green, keep your tee shot to the right-center of the fairway. The second shot is over water to a green that's also guarded by sand in front and a large oak tree near the left front edge.

*6,821 yards/par-72/72.8 rating/130 slope*
*Architects: Lawrence and Roger Packard*
*Fees: $$$*

### *The Blue Nine*

Rick Jacobson's design is more dramatic, with waste bunkering, big elevation changes, forced carries, lots of water hazards, and nice river views. The most imaginative holes come in the middle of the nine.

Two, the cliff hole, is a nifty 393-yard par-four that will create plenty of post-round conversation. Your first shot is from a wooded chute to a tiered fairway that slopes right to left toward some new houses. The second shot is abruptly downhill to a green flanked by trees and large waste bunkers on the left and front and a carved-out cliff on the right. Three, a 436-yard dogleg left par-four, takes you back down into the lowlands along County A. Four, a par-three of 197 yards, introduces you to a vast and dense wetland that dominates the next three holes.

The fifth hole is a 525-yard par-five that demands some strategy. Really big hitters might have to worry about the wetland that divides the fairway about 275 yards out and choose something other than a driver. The second shot must clear about 90 yards of wetland to set up a short-iron approach to a green that's protected on the right by a tongue of the wetland. Six is a 176-yard par-three that comes back toward the wetland. And the seventh hole—a 461-yard monster—features a drive from tees situated on the edge of the wetland. Numbers eight (a 344-yard par-four) and nine (a 512-yard par-five) have a more open feel but feature plenty of water and sand. Maybe someday Jacobson will get a chance to add nine more holes to his Mascoutin masterpiece.

*3,461 yards/par-36/36.5 rating/130 slope*
*Architect: Rick Jacobson*
*Fees: $$$*
*Call: 920/361-2360 or 920/361-2995; Web site: www.mascoutingolf.com*
*Directions: From Green Lake, go north on Highway 49, then left on County A.*

# Tuscumbia
## *Green Lake*

This course completes the best of the Green Lake vacation circuit. It takes you back to a simpler time when golfers wearing knickers carried their clubs from the resort hotel across the street to the course and walked 18 holes. One end of Tuscumbia is a mid-iron from the well-appointed Heidel House, the most famous of Green Lake resorts; on the other end Tuscumbia bumps up to the resort community of Green Lake, where an old wooden band shell sits in a park between the marina and the combination bait shop and liquor store. A well-kept motel sits across the street, and nearby is the newly restored Thrasher's Opera House (it dates to 1910 and is the site of the Green Lake Festival of Music held each summer.).

Tuscumbia, founded in 1896, bills itself as the oldest course in Wisconsin (not without some controversy—the Janesville Country Club traces its roots to 1894). But controversy or not, Tuscumbia is a pleasant trip into golfing past. The entrance is grand—a paved road between holes nine and 18 that's shrouded by tall pines, oaks, and maples. The entry road rises to a handsome clubhouse, where some Native American memorabilia is tucked away in a display case near the dark-paneled bar and painted brick fireplace that serve as part of the Chief Tuscumbia Lounge. Visit the lounge or the outside deck for your 19th-hole libation.

The well-manicured course features gentle elevation changes, small firm greens, grass bunkers, mounds, bumpy fairways, blind shots, and a classic layout that leaves a short walk between tee and green. It's the perfect walking course.

The layout, through century-old hardwoods, towering pines, and parklike grounds, provides a relaxing setting for golf. The front nine is a lot shorter than the back nine—3,090 yards compared to 3,218 yards—and plays a little easier. But if you hit your drives sideways and hate to hit out of greenside bunkers, you might come to a different conclusion. The second and fourth holes (144 yards and 166 yards, respectively) are par-threes surrounded by sand traps. The third hole, a 547-yard par-five, is tough because it slopes to the right, pushing many shots into the trees. The seventh hole is a tough and tight par-four of 388 yards with sand, trees, and a severely sloping green. Nine, a 318-yard par-four, goes uphill toward the clubhouse; watch out for the grass bunkers and trees on the right where the hole takes a slight turn.

The back nine starts off rather rudely with a tough 198-yard par-three and the only water hazard on the course. A big pond lies on the left, the opening to the putting surface is very narrow, and the green slopes hard from the right to the left. A slight downhill shot complicates club selection. Eleven, a 399-yard par-four, is one of the course's few severe doglegs. The hole begins by veering left up a hill to a small plateau. The green is guarded by grass bunkers with long rough. Don't be tempted to cut the corner—high pines about 200 yards out make it tough except for the longest hitters.

Next comes the 556-yard 12th hole, which starts on level ground then drops off at the end to a little green. Out of bounds lines the left side of the fairway. The next hole only measures 119 yards, but it's one of the hardest holes on the course. Number thirteen may indeed be unlucky for many a golfer. It's uphill all the way to a green protected by steep-faced traps on the left, front and right sides of the green and a grove of trees to the rear. The shot is all carry, and at best only the tip of the flag can be seen from the tee. Fourteen is a tree-lined par-four of 402 yards. Next is another long par-five; this 560-yard hole doglegs left uphill then drops off to another tiny green.

The three finishing holes are mid-range par-fours—the best of which is the 345-yard uphill 18 hole that doglegs right around mounds, sand—and trees, of course. The green is quite small, undulating, and shaded by a canopy of trees. The approach is difficult. But just take a deep breath and take solace in the fact you're swinging the sticks on one of the state's oldest golf courses.

*6,308 yards/par-71/70.3 rating/124 slope*
*Fees: $$*
*Call: 920/294-3240; Web site: www.tuscumbiacc.com*
*Directions: South of Highway 23, follow the signs to Heidel House. Located on*
*    Illinois Avenue between the Heidel House and downtown Green Lake.*

## Other Area Courses

A trio of good courses also is available within a short drive of the Green Lake–Berlin area. Two are new courses and the older course has a new nine.

# Two Oaks North

*Wautoma*

This course, in the bucolic countryside south of Wautoma, is the center of a budding real estate development. But the country atmosphere still dominates—a working barn across the road, an old schoolhouse down the road, and mounds of glacier-carried boulders around the course. The course opened in 1992 on a design by "Badger Bob" Lohmann and is known for its well-maintained grounds.

The back nine is longer (3,316 yards to 3,266 yards), more hilly, and features the toughest holes. The four finishing holes measure 543 yards, 443 yards, 223 yards and 528 yards from the back tees. Water can come into play on the two par-fives. This young course will only get better with age.

*6,582 yards/par-72/70.7 rating/120 slope*
*Architect: Bob Lohmann*
*Fees: $$*
*Call: 800/236-6257*
*Directions: Take Highway 73 south of Wautoma to County F; then go 3 miles*
*    east of County F.*

# Waushara Country Club
*Wautoma*

On the east end of Wautoma, this course added nine holes in July 1999. Art Johnson designed the more dramatic new nine, the Lakeview course, which was added to a course first opened in the 1940s. These 27 holes have it all—woods, ponds, wetlands, elevation changes, dramatic water shots (the most scenic being the 154-yard par-three seventh hole on the Bridges layout).

*6,324 yards/par-72/70.8 rating/124 slope (for the Bridges/Lakeview layout, the*
*highest slope and rating combination)*
*Architect: Art Johnson*
*Fees: $$*
*Call: 920/787-4649*
*Directions: Located at the intersection of Highways 21 and 73.*

# White Lake Golf Resort
*Montello*

A visit here is a near up-north experience, from the knotty-pine-paneled interior of the clubhouse, to the comfy cabins, to the tall pines, to the free-roaming peacocks. Peacocks? Yes. The Scharenberg's family resort—far, far off the beaten path (turn right at the white Lutheran church, don't you know)—calls itself the "home of the peacocks." That cry you hear is not a hawk, or a baby, but that showy bird. It seems "Grandma Scharenberg" liked them, and so the family has kept them around since the 1940s.

Golf is a fairly recent addition to this family resort. The first nine was built in 1985. The course runs through rolling hills, oak and pine forests, and spring-fed ponds and is a lot tougher than the yardage implies.

*6,294 yards/par-71/70.6 rating/120 slope*
*Fees: $$*
*Call: 608/297-2255; Web site: www.wisvacations.com/scharenbergs*
*Directions: Follow the signs off Highway 23, between Montello and Princeton.*

## Practice Areas
A convenient family golf practice area is across from the Lawsonia entrance. Far View Golf, 3 miles west of Green Lake, has a driving range, sand-trap practice area and 18-hole mini-golf course; call 920/294-6454.

## More Fun Things to Do

The great outdoors is the draw here. Although it's within easy driving distances of major cities in Wisconsin and the increasingly developed Wisconsin Dells, Waushara, Marquette, and Green Lake counties have kept a country feel. You can fish lakes or streams, go boating, swim along a lovely lakeshore, hike through thick forests, bike along country roads, knock around antique shops, or shop for crafts.

You can do almost all of those things at the Green Lake Conference Center, which caters to vacationers but asks them not to smoke or drink and to keep the family pet in the campgrounds. Rooms and cottages are available for rent, as are bikes, boats, and, of course, golf clubs. Or simply pay a small entry fee and visit for the day to picnic, swim, and see the sights. Pay another modest fee and climb the Judson Tower's 121 spiral steps for a great view, or explore some of the other towers that can be climbed anytime. (For details, call 800/558-8898 or go to www.greenlakeconferencectr.com and www.lawsonia.com).

Venture off the Lawsonia grounds, and you won't be disappointed. For example, a nice trail for hiking or mountain biking runs approximately 10 miles between Ripon and Berlin (call 920/929-3135).

The entire family will like the Mecan River Discovery Center in Neshkoro, a nonprofit wildlife education center on the spring-fed trout stream. Various summer programs are available. You can stay for a day, or overnight in former Department of Natural Resources (DNR) Youth Conservation Corps cabins (visit www.mecanriver.com or call 920/293-8404).

Why not get in the spirit of the region and plan some old-fashioned family pleasures?

- Summer concerts in Green Lake's Deacon Mills Park.
- A July 4 celebration with a parade, music and fireworks along Green Lake at Playground Park.
- Civil War shows during Berlin's "Victorian Days" held in the last weekend in June and Green Lake's "Golden Days Harvest Festival" in late September.
- Fishing off the countless piers in the area, or from a rental boat.
- Horseback riding at several area stables. Guided trail rides are available at Fox River Riding Stable in Princeton (call 920/295-4656).
- Canoeing down the Mecan River (call Mecan River Outfitters near Princeton at 920/295-3439).
- Picking fruit and taking a hay ride at Caron Orchard near Princeton (call 920/295-6730).

# For More Information

Berlin: Chamber of Commerce 800/979-9334, www.berlinwis.com
Green Lake Area: Chamber of Commerce 800/253-7354 or www.greenlakecc.com
Montello Area: Chamber of Commerce 800/684-7199
Greater Princeton Area: Chamber of Commerce 920/295-3877

# V

# Big Lakes: Michigan and Winnebago

**24** Alpine Resort Golf Course, Egg Harbor
**25** Cherry Hills Lodge and Golf Course, Sturgeon Bay
**26** Maxwelton Braes, Baileys Harbor
**27** Northbrook Country Club, Luxemburg
**28** Deer Run Golf Resort, Washington Island
**29** Chaska Golf Course, Appleton
**30** Rolling Meadows Golf Course, Fond du Lac
**31** Whispering Springs, Fond du Lac
**32** Foxfire Golf Club, Waupaca
**33** High Cliff Golf Course, Sherwood
**34** Irish Waters Golf Club, Freedom
**35** Lakeshore Golf Course, Oshkosh
**36** Winagamie Golf Course, Neenah

# 11

# Kohler and Sheboygan Area

If there's a magic golf kingdom in Wisconsin, it must be Kohler. A planned community incorporated in 1912 on the mighty Sheboygan River just a few miles from Lake Michigan, Kohler is a historic company town with Disneyland-like neatness and order. The Kohler version of Main Street U.S.A. features an English garden city laid out by the most prominent American landscape architects of the early twentieth century, a fascinating display of modern bathrooms at the Kohler Design Center, a luxurious inn called The American Club, fine eateries, elegant shops, a wildlife preserve and private land along the often salmon-filled Sheboygan River, and an array of Pete Dye golf courses unmatched anywhere.

For decades, bathroom fixtures manufactured by the Kohler Company made the village famous. Now it's a travel destination, too. The company, which counts yearly worldwide sales of $3 billion, runs the luxurious American Club resort and also produces furniture, small engines, and other things for modern living under more than a dozen brand names. Founder John Michael Kohler got it all started in 1873 when he bought a Sheboygan foundry catering to the farming implement industry; he got into the plumbing business a decade later when he enameled a horse trough and sold it as a bathtub. This prominent Wisconsin family has produced two governors (Walter Kohler Sr. and Walter Kohler Jr.), a history of art patronage for the masses, and some forward-thinking philosophy.

In the early part of the twentieth century, Walter Kohler Sr. created a village plan for an immigrant workforce on the theory that "employees should not only have wages, but roses as well." In the last part of the twentieth century, Herbert V. Kohler Jr., the Kohler Co. chairman and grandson of founder John Michael Kohler, made the most of his late-blooming passion for golf in the 1980s by developing two courses at Blackwolf Run that became the core of his hospitality business; later he added two more up the coast.

You can see a replica of the Kohler family's ancestral Austrian home, Waelderhaus, plus a nice assortment of flowers, on a plot of wooded land sitting above the Blackwolf Run golf complex and its huge log clubhouse.

If it all seems like golf fantasyland ... well, it is. Kohler and Dye have created a golf kingdom unlike any in the Midwest. Kohler once said he wanted to make

The American Club the Pinehurst of the North. Well, who's to argue with this bear of a millionaire who has put so much of his own money into transforming the Wisconsin and Midwest golf scene?

A new bear is lumbering into the area, however. Jack Nicklaus—the Golden Bear—is scheduled to design a course in nearby Sheboygan Falls. The Bull, using the Onion River and part of a 418-acre family farm, is due to open in 2002.

Up and down this middle part of Wisconsin's Lake Michigan coast—easily accessible from Interstate 43 that runs between Milwaukee and Green Bay—great golf is available amid the prosperous dairy farms, interesting port communities, and historic river towns. Or you can travel west toward Fond du Lac in search of golf, following the general route of the former wooden plank road and the railroads, Highway 23. But don't speed—that's reserved for the race cars at Elkhart Lake's Road America track, just north of 23.

Glacial speed is observed south of the Wade House, an old stagecoach stop on that old wooden plank road at Greenbush. In the northern Kettle Moraine State Forest—from Glenbeulah south to nearly West Bend—lie some of the best-preserved examples of glacial formations in the world. You'll find out that a drumlin has nothing to do with a chicken leg.

The Lake Michigan shorelines of Manitowoc and Sheboygan counties have been inhabited for centuries because of their natural harbors and access to prominent water trade routes. In white settlement times, shipbuilding, manufacturing, cheesemaking, woodworking, and other crafts prospered because of the work ethic of European immigrants from German-speaking lands, Holland, and other countries.

Evidence of this heritage is everywhere, from the Waelderhaus in Kohler to the replica of the Dutch windmill located between Oostburg and Cedar Grove. Sheboygan, don't you know, is the self-proclaimed Bratwurst Capital of America. You can sample brats anytime at several local eateries and bars. For the full brat experience, plan your visit around the annual Bratwurst Days in August.

Since the 1980s, Herb Kohler and Pete Dye have created four golf courses—two inland at Kohler along the Sheboygan River and two on the Lake Michigan coast. In 2001, the Kohler Golf Academy—a teaching program—was added to the Kohler golf experience.

All have received kudos, including Blackwolf Run, site of the 1998 U.S. Women's Open won by South Korea's Se Ri Pak on a 6,412-yard, par-71 layout; she won playing the original 18-hole configuration that debuted in 1988. To see those holes, you have to play the Meadow Valleys' back nine and holes one through four and 14 through 18 on the River course. The courses became separate entities in 1990 with the addition of two new nines to the Blackwolf Run complex. But there's one hole you can see but can't play; that's the original 10th hole, a 340-yard uphill par-four that opens with a tee shot over the Sheboygan. It was "retired" back in 1990 but was used in the Open.

The newest course is the Irish course, opened in the summer of 2000. But there's a first among equals—the Straits at the Whistling Straits complex north of Kohler. The Straits course, which opened in July 1998 aside the great inland sea, has received international attention, became the scheduled venue for the 2004 men's PGA Championship, and made the "mentioned" list for a future Ryder Cup.

You can play the Straits and Dye's three other masterpieces—if you're willing to pay the price. Golf at the Kohler courses is the costliest in Wisconsin— ranging up to $220 in 2000 at the walking-only Straits course. That price includes the fee for the mandatory caddie, who could be a young man from Ireland, and for the opportunity to play among a roaming herd of sheep.

But for most of us who live for golf, scratching out a par on an impossible Dye-designed hole on a windswept course next to Lake Michigan is as close to golfing in the British Isles as we can get without being there—and cheaper, too, if you count the air fare and hotel. It can also be said that golfing in the crossroads of Haven, about nine miles north of Kohler and Sheboygan, is as close as we can get to Wisconsin golf heaven. As the company publicists say, all you have to do is add an E to the place name.

Although the Straits garners most of the attention, especially with the upcoming major championship in 2004, Kohler's other courses are more than worthy of a visit. All the courses have tee boxes to suit long and short hitters. The shortest lengths start at a little over five thousand yards. No matter which tee you choose, Dye's devilish designs will challenge your game.

# Blackwolf Run
*Kohler*

### *Meadow Valleys Course*

Rated the sixth best course in Wisconsin by *Golf Digest*, Meadow Valleys is the most underrated of Dye's Kohler courses. But it shouldn't be. This course has a links feel, lying primarily on grassy tiers above the twisty Sheboygan River. Pockets of trees, drastic pitches and draws, and massive sand traps characterize this course. You know some sand traps are big when you have to use stairways to walk in and out of them.

The signature hole on this 18-hole course is 15, dubbed "Mercy." The mesalike green on this 227-yard par-three falls off steeply in every direction. Between

Number nine on the River course at Blackwolf Run, Kohler, Wisconsin. Photo courtesy of Kohler Co.

the tee and the 48-yard-long green, you'll encounter a dry moat filled with wiry vegetation. Mercy!

Valleys 18 is one that will stick in your memory, too. It has two greens, another indication that no expense is ever spared when Kohler and golf are involved. Golfers teeing off from the shortest red tees play this one as a 303-yard par-four to a green in front of the Sheboygan River. Other golfers play a par-four that measures up to 458 yards and doglegs over the wide Sheboygan. The long approach must be hit over the river to a big green surrounded by big trees and overlooked by the huge log clubhouse. So what if you have water to your right and in front of you? So what if you have a lot of people watching you? Just hit away!

GOLF magazine's watching, too. It rated the 18th as one of the 500 "best holes in the world" in its January 2000 issue.

*7,142 yards/par-72/74.8 rating/143 slope*
*Architect: Pete Dye*
*Fees: $$$$*

## River Course

Until the Straits made its debut in 1998, this was by far the premier course in Wisconsin. (*Golf Digest* rated it the best course in the state and 55th in the United States in 2000.) But many good golfers consider this the tougher course, because the penalty for a poorly hit shot here is often a lost ball; at the Straits, you and your caddie can often find the ball amid the dunes. Here, Dye made the most of every twist and turn of the Sheboygan River. The river and associated ponds come into play on 12 of the 18 holes on this heavily wooded track.

Number five is a scenic and tough 419-yard par-four that begins on a wooded bluff above the Sheboygan River and slightly doglegs right. The river flows along the right-side rough. Even if you keep the drive in the fairway (aim toward the left bunker off the tee), the approach is a killer—to a highly elevated green protected by a grassy embankment and a pot bunker. It impressed *GOLF* magazine, too, which placed it among its 500 "best holes in the world" in its January 2000 issue.

The 337-yard dogleg right par-four ninth hole is short but extremely tricky. The river is right. The landing area is split in two by a stand of 100-foot-high aspens. The green is small and protected by sand. The hole goes downhill, tempting really big hitters to go for it all. Don't be tempted. Hit an iron off the tee, and bail out to the left.

A golfer hitting from the long tees of the 205-yard par-three 13th must hit a shot not from bank to bank but down the middle of the flowing river to a bunkered green. Golfers on the shorter tees have big trees to contend with.

The par-five 16th, playing 560 yards from the long tees, combines the best elements of the River course. This double-dogleg begins slightly uphill, with woods to the right and sand to the left. From there, it's downhill, and the river comes into play along the lefthand side. The green's left side falls off into the river, and a big sand trap is on the right side. It's called Unter der Linden, "under the linden tree." Here's hoping your game doesn't go kaput because of too many balls under the trees of the River course.

*6,991 yards/par-72/74.9 rating/151 slope*
*Architect: Pete Dye*
*Fees: $$$$*
*Call: 920/457-4446 or 800/618-5535; Web site: www.kohlerco.com*
*Directions: Interstate 43 to Exit 126. Go west on Highway 23 and exit County*
    *Y and go south through Kohler past The American Club. Go straight at*
    *stoplight and follow signs.*

# Whistling Straits
*Haven*

### *Straits Course*

The Straits has gotten a lot of well-deserved attention since it opened in 1998. The course was rated third best in Wisconsin in 2000 by *Golf Digest. GOLF* magazine rated it the 37th best course in the United States and the 65th best in the world.

This wind-swept gem became a sensation even before it opened on the heels of the U.S. Women's Open. And in this case, the course lived up to the advanced billing. The PGA and the USGA had it on their future majors list early, and the PGA came through with an accepted offer for 2004.

Many American courses advertise themselves as links courses, but only Whistling Straits and a handful of others are true links courses in the British Isles tradition. Dye sculpted a magnificent test of golf on a piece of former military land with 2 miles of lakefront; you can see the lake from part of every hole. High

Number 13 on the Irish course at Whistling Straits, Haven, Wisconsin. Photo courtesy of Kohler Co.

grasses, fescue fairways, dunes, big untended sandy areas, and pot bunkers fill out the treeless scene. Kohler added a few touches to complete the sense of being in the cradle of golf:

- The course can only be walked. "We were trying to bring the essence of golf, the roots of golf ... to the American people," says Kohler, who walks the course despite two artificial hips. "If you're really going after the essence of golf, you have to be walking the course."
- A small flock of Scottish black-faced sheep roam some holes on the back nine.
- The caddie corps is augmented by a contingent of Irish college students participating in a summer exchange program.
- And the two-story stone clubhouse looks like it was moved here from the Emerald Isle.

The ambiance rates a birdie. The golf—a hole in one. About the only thing missing is salt air.

Just about every hole at the Straits is top notch. But the eight holes along Lake Michigan are superb. Four of the most memorable are par-threes—the 183-yard number 3, the 214-yard number 7, the 166-yard number 12 (one of *GOLF* magazine's 500 best holes in the world) and the 223-yard number 17. All feature big, windswept greens perched on a bluff above the lake. But none intimidates more than 17, where even a good shot can land in the lake and ruin a good score. Seventeen is nicknamed "Pinched Nerve," and once you play it, you'll understand.

It's slightly downhill, but that doesn't really help matters much. The left side of the green and fairway drops abruptly off into sand, rocks, and water. The right side is blocked by a sloping piece of rough punctuated by a couple of pot bunkers. Mix in a little wind and a wager, and even those with steady nerves will be twitching a bit.

That's followed up by a monster of a par-four. The 470-yard 18th heads due west and inland to the clubhouse. The trip is an adventurous one. The tee shot from the longest boxes requires a 200-plus yard carry into the prevailing wind uphill over a grass-topped dunescape. The second shot—if you're in position to make a second shot to the green—is over a creek to an elevated green set into an bunkered embankment. Golfers are forgiven if they cry on their caddie's shoulder.

*7,288 yards/par-72/76.7 rating/151 slope*
*Architect: Pete Dye*
*Fees: $$$$ (walking only with mandatory caddie fee)*

## Irish Course

The newest Kohler course isn't right next to Lake Michigan, but it's close enough to give golfers grand lake views and the windy conditions that go along with the territory. Tight landing zones, lots of bunkers, creeks, wetlands, trees, and changeable weather make the Irish course severe. Depending upon how you play, you will think it combines the best—or worst—elements of the inland Blackwolf Run courses and the true links of the Straits. About the only break you'll get is that you can ride a cart if you want.

"I think the potential for disaster is greater on the Irish Course than it is on the Straits," said Dye, the master of disaster himself in the summer of 2000, when the Irish course opened for play. "I've used every trick I've ever learned in designing this course."

Wrapping around the western perimeter of the Straits course, the Irish course features many big bunkers and sand dunes. Plus, four creeks wind through the course, coming into play on nine holes. Add a splash of the "Dye-abolical" and. . . .

How tough is it? How about a blind tee shot on a par-three? Number 13 is a 183-yard par-three with a huge green of more than twenty thousand square feet built in the middle of what Dye calls a "war zone." This no-man's land surrounding the green—fit for neither golfer nor ball—contains countless pot bunkers and big dunes towering as high as 40 feet. In addition, a creek and wetlands run down the left side of the green. To make the hole even more difficult, the tee shot—even from the elevated back tees—can be a mostly blind one because of the dunes. You can see something other than trouble from the 13th tee; it's one of five holes where you can see Lake Michigan.

Eighteen is a finishing hole to remember. This 558-yard par-five requires the preferred tee shot to carry over a lake to a mostly hidden landing area on the left side. From there, the hole doglegs to the right and suggests a lay-up shot in front of a creek. The 120-yard approach uphill and over the creek is to an elevated green, which is protected by sand on the left and an embankment to the right. The 19th hole never looked so good.

*7,201 yards/par-72*
*Architect: Pete Dye*
*Fees: $$$$*
*Call: 920/565-6050 or 800/618-5535; Web site: www.kohlerco.com*
*Directions: Interstate 43 to Exit 128. Go east to Dairyland Road. Turn north*
*    and take Dairyland to County FF. Then go east to the town of Haven and*
*    Lake Michigan.*

**Other Area Courses**

# Autumn Ridge
*Valders*

This mid-1990s creation features an inventive layout and some surprisingly spectacular scenery. It's located inland from the lake, but it has plenty of water hazards—as well as trees, dramatic elevation changes, and yes, ridges. At 16, the 164-yard par-three signature hole, you hit from ridge to ridge over a bog to a green sloping steeply back toward the ravine.

*6,010 yards/par-70/72 rating/126 slope*
*Architect: Ernie Schrock*
*Fees: $$*
*Call: 920/758-3333*
*Directions: Take Interstate 43 to County C. Go west 7 miles to Pigeon Lake*
*Road. Course is on the left, across from a public boat landing.*

# Badger Creek Golf Club
*New Holstein*

Along the old travel route between Milwaukee and Green Bay, this course, opened in 1994, is worth a detour. Bring an extra sleeve of balls. Water comes into play on 11 of the 18 holes. That's in addition to the sand traps and other natural hazards.

*6,804 yards/par-72/121 slope*
*Fees: $*
*Call: 920/898-5760; Web site: www.badgercreek.com*
*Directions: Located 1 mile north of County X on Meggers Road between High-*
*ways 57 and 67.*

# Fox Hills Resort
*Mishicot*

This resort, dating from 1961, has 45 holes. Most were designed by Edward Lockie, but Bob Lohmann designed the main attraction—Fox Hills National. This 18-hole track is an early example of the inland links-style course with man-made mounds and sandy waste areas mixed in with generous water hazards and usually breezy conditions. The 438-yard par-four sixth, a big dogleg left, is a great gimmick hole. It features a peninsula fairway that juts out like an arm of a cactus into a big pond. Fun for wagering, not for scoring. Hotel, condos, restaurants, locker room, two pro shops, meeting facilities, and two indoor and two outdoor pools.

## Fox Hills National

*Architect: Bob Lohmann*
*6,948 yards/par-72/73.8 rating/136 slope*
*Fees: $$$*

## Fox Creek 18 (Red and White)

*6,406 yards/par-72/70.5 rating/123 slope*

## Fox Creek 9

*2,929 yards/par-36*
*Fees: $*
*Call: 800/950-7615; Web site: www.fox-hills.com*
*Directions: From Interstate 43 northeast of Manitowoc, exit at Highway 310 and go 5 miles to County B; turn left and go 6 miles. Course is just south of Mishicot.*

# Quit-Qui-Oc
## Elkhart Lake

This hilly course opened in 1925 on a design by Tom Bendelow, who also designed the initial front nine at Old Hickory near Beaver Dam. Elkhart Lake was a popular tourist destination for rich folks from Chicago and Milwaukee who came north on the train to stay in one of six resorts. The back nine fell into disrepair during World War II; Carl Wiese redesigned the back nine and restored an 18-hole layout in 1961—a half-dozen years after buying it.

Small greens and tight, rolling fairways characterize the course, which gets a lot of play from famous auto racers who are in town to motor at Road America.

The course has some very short holes. But holes five through 10 are as good as you'll find for a public course of this ilk. That stretch includes the 465-yard par-four dogleg left fifth, the 410-yard par-four sixth, the 212-yard par-three seventh, and the 425-yard dogleg left 10th.

A new nine, designed by Bob Lohmann around a hilltop housing development on a dramatic piece of wooded land, was due to open in fall 2001. Water, sand, and nice views will be included. Lohmann also changed two holes on the 18-hole course: 16 was transformed from a long par-three into a par-four, stretching par to 71 and cutting the number of par-threes to five; and the par-five 17th was altered slightly.

*6,178 yards/par-70/69.6 rating/119 slope*
*Architects: Tom Bendelow/Carl Wiese (redesign)*
*Fees: $$*
*Call: 920/876-2833*
*Directions: From Highway 23, go north on Highway 67 for 2.5 miles and then turn west on County J, which becomes County CJ. Go for about 1.5 miles.*

## Best Nine-Hole Course

# Fairview Country Club
*Two Rivers*

This depression-era course is hilly and fun for beginners. Discounts for juniors and seniors on weekday mornings. Make a round here part of a pleasant lakeshore drive on Highway 42.

*3,051 yards/par-36/34.1 rating/115 slope*
*Architect: John Ahrens*
*Fees: $*
*Call: 920/794-8726*
*Directions: Take Highway 42 north from Two Rivers, turn left on County VV, and then left on Riverview Drive.*

## More Fun Things to Do

You might not consider this kind of territory as a haven for art lovers, but the scions of industry in the area have generously helped make it one. You can sample the arts at the John Michael Kohler Arts Center in Sheboygan, home to a contemporary art gallery and a performing arts center, 920/458-6144, and at the Rahr-West Art Museum in Manitowoc, which features fine art in a Victorian mansion, 920/683-4501.

The Old School in Mishicot has displays of Norman Rockwell prints plus craft and collectible shops, 920/755-2291. Although the Kohler Design Center in Kohler may not feature traditional art, you'll marvel at the elegant bathroom displays. Go to www.kohlerco.com or call 920/457-3699.

Nature and history also abound in this part of the state. State parks, forests, and nature centers are readily accessible, and neat historical sites can be found throughout Manitowoc and Sheboygan Counties.

You can sample the area's history by visiting a host of great sites. Pinecrest Historical Village in Manitowoc is a "living history" museum with 23 buildings, 920/684-4445. In Two Rivers, see the Rogers Street Fishing Village, featuring an 1886 lighthouse, and the Great Lakes Coast Guard Museum, 920/793-5905.

Inland, you can see a stark contrast in modes of transportation. For a sense of what it was like to travel in the olden days, visit Greenbush's Wade House, an 1850s stagecoach inn where there's a fine collection of carriages (go to www.shsw .wisc.edu/ or call 920/526-3271), and the Elkhart Lake Depot Museum, where you can learn about local history in a century-old railroad depot (call 920/876-2922). Then fast-forward to Road America, Inc., a racetrack that draws top drivers from around the world every summer to Elkhart Lake (go to www. roadamerica.com or call 800/365-RACE).

You're by one of the Great Lakes, so why not test your sea legs? Kids and most family members will like a visit to the Wisconsin Maritime Museum in Manitowoc—the largest of its kind on the Great Lakes (www.wimaritimemuseum.com or call 920/684-0218). On display are all sorts of ships, a nod to Manitowoc's history as a shipbuilding center. And everyone can climb aboard a World War II submarine, the *USS Cobia*. Or take the family on a leisurely, nostalgic trip to the other side of Lake Michigan on the Great Lakes' last car ferry (go to www.ssbadger.com or call 888/947-3377). The ferry runs from Manitowoc to Ludington, Michigan, giving travelers great access to various public dunes up and down the Michigan coast.

Take another trip into the past with a visit to Manitowoc's downtown, where the family can find treats at a candy store and antique soda fountain.

In nearby Two Rivers, which claims to be the birthplace of the ice cream sundae, first served there in 1881, stop at the Washington House for a taste of that treat. In Sheboygan, a spruced-up downtown includes a children's museum and a riverfront boardwalk featuring galleries, shops, and restaurants.

Several state parks and recreation areas preserve some of the best of what's left of undeveloped Lake Michigan shoreline. Beachcombers of all ages are welcome. And if you have a surfboard, bring it. The Sheboygan-area shoreline is considered one of the best spots for surfing in the Great Lakes, with waves up to 24 feet. The annual Dairyland Surf Classic draws surfers and the occasional film crew. Other fine recreation areas include:

- Fischer Creek State Recreation Area, Manitowoc. Nearly a mile of shoreline. 920/683-4185.

- Kohler-Andrae State Park, Sheboygan. Two miles of sandy beach, wooded campsites and an adjacent wildlife refuge. 920/451-4080.
- Point Beach State Forest, Two Rivers. Six miles of beach. 920/794-7480.
- Woodland Dunes Nature Center, Manitowoc. Exhibits and hiking trails. 920/793-4007.

Inland, the entire family can take a walk on the wild side with a hike on the Ice Age Trail, a national scenic trail in Wisconsin that hopes to trace the 1,000-mile outline of the advance of the last great glacier more than ten thousand years ago. A good place to start is the Ice Age Visitor Center in Campbellsport, a gateway to the 29,000-acre Kettle Moraine State Forest–Northern Unit, 920/626-2116.

At the Natural Ovens Bakery in Manitowoc, children can visit a petting zoo after a tour of the bakery (go to www.naturalovens.com or call 262/758-2500). For animals without the calories, try the Lincoln Park Zoo (in Manitowoc, not Chicago). Call 920/683-4537.

## For More Information

Sheboygan: 800/457-9497; www.sheboygan.org
Kohler: 920/458-3450
Manitowoc: 800/627-4896; www.manitowoc.org/tourism.html
Two Rivers: 888/857-3529

# 12

# Green Bay and Northeastern Wisconsin

G reen and gold rules Green Bay, but we're not talking about the fall colors. The Packers, the storied community-owned franchise in the NFL's smallest market, dominate the local scene.

The Packers are always news in Green Bay. If the Packers aren't playing at Lambeau Field or on the road, then they're getting ready for the season—drafting new players, signing current players, putting players through the rigors of training, or staging some preseason games. So in "Titletown," there are only two seasons: the football season and the off season, where golf sometimes is squeezed in between spring and preseason drills.

But there's more to Green Bay than the Packers. This city of more than 102,000 people is a paper-making center. It also has lively museums, zoos, and a thriving Native American community known primarily for its casino. This is also one of the first European settlements in Wisconsin. The French settled in around 1680, called it La Baye, and made it a center of their New World fur-trading empire.

Green Bay, in addition, is a gateway to the north Lake Michigan shore and Michigan's Upper Peninsula. Along the shore, sailing enthusiasts ply the waters during breezy summers. Inland, sports anglers pursue fish in the lake and river country almost any time of year. Major stops going north include Oconto, site of Copper Culture State Park and a 2,000-year-old Native American burial ground; Peshtigo, site of a massive wildfire in October 1871; and Marinette, which shares a great lumber-milling history with sister city Menominee, Michigan.

Lately, this area is becoming known for its great golf, too. Can't find a tee time in your town? Come to Green Bay and tee it up on a Sunday when the Packers are playing. You won't have much competition.

## Brown County Golf Club
*Oneida*

T his layout has aged well since its August 1958 opening. Flashier courses have opened in the years since, but Brown County stands as one of the best—its subtle design taking advantage of rolling terrain characterized by healthy stands of mature hardwoods and ample flowing waters in the form of Duck and Trout creeks. These waters can come into play on eight of the course's 18 holes, luring plentiful waterfowl as well as golf balls.

Credit Lawrence Packard, a former Chicago-based architect who had a hand in many fine Wisconsin golf courses. He's best known now for the courses at Innisbrook, the resort north of Tampa–St. Petersburg, Florida. "We were just getting started," Packard once recalled. "It was one of our first 18-hole, regulation, big-time jobs."

Packard didn't disappoint. "We knew we had an excellent site," said Bob Barclay, a citizen and self-described "golf nut" who led the lobbying effort for the municipal golf course. "The architect really convinced us it had everything. The course has proved it's true." The locals came to love the course and dubbed it "the County." Said Packard: "I definitely consider it one of the top courses we've ever done."

Packard added more than fifty sand traps to the prime golf course property. Good, consistent course maintenance over the years has enhanced Packard's Wisconsin masterpiece.

The fourth hole is a 423-yard par-four dogleg left around trees and Duck Creek. It's the first of three par-fours over 400 yards. Number 9 is the second, and at 444 yards it's even tougher. You must hit a long drive to the corner and then hit a fairway wood or long iron uphill and over Trout Creek to a severely sloping green. Number 11, also 444 yards, begins a stretch of crucial holes the locals call their own "Amen Corner."

From the 11th tee, take in the grand view. Now get serious about placing the drive in the fairway, which runs downhill and to the right next to thick woods. The 12th hole is a tricky, 399-yard par-four that uses Duck Creek and a stand of gnarled trees as it takes a slight turn to the right.

Number 13 is the shortest par-four on the course at 349 yards, but it might be the toughest. Duck Creek and trees lie along the right side, and there's trouble everywhere. This is definitely a hole to keep the driver in the bag. Play for position, and hit two irons. This hole takes a severe lefthand turn and then comes up on a set of three ponds that make the putting surface appear like an island green. Sand also guards the severely sloping green, just in case the water hasn't made you nervous enough. If you manage bogey or better, say "Amen."

The course is capped off with a classic finishing hole, a 397-yard par-four that runs uphill and doglegs around tall trees at the corner. A shot far left tumbles into Trout Creek valley. A shot too far right will find you in the midst of some of the course's towering oaks.

Too tough? Some said that after the course opened. But in 1959, some of Wisconsin's best golfers competed at Brown County in the State Open Championship. Bobby Brue, a trick-shot artist who later played on the Senior Tour, put that to rest by shooting a sizzling 64. "He kind of bailed us out," Packard said.

*6,749 yards/par-72/72.1 rating/133 slope*
*Architect: Lawrence Packard*
*Fees: $$*
*Call: 920/497-1731*
*Directions: From Green Bay on Highway 29/32 go to County J; turn left and*
*    go about 4 miles and then left over the railroad tracks.*

# Thornberry Creek Country Club
*Oneida*

Years before Tiger Woods and the golf boom, Green Bay developer Jack Schweiner bought a 90-acre sand pit, envisioning it as part of an upscale subdivision on the western side of Green Bay. Walking through the property one day, he saw scores of golf balls that had been hit into the pit over the years by nearby residents. Somebody said to him, "Why not build a golf course?"

Schweiner wasn't a golfer, but he was a businessman. He saw a business opportunity and followed through. He got an up-and-coming designer—Rick Jacobson of Libertyville, Illinois. Jacobson crafted an unusual design—a 3,000-yard course with double greens that opened in July 1994. Plenty of sand—of course—plus water and a surprising number of mature trees make this a neat course. You hit from the first tee down into the old pit and don't emerge until you play the 156-yard par-three ninth hole and walk up the hill. The par-36 course is short—about 3,097 yards—but it's no pushover. We like the back-to-back water holes—the 168-yard par-three fourth hole and the 494-yard par-five fifth hole.

Then Schweiner bought more land—about five hundred acres this time—and Jacobson mapped out a more conventional 3,200-yard layout on a landscape of thick woods, water, and hills. New homes popped up within view of the course, which opened in June 1998. The public and local homeowners, who get a discount on a membership, gave it good reviews.

This par-35 nine is generally tight. Numbers 10, 428 yards from the back tees, and 18, 409 yards from the blue tees, are two solid par-fours with little room for error. Number 10 begins atop the same wooded lofty ridge where 18 finishes after a dogleg left between woods and water. You'll like teeing off from that elevated ridge on 10, but hitting to the elevated 18th green is tricky. The toughest hole may be the 218-yard 17 hole, a par-three cut out of the forest.

Finally, Jacobson went to work on a third phase of the project—a new nine that will measure about 4,000 yards. It's set around a monster, $1 million man-made lake in open terrain. Water will come into play on five of the nine holes, creating a lot of risk-and-reward golf strategy. The new third nine will be mixed in with the second nine, and the 18 holes will be renumbered. All will have bent grass greens, tees, and fairways.

When the new nine opens for play in spring 2001, Thornberry Creek will boast 27 holes that can play like 36 holes. There will be the low-priced course (the nine-hole course with double greens) and the higher-priced course. And players will relax in a 40,000-square-foot glass-and-stone clubhouse featuring locker rooms, a supper club, and banquet facilities. A new driving range will round out the complex.

"That's it," says Frank Guarascio, the general manager. "We'll have two very different golf courses." Not bad for a development by a businessman who still doesn't play much golf.

*6,381 yards/par-71/71.3 rating/127 slope (longest yardage of current 18)*
*Architect: Rick Jacobson*
*Fees: $$*
*Call: 920/434-7501*
*Directions: From Highway 41, go west on Highway 29. Take a left on Sunlite Road and then take another left on Pine Tree Road.*

# Cathedral Pines Golf Club
*Suring*

Beginning in 1962, Suring's golf course was the nine-hole Maple Valley Golf Course. The 5,284-yard track didn't attract much attention outside of Suring. Bob Lohmann, the Marengo, Illinois, designer, is changing that with the encouragement of owners John and Linda Saletri, who once farmed the land.

Maple Valley is no more. Golfers now are noticing its successor, Cathedral Pines. A new nine was built and opened in 1999, and the old nine someday will be transformed. "When we're finished, what had been a fairly ordinary nine-hole layout will be a new 18-hole golf course and one of the state's best daily fees," Lohmann said. "It's such a great site—lots of sand and natural contours. I loved it the moment I laid eyes on the sandy blowouts and spectacular vegetation." In the meantime, golfers can see a great work in progress.

The Lohmann-designed holes work through 170 acres of wetlands and pines. Lohmann says the parcel has a "Pine Valley feel to it," referring to the New Jersey course rated the toughest and most exclusive golf course in the United States. "This is not a densely populated region. In order to draw players from a wide area—especially from Green Bay—the owners realized we needed to create something special. That's why we went with bent grass tee to green, which is unusual for this part of the country," says Lohmann, a Wisconsin native who has designed other courses around the state.

The name of the new course comes from the Lohmann design, which carves new holes from a hardwood forest and pine plantation. "When you walk down the fairways, you really feel like you're walking down a church aisle," says Linda Saletri.

Three of Lohmann's best come in a cluster. The 12th hole is a 386-yard par-four dogleg left to a green set in dense woods. Number 13 is a 403-yard par-three with a tight landing area pinched by trees and bunkers. And 14, a 566-yard par-five, sweeps left around a wetland.

The difficulty of the new nine must have impressed the course raters: They gave it a slope rating of 141, one of the highest in the state.

Golfers traveling to Suring in 2000 played the new back nine (a 3,463-yard par-36 layout) at a higher fee than the old nine (2,678 yards, par-35). At some point, the old nine will be shut for renovation.

*6,926 yards/par-72/74.6 rating/141 slope*
*Architect: Bob Lohmann*
*Fees: $$*
*Call: 920/842-4653; Web site: www.cathedralpinesgolf.com*
*Directions: Take Highway 32. A half-mile east of Suring, turn north on Golf*
   *Course Road and go 0.25 mile.*

# Hunter's Glen

*Crivitz*

R ick Jacobson joined forces with the golfing Gruszynski family of Crivitz and co-owner Glen Mursau to craft this new 18-hole golf course in the sparsely populated vacation area of northeast Wisconsin. Jim and Sharon Gruszynski bought 179 acres on the east side of Crivitz around 1980, thinking they'd build a housing development some day. But their two sons urged them to build a golf course instead. The boys won out.

Opened in fall 1998, the course soon drew a steady stream of golfers from Green Bay and Appleton looking for good golf and open tee times at an afford-able price. Hunter's Glen, built at a bargain rate of $2 million through woods and former farmland, fits the bill.

And the course has a plan to keep improving. More sand and water will be phased in over time. But don't wait until the tinkering is finished. Hunter's Glen is a worthy golf course right now.

The open front nine features rolling hills and tall native grasses in the wide spaces between the fairways. The back nine is characterized by tree-lined fair-ways. Not quite a prairie course, not quite a links layout, not quite your typical North Woods layout, but it's enough of all three to draw local and traveling golfers. The 356-yard par-four fifth hole combines the elements. Trees line the left side; the native grasses line the right side. The elevated green is set back in the woods.

To score well here, you don't have to hit the ball far, but you do have to land it in the right place. Three of the best and most demanding holes work around a big wetland.

First in the trio is the narrow, tree-lined number 12, a 496-yard par-five. The drive comes to rest in front of a pond that stretches across the fairway. But a long driver thinking of getting home in two shots risks hitting into trees around the hilly green.

Number 13, a 182-yard par-three, features a tee shot over a tongue of the wetland to a gently sloping green flanked by a thick birch forest and underbrush. Number 14 is another par-five. This one is longer, 530 yards, and requires a tee shot over another part of the wetland to a narrow landing area with trees on both sides. Bunkers along the right side complicate the task of getting around the short dogleg right and to the green.

But the hole everybody will be talking about is 18, an uphill, dogleg right par-four of 400 yards that will be even tougher when a planned pond is built to the right of the tee. It's tough enough now—with a big bunker in the middle of the landing area. You'll like Hunter's Glen, even if you spend a lot of your round hunting balls in the grasses of the glen.

*6,395 yards/ par-72/70.5 rating/121 slope*
*Architect: Rick Jacobson*
*Fees: $$*
*Call: 715/854-8008; Web site: www.golfhuntersglen.com*
*Directions: Take Highway 41 to Crivitz and turn right at the stoplight. Take*
    *County W to Old W and then proceed 0.5 mile to the course.*

**Other Area Courses**

# Crystal Springs Golf Course
*Seymour*

T his is a well-maintained, pretty course in Outagamie County west of Green Bay featuring a new clubhouse and a three-hole family course. Water and sloping greens dominate this course, opened in 1969. One par-five measures 601 yards.

*6,595 yards/par-72/70.9 rating/119 slope*
*Fees: $*
*Call: 920/833-6348; Web site: www.crystalspringsgolf.com*
*Directions: From Green Bay, take Highway 54 west 15 miles through Seymour; then go right on French Road 2 miles.*

# Golden Sands Golf Community
*Cecil*

A pleasant course on the east shore of Shawano Lake, Golden Sands was designed by Homer Fieldhouse and opened in 1971. Lodging packages are available. Near the Menominee Casino.

*6,178 yards/par-71/69.4 rating/118 slope*
*Architect: Homer Fieldhouse*
*Fees: $*
*Call: 715/745-2189*
*Directions: Take Highway 29 northwest from Green Bay for 35 miles to Highway 117; turn right on Highway 22 and then go to County R.*

# Little River Country Club
*Marinette*

T his is a short but tricky course with woods, water, and six par-three holes. It opened in 1927.

*5,748 yards/par-69/66.5 rating/110 slope*
*Fees: $*
*Call: 715/735-7234*
*Directions: From Highway 41, take County T south, then east, to Shore Drive; turn right and go about 2.5 miles.*

# Mid-Vallee Golf Club
*De Pere*

F irst opened in 1964, the course now has 27 holes that are getting better and better each year as trees mature. Some 15 holes were built or remodeled in 1997.

*Red nine: 3,019 yards/par-35*
*White nine: 3,164 yards/par-35*
*Blue nine: 3,220 yards/par-35*
*White and Blue 18: 6,225 yards/par-70/69.5 rating/119 slope (toughest combination)*
*Fees: $*
*Call: 920/532-6644*
*Directions: On Highway 41 about halfway between Appleton and Green Bay.*

# Mystery Hills Golf Course
*De Pere*

F irst opened in 1971, the course now has 27 holes, a regulation 18 and a par-32 nine-holer measuring 1,851 yards. Nice views of Green Bay and De Pere are available on a redesigned course with more than forty new sand traps and several ponds.

*6,249 yards/par-72/70.1 rating/120 slope*
*Fees: $*
*Call: 920/336-6077*
*Directions: From Green Bay, take Highway 172 east; exit on County GV south and then left on County G 1.5 miles.*

# Royal Scot Country Club
*New Franken*

D on Herfort designed this course, which opened in 1971. Water dominates, especially on the back nine.

*6,571 yards/par-72/70.7 rating/122 slope*
*Architect: Don Herfort*
*Fees: $*
*Call: 920/866-2356*
*Directions: Three miles north of Green Bay off Highway 57. Go south on Church Road 2 miles.*

# Shawano Lake Golf Club
*Shawano*

On the north side of Shawano Lake, this course was opened in 1922, and the old clubhouse revealed within the cement block addition shows that it was the old Shalagoco (not an Indian word but a combination of letters from *Shawano Lake Golf Course*). It features small, well-tended greens and long par-fours, typical of the vintage. Numbers four, eight, and 17 each measure 445 yards over hilly terrain. Look for the osprey nesting platform in back of the number eight green.

*6,201 yards/par-70/68 rating/124 slope*
*Fees: $*
*Call: 715/524-4890*
*Directions: On County H north of Highway 29 about 45 miles from Green*
   *Bay.*

**Nine-Hole Course**

# Shorewood Golf Course
*Green Bay*

When the University of Wisconsin–Green Bay was built, nine holes of this course fell to the bulldozer. But somebody had the foresight to leave nine holes on a bluff overlooking Lake Michigan's Green Bay for the student, faculty, and public golfer. This course is short and old (dating from 1932), but its towering oak trees, small greens, and extra-tight fairways always make for a challenging round.

*2,792 yards/par-35/33.7 rating/117 slope*
*Fee: $*
*Call: 920/465-2118*
*Directions: From Green Bay, take Highway 54/57 north to Nicolet Drive. Take*
   *the third campus entrance.*

**Practice Facility**
The Golf Shack along Highway 41 near De Pere (Exit 8 along the frontage road) offers a good driving range (with heated stalls for those cold Green Bay days), a well-stocked pro shop, a bar and grill, and indoor golf simulators for those days when even hardy Wisconsin golfers must stay inside. Call 920/339-3139.

## More Fun Things to Do

You don't have to love football to have fun in Green Bay. Art lovers, train fans, history buffs, and nature lovers can have a field day in and around Green Bay and up the coast to Marinette.

The Neville Public Museum near the Fox River in Green Bay is one of Wisconsin's best museums, featuring history, art, and science exhibits. Call 920/448-4460.

Nature trails can be found at the L. H. Barkhausen Waterfowl Preserve in nearby Suamico (920/448-4466), which is also close to the New Zoo, a 43-acre natural area with animals from around the world (920/434-6814). Also try the Bay Beach Wildlife Sanctuary on the Green Bay shore, a 700-acre refuge for many native Wisconsin animals. Stop and smell the flowers at the Green Bay Botanical Garden (920/490-9457), where there's also a children's garden with a tree house and frog pond.

Families also will like two museums with outdoor exhibits. The Heritage Hill Living History Museum is set on a hill overlooking the Fox River (www. netnet net/heritagehill/ or 800/721-5150). The 66-acre park includes historic buildings moved there from other locations and staffed by folks in period costumes. The National Railroad Museum features warehouses full of historic trains in various stages of restoration (www.nationalrrmuseum.org or 920/437-7623). Some 75 train cars are on the 40-acre site, including the locomotive and two sleeping cars used by General Dwight D. Eisenhower during World War II in Europe. Families also can enjoy a short ride along the mighty Fox River on an old train.

Feeling nostalgic for simpler times? Don't miss the Bay Beach Amusement Park, a throwback to a bygone era that is still entertaining—for a fraction of the price of today's green fees. In 2000, most rides were one ticket, and tickets were five for $1.

Smaller kids will love the small-scale train, Ferris wheel, merry-go-round, and kiddy rides. Bigger kids have bumper cars, go-carts and old favorites such as the Tilt-a-Whirl. Older adults may like to twirl in the old, stately Bay Beach Pavilion, the site of frequent ballroom dancing. Near all of this is a wildlife sanctuary, a 700-acre zoo featuring timber wolves, coyotes, deer, and lots of water in a wooded setting along a 6.2-mile trail. There's also a Nature Education Center and other indoor exhibits. Call 920/391-3671.

Football fans flock to see the Packers practice at their outdoor facilities near Lambeau Field. Kids and football fans of all ages also will get a kick out of a visit to the Green Bay Packers Hall of Fame (www.packerhalloffame.com or 920/499-4281) and the Packers' Experience (www.greenbaywi.com or 920/494-3401).

If you have the penchant to gamble off the golf course, try the Oneida Bingo and Casino across from the entrance to the airport. Blackjack, bingo, slots and on-site lodging (www.wisconsingaming.com or 800/238-4263).

While you're there, sample the history of the Oneida tribe, which has distinguished itself as among the leaders in establishing tribal businesses other than gambling. The Oneida National Museum has what's billed as the largest exhibit of Oneida history and artifacts in the world. Call 920/869-2768.

More casinos and history await in Shawano and Menominee counties to the west. Two tribes—the Menominee and the Stockbridge-Munsee—operate casinos in Keshena and Bowler, respectively. But the outside attractions trump what casinos can offer. Some of the best pleasure drives in Wisconsin await.

For example, take the drive from Shawano north on Highway 55 through Keshena and then along the Wolf River to Langlade. You'll get a glimpse of the great pine forests that used to cover all of northern Wisconsin before the land was stripped by loggers. The history of those days can be seen at the Heritage Park Museum in Shawano (call 715/526-3323) and the Menominee Logging Museum in Keshena (call 715/799-3757). The Wolf River, one of the best-known trout fishing venues in the state, also offers some of the best whitewater kayaking and rafting around.

There's also a lot of undeveloped territory, good fishing, and more whitewater rafting in Oconto and Marinette counties to the east. For a picnic, some fishing and a taste of the great North Woods, try two Marinette County parks—Goodman and McClintock, with sturdy log buildings built by the Depression-era Civilian Conservation Corps.

But find time to explore a little history, too. In Oconto, go to Copper Culture State Park, where you'll see Native American mounds and a museum with artifacts from a 5,000-year-old Indian civilization (call 920/492-5836). In Peshtigo, learn about what's billed as the greatest fire disaster in American history at the Peshtigo Fire Museum (715/582-3244). On October 8, 1871, the same windy day of the more famous Chicago fire, a wild blaze destroyed the logging town and killed some twelve hundred people.

You can also take another side trip outside of greater Green Bay to pay homage to an all-American dish at the Hamburger Hall of Fame in Seymour (920/833-9522).

## For More Information

Green Bay: 888/867-3342 or 920/494-9507; www.greenbay.org
Peshtigo: 715/582-0327
Marinette: 800/236-6681; www.mari.net/marinette
Shawano: 800/235-8528

# 13

# The Door Peninsula

The Door Peninsula has so much going for it that golf often has been a secondary consideration. People didn't travel all the way to one of the prettiest peninsulas in the Great Lakes region just to play golf. And the golf courses generally were built for that very kind of player. Courses were short and forgiving, so the twice-a-year player could enjoy a rare round.

That's changing. The year 2000 saw the opening of two new golf courses near Egg Harbor on the Green Bay side of the peninsula. Now serious golfers can justify a trip built around golf.

The Horseshoe Bay Golf Club and the Orchards at Egg Harbor have been a long time in coming. Come just to play golf. It's worth the trip. And if you're coming up the Lake Michigan coast, you can easily sample some of Wisconsin's best golf, beginning with Brown Deer in Milwaukee and including The Bog, the Dye courses around Kohler and Brown County in Green Bay.

Of course, tourists have been making that northern trip to the Door Peninsula since the early twentieth century. You understand why as soon as you glimpse the water from one of the coastal roads. Pull over, get out of the car, and take it all in. You'll really get in the mood when you cross the drawbridge over the Sturgeon Bay canal, where sailboats, pleasure boats, and working boats tie up for the night. And you'll lower the blood pressure significantly by simply going to the tip of the craggy peninsula and gazing through the haze at Washington Island.

The rocky peninsula is part of the Niagara Escarpment, the dolomite ridge that runs up the right side of Lake Winnebago, turns right before Green Bay, and runs toward the big falls on the New York–Canada border.

But long before tourists, condo resorts, golf courses, and housing developments entered the scene—changing the landscape and life for the local people forever—the peninsula prospered as a center for Great Lakes fishing, lumbering, and trading.

Trading is a centuries-old activity—dating back well before Marquette and Joliet passed through La Baye Verte (Green Bay) in 1673 and before LaSalle journeyed here in 1680. The Potawatomi, Fox, Ho-Chunk, and Menominee tribes all have long histories here.

Elements of the old economic mainstays linger—especially in wonderfully out-of-the-way places such as Washington and Rock islands and in still-rural parts of the peninsula's interior. State parks, numerous county parks, large nonprofit conservation holdings, and big blocks of private land also have helped preserve some of the best of what Mother Nature gave the peninsula and what many tourists come to see. The Door County part of the peninsula—only 75 miles long and 10 miles wide—boasts 250 miles of shoreline, acres of cherry and apple orchards, a rich maritime history punctuated by more lighthouses (10) than any other county in the country, and five state parks.

Door County history and golf are best linked at the appropriately named Peninsula State Park, a 3,776-acre recreation area near Fish Creek and one of the most-visited of Wisconsin's state parks. Golfers for years have patronized the short but quaint and tricky golf course—the only state park course in Wisconsin. And anybody who plays there remembers the 69-yard par-three over a 50-foot cliff toward a 30-foot-high totem pole.

The totem pole has a story. It was unveiled on the site by Potawatomi Chief Simon Kahquados in 1927 to honor the peninsula's first inhabitants. Four years later, he died and was buried there under a huge glacial boulder that became part of the golf course growing up around it. The inscription tells us that he was "a true and worthy Indian." The pole you see today is a reproduction, put in place in 1970. The artisan, summer resident Adlai Hardin, did a fine job, capping it with a black bear—a clan symbol for the Potawatomi tribe.

For many years, Peninsula State Park Golf Course was the most-recognized place to play in Door County. True championship golf courses weren't part of the mix until the turn of the twenty-first century, when developers saw a growing market for the game. Now golfers have more of a choice, but they shouldn't forget to squeeze in a round at Peninsula, where they can hit over a cliff and pay respects to a worthy chief.

# Horseshoe Bay Golf Club
*Egg Harbor*

Horseshoe Bay isn't just one of those nice names dreamed up by the publicists for a big California development company. It's a name with historical standing in these parts. It means Murphy lumber, apples and cherries, prized Holstein dairy cows, and well-kept farm buildings like you'd see on venerable Kentucky horse farms. So the name of the golf club, on the site of the old Horseshoe Bay Farms, perfectly fits this homegrown development on a broad ledge above the waters of Green Bay.

The old farm buildings down by the waterfront are close to where white settlers traded cordwood, built barrels, and cut ice in what was once known as Cooperstown. The later village of Horseshoe Bay declined by the 1890s.

Horseshoe Bay Farms followed in 1917 on land logged by Murphy lumber. Frank Murphy, a scion of the logging family behind the new development, once started a country club at the family's Horseshoe Bay Farms.

Frank, his nephew, and some other Green Bay investors formed a board to create a country club. They built a clubhouse, paved streets, and built a number of cottages—advertising the place as the "California of the north." But it didn't work. So the Murphys shifted their attention to Holsteins (a cow named Johanna Star Reka once was known as the third-largest milk producer in the world), and the clubhouse came to be used for a "cherry camp" that paid teenage boys to do the pickings. The old farm buildings, minus the cherry camp, still stand, neatly kept.

The Frank Murphy Cowles family says Frank Murphy's dream of a country club now is being realized by this housing and golf development. Today's golfing public surely must acknowledge that the result would agree with a businessman like him. The golf course and accompanying amenities make it a must-see stop on any Wisconsin golfing tour.

You'll pay richly for the privilege of playing (just below $100 in the first year for nonmembers). But you won't be disappointed—unless you expect fantastic views of Lake Michigan on every hole. In fact, there are only two.

Still, Rick Robbins and Brian Lussier, the North Carolina golf course architects, crafted a course with many memorable holes. And they did it with few of the gimmicks and little of the punishment inflicted by many new courses. There are few forced carries, and a player can often play a safe bump-and-run—which is advised if one of those breezy Door County days is encountered. In addition, five tee markers provide ample flexibility for a vacationing group of occasional golfers.

All of that being said, this is a tough test of golf—especially from the black tees, which measure 7,101 yards. How tough? Nancy Lopez, who works with the architects, helped open the course in 2000 and shot a 75.

Robbins, Lussier, and the developers moved a lot of dirt and blasted the dolomite limestone bedrock (never far from the surface in the Door Peninsula) to establish one of the best courses in the state. They created unique holes by using rock outcroppings, remnants of the orchards, stands of pines, and stately, mature deciduous trees. To complete their fine work, the architects built greens with two or more tiers to allow for some very tricky pin placements; on some holes, the pin sits on a shelf no bigger than your backyard deck.

It's a course that defies the usual labels. It has lots of amber-colored natural grasses waving in the breeze, but it's not really a links course. It has many trees, but it's not a typical North Woods course. Well-watered fairways flow through old pastureland, but it's not a traditional inland course, either. Let's just call it well worth playing.

After an open 402-yard par-four to start, number two throws a surprise at you. A pond, hard to see from the tee, sits at the corner of this 403-yard dogleg right, setting up a touchy shot over water to a narrow, two-tiered green. The third hole, a 174-yard par-three, also features water, but only those from the very back tees must hit over a substantial piece of the pond. The fourth and fifth holes (a par-five of 521 yards and a par-three of 207 yards, respectively) are wide open again. But this was not the architects' call. Mother Nature sent a powerful twister through these holes in August 1998.

Number five looks nasty, and it is. Big traps and a big waste area lie to the right; you can't enter the waste area because it's classified as environmentally sensitive. A corn field and fence row are on the far left. And the green has enough rolls to fill a bakery. There's some sand-free fairway and mounds on the left part of the hole, so aim to the left side of the green and take a par gladly.

Number six, a tree-lined 361-yard par-four that doglegs sharply left and down over a rise, gives you a glimpse of the rock outcroppings to come. Number seven is a fairly open par-four of 407 yards that doglegs a little right. Then comes eight, a one-of-a-kind 535-yard par-five that is the premier handicap hole on the course. The fairway is split in two laterally at the drive landing area by a rocky ridge. On either side lie tall grasses and pine trees. Two fairway traps and four greenside traps complicate the approach on this sweeping dogleg left. The upper half of the fairway offers the better angle, and if you're a good player hitting downwind, you can get home in two.

Number nine—finally—offers a lake view. At the end of the 415-yard slight dogleg right par-four, you spy the lake over the wooded cliffside to the left of the members' clubhouse. The area below was the busy port of Cooperstown, and on September 16, 1900, one of the port's frequent visitors—a scow named the *Farand H. Williams*—sank in Green Bay. We hope you sink your putt.

Number 10 and many of the back nine holes travel through former apple orchards, allowing a late-season snack of the fruit that helped make Horseshoe Bay farms the largest fruit producer in the county and a major force behind the Sturgeon Bay Fruit Growers Cooperative. Taste one for yourself. It's hard to concentrate on golf under those circumstances, but you must. The 10th hole is a tough 419-yard par-four with strategically placed traps.

Number 11 is a hole you won't forget. The 408-yard par-four dogleg right features numerous rock outcroppings exposed during extensive blasting. The uphill tee shot must carry an exposed rock ridge crossing the fairway and then avoid a trap right—and mounds, thick rough, and a trap on the left. Hit too far left, and a big birch tree could present trouble in hitting to the small, shady green back in the trees.

After a pleasant journey through more apple trees at the 398-yard, par-four 12th, you come upon one of the most unusual par-fives in the state. It's liable to be one of the holes that occupies a lot of post-round talk in the sprawling clubhouse that mimics the great old barns of Horseshoe Bay Farms. Number 13 is a par-five of 584 yards that begins on an elevated tee and ends on a windswept multitiered green. How you get from tee to green is up to you. After a drive over tall grasses to a wide landing area, things get awfully complicated. The choices for your second shot are too many. That's because the fairway splits ahead of the trap on the left—with the left side of the fairway ahead far below the right side. The lower-left approach is deemed a better uphill angle to the green, but getting there is tough because two big leafy trees shade the middle and left. The right side is more open, but fail to land the lay-up shot on the narrow peninsular fairway, and you'll squander par. The right fairway ends just beyond the fairway trap on the right, about 130 yards from the green. Even if you place the second shot correctly on the right, upper shelf, you're left with a downhill shot. Those on the lower shelf have to hit over a massive, grass bunker below a steep 10-foot embankment on the left front of the green.

The upcoming holes are more typical but no easier. Numbers 14 and 15 are two long and difficult par-fours of 449 and 455 yards, respectively. Between them is a 164-yard par-three that demands an accurate iron to a multitiered green. Don't be fooled by the traps in the foreground; take an extra club and hit long. Likewise, the 195-yard par-three 17th over water requires some thought, depending upon where the pin is set on this multilevel green.

The 18th hole is the pièce de résistance of the Robbins-Lussier effort. From the very tips, it's a 604-yard monster that sweeps left to right and downhill to a green with a most spectacular view. But pay attention to the task at hand. Hit your drive toward the big flag at the barn clubhouse while avoiding the four traps at the corner. Now try to hit the second shot to the narrow fairway between the lateral rock ledge on the right and trees on the left. On your third attempt, you're bound to think a long shot will land you in Green Bay. But the green is pitched to handle a long iron, so take all the club you need.

Once you putt out, pause briefly to take in that view. Below is Frank Murphy County Park, which preserves a good chunk of the waterfront where fruit from Horseshoe Bay Farms was shipped to Peshtigo and Dyckesville for transportation on the rails. To the left is the members-only clubhouse, and up the rise a bit is the re-created barn, golf shop, grill, and real estate offices. Frank, you finally got your country club.

*7,101 yards/par-72/74 rating/134 slope*
*Architect: Rick Robbins, Brian Lussier*
*Fees: $$$$*
*Call: 920/868-9141*
*Directions: On Highway G, just south of Egg Harbor, east of Highway 42.*

# Idlewild Golf Course
*Sturgeon Bay*

The old Lost Creek Golf Course, opened in 1976, has come back after years of neglect. A group of Sturgeon Bay businessmen bought the course in the 1990s and has invested heavily to restore a fine layout to good condition. Improving the course's bunkers was the main agenda item in 2000. Most Door County visitors rush through Sturgeon Bay. But they're missing something, including this golf course and the Potawatomi State Park next door.

This is one tough golf course from the back tees, with plenty of opportunity for penalty strokes. As many as a dozen holes have hazard stakes, and eight of the 10 par-fours measure more than four hundred yards up to as long as 440 (number two, a dogleg left).

There's no view of Lake Michigan's Green Bay, even though the course is only about a half-mile away from the big water. But there's plenty of water within easy reach (alas, sometimes a little too easy to reach). Water comes into play on at least 10 holes. Most notable is the big pond in view of the beach-styled clubhouse, partially built on stilts.

The pond affects play on four of the course's best holes—the first, fourth, ninth, and the 18th holes. The first hole gets you thinking of trouble right away. The 411-yard par-four doglegs right with a tee shot over a creek bed. A bad tee shot far to the left will get your ball wet in the big pond. The fourth hole, a sweeping dogleg left around the pond, begins on an island tee and ends 428 yards later at a well-bunkered green.

Number nine—a 499-yard par-five dogleg right—features an island green; it's not as severe as 17 at the Tournament Players Club (TPC) at Sawgrass, but it's intimidating nonetheless. Number 18, a 407-yard par-four that doglegs slightly to the right, also has a green nearly surrounded by water.

Lost Creek (a Lake Michigan tributary that partially dries up in drought years), other ponds, and streamlike pond connectors provide the other water hazards. And when water isn't present, trees and sand are. Number five, a 424-yard par-four, is one of those holes where bad shots are not forgiven; the dogleg right has water near the tee, along the right side and then in front of the green.

State pros who have played the course like the layout, the bent grass greens, and the improved range. You'll like this course, too, but you might try it from the short tees the first time out. Door County is too nice of a place to get mad about a golf score.

*6,825 yards/par-72/72.4 rating/128 slope*
*Fees: $$*

*Call: 920/743-3334; Web site: www.idlewildgolf.com*
*Directions: Next to Potawatomi State Park, about 2.5 miles east of Highway*
   *42/57. Off of the highway take Park Drive to Hainesville Road to Golf Valley*
   *Drive.*

# The Orchards at Egg Harbor
*Egg Harbor*

Jack Jackson used to operate a driving range on the ridge above bustling Egg Harbor. His customers used to complain that Door County courses were too busy and not up to the standards of the courses they were used to playing in suburban Milwaukee and Chicago. Now as managing partner, he's operating a golf course that fills a niche in the Door County golf scene. Something must be going right. The new course opened in 2000, and the group already is planning another nine holes.

Here's why. The Orchards is a very good course with a comfortable clubhouse that costs less than the semiprivate Horseshoe Bay but gives you much more yardage and more acreage than your average resort course.

William Newcomb of Ann Arbor, Michigan, made the most of the elevation changes and the working orchards when designing this inland track, set on 200 acres of prime real estate. Newcomb, who used to work with Pete Dye, has designed courses at Boyne Highlands and Grand Traverse resorts on the other side of Lake Michigan.

The front nine runs through a forest dominated by birch, maples, and evergreens. A man-made, five-acre lake near the clubhouse and the fruit orchards are the main features of the back nine, which runs on the clubhouse side of the road. Before or after the round, a stop in the handsome 7,500-square-foot clubhouse—stained dark with green shingles and dormers—is in order.

Ah, now to the course, which will only get better as it matures. Four sets of tees provide flexibility for the high-handicappers in the group. From the back tees, it's 7,060 yards. The par-five measure 550 yards or more. The par-threes measure 175 yards up to 233 yards.

The mostly wooded front nine is not so tight as to hamstring the long drivers, but you can't spray it around either if you want to score well. Two of the better holes here are the 175-yard third and the 436-yard fifth.

The par-three third has a big maple tree guarding the left side of the green and a big bunker guarding the right side of the green. And the par-four fifth has length (it's the longest par-four on the course at 436 yards), slope, trees, and sand (a long trap runs along nearly the entire right side).

The scenic back nine is more open and has several downhill drives. But it seems to play tougher, especially in the wind. Number 11 is a monster 233-yard par-three to a green protected by trees and a big trap on the left side. That's followed by four par-fours. The shortest—the dogleg left, 315-yard 13th—plays longer because it demands a drive to a fairway target 20 feet above the tees. Accomplish that, and you've got a short iron to a well-trapped green that slopes sharply right. Par here certainly isn't as easy as it looks on the scorecard.

Then comes a trio of great finishing holes, all featuring the man-made lake. Number 16 is a 577-yard par-five that dips in the middle. Sand comes into play along the left side, and water comes into play on the right side for the third shot—or the second, if you're a big hitter aided by the wind. Play it smart and take a par if you can. Number 17 is a picture-perfect par-three of 195 yards. You tee up 50 feet above the green and hit down to a fairway and putting surface surrounded on three sides by water and sand. Yes, you'll want to hit it straight.

Number 18 is another backbreaking par-five. This one measures 550 yards but plays a little shorter because the tees once again are elevated. All but the most left-leaning shots have to get over part of the lake to an extra wide fairway. The hole narrows on the second and third shots; sand lines the lefthand side as the fairway juts left at the every end. There's more sand around your final destination.

After this hole, you might shy away from the Door County beaches for the rest of the trip.

*7,067 yards/par-72*
*Architect: William Newcomb*
*Fees: $$*
*Call: 920/868-2483 or 888/463-GOLF; Web site: www.orchardsateggharbor.com*
*Directions: Just north of Egg Harbor on Highway 42, right on County FF.*

# Peninsula State Park
*Fish Creek*

In many ways, this is the perfect family course—easy enough for those of varying skills but hard enough to keep the skilled golfer interested and challenged. This course is a Door County original—about the only thing missing is a 19th-hole fish boil! Golfer or not, you've got to like the setting and the spectacular views of Eagle Harbor and the town of Ephraim.

Some of the loveliest views come on the 12th and 17th holes, perhaps the best holes on the course. The 12th, a par-four of 394 yards, is an uphill dogleg left featuring a tiny landing area that's unseen from the tee. The second shot is uphill to a green cut into a steep hillside. Miss left, and your ball could roll a long way down the grassy slope, leaving another full approach shot. The best view here is from the green.

The 17th hole takes advantage of that same steep hillside. A par-three of 179 yards from the back tee, it's all downhill to a fairly level green backed by trees. No matter how you hit the tee shot, stop to admire the view. On a clear day, you can see over Eagle Harbor, past Ephraim, and up the coastline into the upper end of Lake Michigan's Green Bay.

This has always been a prime piece of real estate, according to the following passage from *Old Peninsula Days,* a book of local history written by resident Hjalmar R. Holand and first published in 1925: "The finest farm on the peninsula, and perhaps in all of Wisconsin was the old Hanson farm, across the harbor from Ephraim. It had rich deep soil, well drained, and was protected from strong winds by high, wooded hills on the north, west and south sides. There was never a crop failure on this farm. In addition, it had an unsurpassed scenic location. It is now no longer a farm but a first-class golf course in Peninsula State Park."

As Holand tells it, the Hansons settled here in 1854, cleared the land, planted many apple trees, and operated the first profitable farm in the county. The state acquired the Hanson parcel in the early 1900s, paying Olaf Hanson a mere $8,000 (about $1,000 of which went to a Green Bay lawyer). "Could anyone blame Olaf for being sore?" wrote Hanson. By 1910, the state had acquired the lion's share of the park land for about $80,000—a keen investment judging by today's real estate prices.

In 1921, a six-hole course was opened on the old Hanson farm—laid out by W. R. Lovekin of Green Bay on land leased from the state by the Ephraim Men's Club, according to Peninsula Golf Associates, the nonprofit group that helps the Department of Natural Resources maintain the course. In 1926, the courses added three more holes—these laid out by Alex Cunningham, the first course pro. Among the new holes was Peninsula's trademark par-three number eight over the cliff.

In 1929–1930, the course became an 18-hole layout, expanding to the wooded plateau above the clubhouse. Here, you'll experience a feel of what the deep peninsula forests must have been like in pre–white settlement times. Maple, pine, and cedar trees are notable.

Lawrence Packard, who designed many of Wisconsin's favorite layouts, did a major overhaul of the course in the early 1960s, creating 11 new or drastically changed holes. Packard, who used to spend some summer vacations in Door County, had the good sense to leave number eight intact. Chances are it will never be changed. And while Olaf still may be sore, that'll be just fine with the rest of us.

*6,308 yards/par-71/69.8 rating/123 slope*
*Architect: Lawrence Packard (redesign)*
*Fees: $$*
*Call: 920/854-5791*
*Directions: Off Highway 42 between Ephraim and Fish Creek.*

## Other Area Courses

# Alpine Resort Golf Course
*Egg Harbor*

Three fun nines make this a favorite of Door County visitors, who never tire of taking the tram to the top of the bluff for a spectacular view of Green Bay. The 268-yard par-four ninth hole on the Blue course—where you enjoy a spectacular water view before teeing off to the green below—is worth the price of admission. But the 365-yard first hole on the blue nine is something to remember, too, as it runs along the base of a limestone cliff. Fritz Schaller designed the "upper nine" (blue) in the 1970s. The rest dates from the mid 1920s.

A nearby resort on the water offers a restaurant, beach, tennis, and heated pool. Golf packages available.

*Red: 2,849 yards/par-35/67.9 rating/109 slope*
*White: 3,198 yards/par-35/69.4 rating/117 slope*
*Blue: 3,009 yards/par-36/67.6 rating/114 slope*
*Fees: $$*
*Call: 920/868-3000*
*Directions: Located just southwest of Egg Harbor on County G.*

# Cherry Hills Lodge and Golf Course
*Sturgeon Bay*

This resort course, opened in the mid-1980s, features small, undulating greens and difficult stances. The front nine is hilly. The back nine is flatter but has more trees. The signature hole here is the 15th, a 409-yard par-four broken in two by a cliff (about 245 yards from the back tees and about 185 yards from the white tees). Hit to the edge of the cliff and then hit the downhill, 175-yard shot to the green below. Golf instruction schools. Golf packages at the sister nine-hole course, Bay Ridge, a 2,849-yard layout in Sister Bay.

A picturesque hole at the Alpine Resort Golf Course overlooking Green Bay.

*6,110 yards/par-72/69.2 rating/121 slope*
*Fees: $$*
*Call: 920/743-4222*
*Directions: Four miles north of Sturgeon Bay on Highway 42. Turn left on
    County P.*

## Maxwelton Braes

*Baileys Harbor*

Opened in 1931, this resort course is situated on open terrain on 200 pleas-
ant, rolling acres on Door County's quiet side. Hotel, restaurant, and heat-
ed pool on site. Golf packages available.

*6,019 yards/par-70/67.7 rating/111 slope*
*Architect: Eric Van Holst*
*Fees: $$*
*Call: 920/839-2321*
*Directions: One mile south of Baileys Harbor on Highway 57.*

# Northbrook Country Club
*Luxemburg*

A well-manicured course, opened in 1970, with plenty of woods and hills. Leave the driver in the bag. The most talked-about hole here is the 10th, a demanding par-four requiring an accurate downhill tee shot and then an uphill approach over School Creek to an elevated, sloping green tucked into the woods.

*6,220 yards/par-71/69.4 rating/121 slope*
*Architect: Fritz Schaller (did much of the design and building)*
*Fees: $*
*Call: 920/845-2383*
*Directions: From Green Bay, go 14 miles east on Highway 54 to Luxemburg*
*and then turn left on County A.*

## Best Nine-Hole Course

# Deer Run Golf Resort
*Washington Island*

It's not often you have to take a ferry ride to get to the golf course, but that's the case if you take a day trip to the nine-hole Deer Run Golf Resort on Washington Island. The old Maple Grove course, though recently redesigned and renovated, doesn't quite compare to Wisconsin's other Great Lakes island course, the Robert Trent Jones–designed layout on Madeline Island.

But it's a bargain, even when you roll in the cost of the ferry ride. The remodeled resort offers a free shuttle from the ferry dock to the golf course. That way, you can leave your car on the mainland and carry your bag and shoes on the ferry.

The resort offers three bed-and-breakfast styled rooms with discounted golf, golf packages for motel guests, club rentals, motorized and pull carts, a pro shop, and full restaurant and bar service. Beaches and other attractions are nearby, including a recreation center with an indoor pool, whirlpool, and exercise room.

*2,700 yards/par-36/33.1 rating/106 slope*
*Fees: $*
*Call: 920/847-2017*
*Directions: On Main and Michigan Roads, Washington Island.*

## Practice Facility

If you're just in the mood to practice, try 27 Pines Golf Course, south of Sturgeon Bay. It has what's billed as "Door County's first championship par-three golf course" plus extensive practice facilities including a driving range, practice bunkers, and a putting green. Pro shop and lessons available. A clubhouse serves refreshments. Call 920/746-8762.

## More Fun Things to Do

If you do nothing else but sit on the shoreline for one hour and watch the waves of a great inland sea, your trip will be worthwhile. Door and Kewaunee counties offer many places to contemplate the good things in life, but the places that should be at the top of your list are the state parks, the two lighthouses with public tours, and Gills Rock at the very tip of the peninsula overlooking the Ports Des Mortise ("Death's Door") passage.

The five state parks and their nearest communities are:

- Peninsula, Fish Creek, featuring a Door County sampler—golf course, lighthouse, observation tower, summer theater, high bluffs, sandy beaches, camping, and hiking trails (920/868-3258).
- Potawatomi, Sturgeon Bay, with two miles of shoreline and an observation tower overlooking Green Bay plus camping and hiking trails (920/746-2890).
- Whitefish Dunes, Jacksonport, with 6,000 feet of sandy beach, the state's highest sand dunes, hiking trails, and features for people with disabilities (920/823-2400). Also check out Cave Point County Park on this less-developed stretch of the peninsula. Anglers should try their luck casting into the big lake from shore or by wading tributaries.
- Newport, Ellison Bay, featuring 2,370 acres of forests, 11 miles of Lake Michigan shoreline, camping, and hiking trails (920/854-2500).
- And then there's Rock Island, a once privately owned investors' retreat where primitive camping is available (920/847-2235). The two lighthouses with public tours are the Eagle Bluff Lighthouse in Peninsula State Park and the Cana Island Lighthouse in Baileys Harbor.

These state parks listed previously are fun for kids who like to explore beaches, ride bicycles, or run up observation towers and lighthouses (with or without weary parents).

Those who like amusement parks more than the natural ones can go to Thumb Fun Park and Waterworks on Highway 42 in Fish Creek. It has water slides, go-carts, bumper boats, and other such fare. Call 920/868-3418.

Kids—and anglers of all ages—like to watch salmon and trout at the Kewaunee fish ladder and egg-gathering station. Call 920/388-1025. Preschoolers will like the petting zoo at the Farm, in Sturgeon Bay, which also features nature trails and gardens. Call 920/743-6666.

Go to Gills Rock to pick up ferries and cruise ships. You can take your car to Washington Island, but no wheeled vehicles are allowed on Rock Island. For cruise information, go to www.concertcruises.com or call 920/854-2986. For ferry and passenger boat information, go to www.wisferry.com/index.html.

Sturgeon Bay, the county seat and commercial hub, is a ship watchers' paradise. Shipbuilding is still done here. And why not? A 7,400-foot canal, built in 1881, provides a 100-mile shortcut from Green Bay to the main part of Lake Michigan. Sturgeon Bay also is a center for cherry packing and processing. Try the Door County Maritime Museum and the Door County Museum for local history. Each August, a maritime festival is held.

Kewaunee and Algoma, fishing towns down the Lake Michigan coast, offer pleasant walking tours of their historic sites. Kewaunee, which experienced a brief and false gold rush in 1836, thrived on the lumber trade in the 1840s. More than 40 houses and buildings are listed on the National Register of Historic Places. Algoma is home to one of the state's largest charter fishing fleets. These boats take anglers on Lake Michigan trolling for big salmon and trout that group in the lake and take spawning runs up tributaries that are their home waters.

Take a side trip into the interior of Kewaunee County, where a group of towns between Brussels and Dyckesville represents the largest Belgian rural settlement in the United States. Other parts of Kewaunee County have a strong Bohemian flavor—what would you expect in a hamlet called Slovan?

Rainy or foggy days on the Door Peninsula—not all that unusual because of Lake Michigan's weather-changing power—aren't cause for boredom. The area boasts shops, fine restaurants, cozy coffee shops, wineries, history museums, and art and craft galleries. Check out the Jacksonport Craft Cottage, a former lumbering office, and the Fieldstone Gallery, both near Jacksonport. Or find a comfy spot in your B&B and read a book—preferably this one!

## For More Information

Door County: 800/52-RELAX or 920/743-4456; www.doorcountyvacations.com
Sturgeon Bay: 920/743-6246
Kewaunee: 800/666-8214
Algoma: 800/498-4888 or 920/487-2041

# 14

# Fox Valley
# and the Chain O' Lakes

Native Americans found Lake Winnebago, the Fox River, and the surrounding area to be prime hunting and fishing grounds, and they left us names such as Oshkosh (a Menominee chief).

The colonial French in the late 1600s took a liking to the area, too, mostly because of a water-loving mammal prized for its pelt; they left us beaver-trapping and trading lore and names such as Fond du Lac ("End of the Lake") and Lake Butte des Morts ("Hill of the Dead").

Next came the lumbermen who culled great pine logs and shipped wood products down the turbulent Fox River and the 170-foot drop to Green Bay. A thriving paper industry followed, cementing the Fox Valley's image as an industrial corridor.

But there's a softer side to the Fox Valley and Lake Winnebago region. The wealthy citizens of the Fox Valley have always liked to escape the industrial grind, and that made the nearby Waupaca's "Chain O' Lakes" a major location for weekend cabins and small resorts. You can cruise a good part of the 22-lake chain aboard a sternwheeler or a motor launch.

The entire region has become a recreational center for outdoor water sports of all kinds—from pleasure boating and sailing to fishing. In winter, thousands of hardy ice anglers set up shanties and cut big holes in the ice on Lake Winnebago, Wisconsin's largest inland lake, to spear a huge and ancient fish called the sturgeon. They're in the right place; state officials call this the largest single concentration of sturgeon in the world.

During the spring, summer, and fall, anglers use more conventional gear to fish from boats or along shore for a variety of warm-water fish, including walleye. Good trout fishing can be found in the cold-water tributaries that feed these big waters. Waterfowl hunters never have to go far to find a blind where they can shoot plentiful ducks and geese winging their way south each fall along one of North America's biggest flyways.

The region's recreational assets often are overlooked because of their proximity to more famous Wisconsin resort spots—Door County, Green Lake, and the Lake Michigan shore. But you're missing something if you don't wander a bit in this east-central part of Wisconsin. One of the best views in Wisconsin is look-ing west from the Niagara Escarpment, a 200-foot-high dolomite ridge that runs along the eastern shore of Lake Winnebago and then northeast through the Door Peninsula into the Upper Peninsula of Michigan and all the way to Nia-gara Falls. Go to High Cliff State Park in Sherwood and take in the view from limestone cliffs sacred to Native Americans. The park features effigy mounds from the pre–white settlement times and a lime kiln and a quarry built by early white settlers. Near this historic site is an important example of twentieth-century civi-lization—a scenic 6,142-yard, par-71 golf course named—appropriately enough—High Cliff.

All of the inland Fox Cities have their attributes, but the biggest one is Appleton. It's a great jumping-off spot for those after fish, fowl—or golf. When in Appleton, make sure to see an exhibit devoted to native son Ehrich Weiss, aka Harry Houdini. This escape artist can help get you in the mood to escape to one of a growing number of good golf courses nearby. But alas, even that great illu-sionist couldn't free a golf ball from one of the region's many water hazards with-out a penalty.

# Chaska Golf Course
*Appleton*

Lawrence Packard, one of Wisconsin's most prevalent designer names, laid out a fine course on gently rolling terrain that at the 1975 course opening was considered far west of Appleton. Now there's a big mall and associated sub-urban claptrap 3 miles away at the Highway 41 exit you take to go to the golf course. The course is also close to the local airport, which makes it convenient for air travelers. But Chaska—a Native American name meaning "Great White Deer"—is sufficiently "in the country" to get away from all of that and even see a tan-colored deer or two.

Like some of Packard's other Wisconsin creations—Brown County near Green Bay and Naga-Waukee in Pewaukee—Chaska brings golf into harmony with nature. Packard didn't have quite the piece of land he had with those scenic, hilly courses. But it's a pretty place with a lot of water, big traps, and young trees. And it plays long—especially into the prevailing westerly wind whipping across the farm country to the west.

You better hope the wind is behind you when you tee off on the 465-yard par-four 16th hole, a slight dogleg right with a big trap at the corner. A second shot from the front of the trap measures 216 yards. The 16th is among five par-fours of more than 400 yards.

Another tough par-four is the finishing hole, a 425-yarder that doglegs severely left around a big willow tree at the edge of a big pond. That part of the pond and a trap on the other side almost meet in the fairway, about 190 yards from the green. The very narrow opening gives the big hitters pause as they contemplate their drives on this terrific finishing hole. Four big traps surround the green, a pitch shot away from the distinctive clubhouse.

The par-threes are pure Packard—understated but penalizing to the overconfident. Water comes into play on two of the best—the 229-yard 13th and the 155-yard 17th.

Chaska also has one of the best practice areas in the region, with a driving range, practice chipping area, and practice putting green available. The clubhouse has a snack bar and locker rooms. On top of all of that, Chaska offers affordable green fees, making it a great golf bargain.

*6,912 yards/par-72/72.8 rating/129 slope*
*Architect: Lawrence Packard*
*Fees: $$*
*Call: 920/757-5757*
*Directions: Take Exit 138 off of Highway 41. Go west 3 miles on Highway 96.*

# Rolling Meadows Golf Course
*Fond du Lac*

First established in 1960, this used to be your average municipal course—open and easy to score on. But that changed in the mid-1990s with a big renovation project that turned Rolling Meadows into something quite different from its serene name. Illinois architect Dick Nugent—who has had a hand in many Wisconsin courses—turned Rolling Meadows into one of the state's finest and toughest muni layouts. Now the complex just southwest of the intersection of two major highways (41 and 151)—just drive to the big barn—boasts 27 solid holes featuring plenty of water (12 ponds), sand (some 50 traps), and long carries over trouble (a 10-acre wetland comes into play on four holes).

The holes are numbered one through 27 so you can actually play a 19th hole (a 361-yard par-four) instead of merely bellying up to it. No matter which 19th hole you've visited first, you'll remember seven—a 462-yard dogleg right par-four that demands a straight drive and a long approach over a big swamp to a green guarded by sand.

The architect added features other than expanded water hazards. Gentle mounds and nicely shaped traps give the course the feel of a more expensive, upscale layout. You get that feeling immediately on number one, a hook-shaped 397-yard par-four that features a big pond to the right of the fairway and in front of a green also protected by a "beach" bunker.

Nugent also added length to the course, pushing any 18-hole combination of the three nines to more than 6,900 yards from the back tees (the yardages listed here). The first and third nines measure 7,014 yards from the tips. Two par-fives—numbers nine and 17—are tough holes measuring more than 580 yards. Nine is a memorable hole because of the second and third shots—the second must negotiate a big tree in the fairway, and the third presents a short-but-tough approach over water to an elevated green. It's a good course that demands accuracy above all. It's a good example of Nugent-styled target golf.

All of Nugent's work comes together on the 26th and 27th holes. Number 26, a 547-yard par-five, features a waterway flowing diagonally through the last third of the hole. The hole sweeps right, and in addition to the creek there's a pond to the right of the green. The 27th is a 467-yard par-four that doglegs right around—what else?—water in the form of two ponds. It ends at one of the most contoured greens on the course.

*Numbers one through 18: 6,990 yards/par-72/73.5 rating/129 slope*
*Numbers 10 through 27: 6,988 yards/par-72/73.5 rating/129 slope*
*Numbers one through nine and 19 through 27: 7,014 yards/par-72/73.6 rating/129 slope*
*Architect: Dick Nugent*
*Fees: $$*
*Call: 920/929-3735*
*Directions: On Rolling Meadows Drive, southwest of the Highway 41 and 151 intersection.*

# Whispering Springs
*Fond du Lac*

Opened in 1997, this scenic golf course–housing development lies atop the western edge of the Niagara Escarpment overlooking Fond du Lac, Lake Winnebago, and the gothic-looking Taycheedah women's prison.

Treasure your freedom when you take in the views to the west. But pay attention. While not as penal (or as expensive) as the Kohler courses, this Bob Lohmann design can force plenty of penalty strokes from the back tees. One of the owners, Ed Huck, once remarked that Whispering Springs is a course "where you can dial up as much punishment as you want."

Take a little pressure off the first time you visit; play something other than the black tees. There are five tee sets to choose from, so there's a teebox for everybody's game.

The course is in country club condition. One amenity is lacking, however: a full-fledged clubhouse befitting the course had yet to be built as of 2000.

The course has two distinct nines—a relatively open front with a links feel and a heavily wooded back. Few holes are alike. The greens come in all shapes and sizes and surfaces, with grassy mounds and grassy bunkers framing many holes. Add four ponds and flowing creeks, and you've got the recipe for a great golf course.

Things get rolling fairly quickly. Number two, a 576-yard par-five from the very back tees, wiggles through some gentle country until the approach shot. Bunkers and mounds lie on the right. And a pond and a big trap hug the left side of the two-tiered green, with the low part of the green in the back-left corner. We hope you don't have to contend with *that* back left-corner pin placement so early in the round.

Number three, a nice 165-yard par-three, introduces the creek, which goes in front of the green. Woods lie to the left. The creek also presents plenty of trouble on the 512-yard fourth hole, crossing in front of the tee and then running along the left side until it divides the fairway.

A pond comes into play off the tee on the 371-yard dogleg fifth hole, which also features a sandy wasteland to the right. Another pond lurks on the approach at the 407-yard eighth hole.

Number nine, at 445 yards, is one of two very long par-fours. It's probably the toughest. You start in a wooded chute and hit straightaway to a fairway with trees on both sides. If you can, keep the tee shot to the right of the hickory tree in the fairway for the best angle to the green. Then things really get tough. The long approach is to a narrow green bordered on the right side by a big pond.

It doesn't get any easier on the back nine. Number 10, a 532-yard par-five, has a tree-lined creek to the right that crosses in front of the green, and the 412-yard 11th uses the same hazard.

Numbers 14 and 15 lie on the western edge of the property at the edge of the ridge. Lohmann used dramatic sandy areas to highlight these two holes, which begin a tough finishing stretch. The 14th, measuring 350 yards, demands an all-sand approach to a green surrounded by trees. The 15th, at 166 yards, starts on a tee in the woods and requires another long sand carry to an oasislike green.

Number 16 is the other long, long par-four—measuring 441 yards from the tips. The 17th, at 407 yards, doglegs right sharply at a set of fairway bunkers and around a line of trees to a green surrounded by more timber. Number 18 is another fine Lohmann par-five—high on hazards not on length at 529 yards. Trees are on both sides of the fairway, which jogs at the very end to the left over a creek and toward the pond on nine. The approach over the whispering springs can be very testy if a shouting wind is playing across the open green.

*6,961 yards/par-72/73.9 rating/134 slope*
*Architect: Bob Lohmann*
*Fees: $$*
*Call: 920/921-8053*
*Directions: Go east of Fond du Lac on Highway 23; on top of the ridge, go left on Whispering Springs Drive.*

# Foxfire Golf Club
*Waupaca*

For decades, the Waupaca area has been a popular weekend escape for Fox Cities dwellers. But golf—at least 18-hole golf on something other than a putt-putt course—wasn't in the plans of most weekenders.

That was until two Wisconsinites with golf backgrounds—David Truttman and George Stoffel Jr.—came along with a good golf idea. They helped create and sustain Foxfire, which upon its 1996 opening was hailed as the first 18-hole golf course in Waupaca County. Truttman designed the course and got it built. Stoffel, also the resident teaching pro, led a group that bought the course.

The compact course is on a former farm surrounded by wooded lots and a residential development; the par-70 course occupies only about 105 acres, small in comparison to most new golf courses. But there's room enough for 18 nice golf holes plus room for meeting facilities, a practice area, and a nice clubhouse with snack bar.

The course combines the feel of a links and parkland course. Numerous mounds topped by wild fescue provide the links feel. The bent-grass playing surfaces, a bevy of new trees, and the three big lakes provide the parkland feel.

You'll feel great if you negotiate Foxfire's tough holes. There's only two par-fives. But Truttman, a former golf irrigation system salesman, made up for that with

- Two back-breaking par-fours in a row ... the 443-yard ninth and the 453-yard 10th
- The 230-yard par-three number two hole
- The 554-yard par-five 18th, where golfers play up a narrow peninsula fairway and then have to hit the final approach over water. The 18th is the eighth Foxfire hole where water comes into play.

But one of the most notable holes isn't all that long. The 159-yard 16th is reminiscent of the 16th hole at Augusta National. In both cases, the distance between golfer and pin over water can vary a lot depending where the flag is put on the tiered green. You'll feel like you've won a green jacket if you birdie this hole and master Foxfire.

*6,449 yards/par-70/70.9 rating/124 slope*
*Architect: David Truttman*
*Fees: $$*
*Call: 715/256-1700*
*Directions: West of Waupaca on Highway 54, just west of where Highways 10,*
*    54, and 49 meet.*

## Other Area Courses

# High Cliff Golf Course
*Sherwood*

This is a short but scenic course near a state park and beautiful bluffs.

*6,118 yards/par-71/68.1 rating/115 slope*
*Architect: Homer Fieldhouse*
*Fees: $*
*Call: 920/989-1045*
*Directions: On Lake Winnebago's northeast shore about 10 miles east of*
*    Appleton and 1 mile west of the intersection of Highways 114 and 55.*

# Irish Waters Golf Club
*Freedom*

This 1990s course is laid out along Duck Creek about 15 minutes from Appleton. Number 12 has an island green.

*6,015 yards/par-71/68.9 rating/114 slope*
*Architect: Gilmore Graves*
*Fees: $*
*Call: 920/788-7444*
*Directions: About 1.5 miles west of Highway 55 on County S.*

# Lakeshore Golf Course
*Oshkosh*

Here's another fine municipal course, slated for a much-needed major overhaul to fix a perennial drainage problem. The hilly course first opened around 1920, and although short, it was a local favorite because of its easy access off Highway 41 and the number of holes along Lake Butte des Morts.

Number nine, for example, is a 220-yard par-three that starts on a tee jutting out on the water and goes uphill to a small, sloping green. The old course also featured some monster par-fours including the 454-yard number one and the 452-yard 18th hole.

Garrett Gill of River Falls handled the redesign work, which calls for tweaking the best holes; improving drainage; adding yardage, mounds, ponds, and traps; and redoing some holes such as 12, 13, and 14. The project broke ground in October 2000, and the full 18 should be ready to play by late 2001 or early 2002. "It's going to look good and play a lot better," said Gill.

*Architect: Garrett Gill (redesign)*
*Fees: $*
*Call: 920/235-6200*
*Directions: Exit Highway 41 and go east on Highway 21 for less than 1 mile;*
*    then go left and north on Punhoqua Drive.*

# Winagamie Golf Course
*Neenah*

This course got a makeover in 2000. The new Winagamie has an improved regulation course and a nine-hole beginners' course. Nice views.

*6,355 yards/par-73/69.5 rating/115 slope*
*Fees: $*
*Call: 920/757-5453*
*Directions: Six miles west of Highway 41 on County BB.*

## More Fun Things to Do
Water and other outdoor sports are first-rate options given the natural assets of the area. State parks include Hartman Creek on Waupaca's Chain O' Lakes

(715/258-2372) and High Cliff State Park on the east side of Lake Winnebago (920/989-1106). And there are these nature centers with hiking and other attractions:

- Mosquito Hill, New London, 920/779-6433
- Gordon Bubolz Nature Preserve, Appleton, 920/731-6041
- Memorial Park Arboretum, Appleton, 920/993-1900
- 1,000 Islands Environmental Center, Kaukauna, 920/766-4733
- Kaytee Avian Education Center, Chilton, 800/669-9580
- Ledgeview Nature Center, Chilton, 920/849-7094

Once a year, Oshkosh is the location of one of the busiest airports in the world during EAA AirVenture Oshkosh. Each summer it attracts more than twelve thousand experimental and other airplanes and some eight hundred thousand spectators. Year-round you can view historic civilian and military aircraft at the EAA Air Adventure Museum. Go to www.eaa.org or call 920/426-4818.

If baseball is your bag, take in a Timber Rattlers minor-league baseball game at a fine ballpark, Fox Cities Stadium, just off Highway 41 in Appleton. Go to www.timberrattlers.com or call 920/733-4152. You can watch drivers speed legally at the Wisconsin International Raceway in Kaukauna (call 920/833-9522).

Take in some performing arts at the restored Victorian-styled Grand Opera House in Oshkosh (920/424-2355).

For a rainy day, the region's museums cater to a wide variety of tastes. Discover local history and secrets about Houdini at the Outagamie Museum in Appleton (call 920/735-9370). See a spectacular collection of glass paperweights at the Bergstrom-Mahler Museum in Neenah (call 920/751-4658).

See regional and natural artifacts at the Oshkosh Public Museum (go to www.publicmuseum.oshkosh.net or call 920/424-4730). And see more than twenty well-preserved buildings at the Historic Galloway House and Village in Fond du Lac (call 920/922-6390). And if you want to get a jump on Christmas shopping, try the Kristmas Kringle Shoppe in Fond du Lac, a two-story Bavarian-styled building housing many Christmas shops (call 800/721-2525).

Kids have plenty to do in the area. A dependable stop is the Fox Cities Children's Museum in downtown Appleton (go to www.funatfccm.org or call 920/734-3226). Or they—and you—can learn about the universe at Barlow Planetarium at the University of Wisconsin at Fox Valley, Menasha (call 920/832-2848).

At sunset, why not a stroll at the end of the lake? Lakeside Park at the north end of Main Street in Fond du Lac features a lighthouse, antique carousel, petting zoo, and canoe rental (call 800/937-9123).

## For More Information

Waupaca area: 888/417-4040

Appleton and the other Fox Cities: 800/2DO-MORE or 920/734-3358; www.fox cities.org

Oshkosh: 877/303-9200 or 920/303-9200; www.oshkoshcvb.org

Fond du Lac: 800/937-9123 or 920/923-3010; www.fdl.com

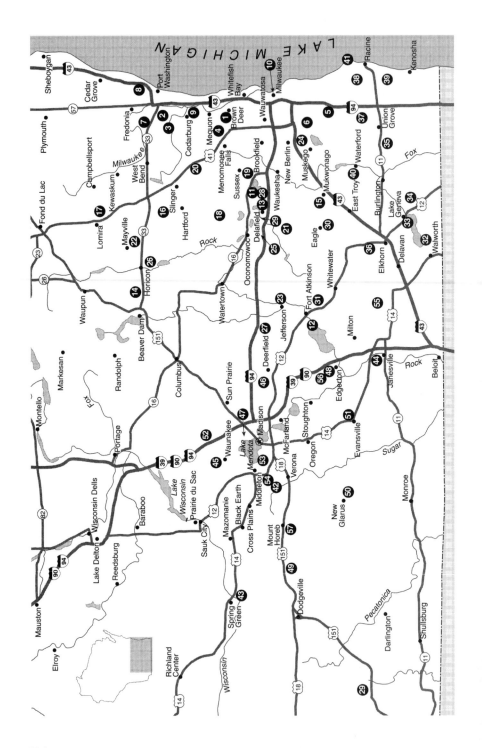

# VI

# Southern Wisconsin Lakes

# 15

# Milwaukee and Ozaukee Counties

Golf has long been a mainstay on the most populated part of Wisconsin's east coast. Gene Sarazen, one of golf's all-time greats, won the 1933 PGA title—then a match-play championship—at Blue Mound Country Club in Wauwatosa, in western Milwaukee County.

You can't play Blue Mound Country Club without an invitation. But you can play at an old municipal course where the male pros play—Brown Deer Park, a Milwaukee County course that's the site of the annual PGA's Milwaukee Open. And you can play one of the best public-access courses in the state—The Bog, in Saukville.

And someday, you'll be able to play a lakeside county course in Oak Creek's Bender Park, if all the government and financing falls into place. Bender Park, a great piece of golf property on Lake Michigan near the Milwaukee County–Racine County line, could be the location of Milwaukee County Parks' 17th course and eighth regulation 18-hole layout. Some golf fans envision a course on the scale of the Kohler courses; others say a more affordable course would be appropriate. Either way, Bender Park would build on a legacy that began in 1903, with the opening of the first county course—a six-hole layout at Lake Park.

Milwaukee County and its northern neighbor, Ozaukee County, offer a lot of golf options—from fine executive courses to top-notch practice facilities where you can satisfy your golf obsession even when the snow flies. And all of this is available amidst the attractions of the state's largest urban environment and a well-developed Lake Michigan shoreline.

The Milwaukee area is more than beer, brats, bowling, polka dancing, and cheap hamburgers at George Webb's—although those are five good reasons to visit. Take in a big-league ball game in new Miller Park. See fine art at the expanded and redesigned Milwaukee Art Museum right on the lake. Sample the best in modern music or an ethnic festival at the Summerfest grounds. Stroll the Riverwalk along the Milwaukee River. Picnic or jog in the many municipal parks. Gamble in the expanded Potawatomi casino. Visit the quaint shops of Cedarburg to the north. Launch a sport-fishing expedition from Port Washington's scenic harbor, guarded by a lighthouse. The possibilities, you see, are practically endless.

It wasn't always so. Although the meeting of three important rivers—the Milwaukee, Menomonee, and Kinnickinnic—made the area a natural spot for Native Americans, white fur traders concentrated their activities well up the coast. That made Green Bay much more important in the early white-settlement days than Milwaukee.

But that changed after the Black Hawk War, when land speculators and immigrant groups began to stream into Milwaukee. Irish, German and Slavs came in great numbers throughout the nineteenth century, helping to swell the population of a city incorporated in 1846. So many Germans settled in Milwaukee that a healthy contingent of German-language newspapers once competed for their attention. Chancellor Helmut Kohl, who reunited East and West Germany after the Cold War, visited Milwaukee with President Bill Clinton because of that heritage. Today, it's most easily sampled at the city's eateries that feature German food and beer, brewed at home and abroad. If nothing else, take in the fish fry at Turner Hall, an 1882 brick building that once housed the local German gymnastic society. This landmark, across from the Bradley Center, has been spruced up to show off its Romanesque Revival architecture and distinctive tower.

> Before teeing off at Forest Hills in La Crosse, put your ear to the ground. Train tracks cross the first fairway, and it's against the rules to hit the train or to try to hit over it.

But you can find great African-American and Mexican dishes, too, not too far away from Serbian and Italian food. This melting pot flavor of modern-day Milwaukee also is evident in its eclectic variety of architecture—from Romanesque to Flemish and everything in between. Modern buildings mix well with the handsome old buildings. Milwaukee's skyline is dominated by a few skyscrapers, including the tallest building in the state; Old World–styled City Hall; magnificent spired and domed churches; and several tall hotels. The new Midwest Express Center, across from the refurbished and expanded Marcus Hilton on Wisconsin Avenue, blends the new and old architecture.

Miller Brewing, Midwest Express Airlines, Harley-Davidson motorcycles, and Marcus Corp. (a hotel, theater, and resort company) are some of the city's most prominent corporations. They're changing the image of a corporate legacy that once got Milwaukee labeled a mere factory town.

But that image, bolstered by TV's *Happy Days* and *Laverne and Shirley,* has given way to a more cosmopolitan one where golf—not bowling—is often the sport of choice.

# Brown Deer Park
*Milwaukee*

The Milwaukee County Park System has 16 golf courses, but Brown Deer is the one that even the pros know about. Although it fell into neglect in the 1980s, the venerable course was spruced up and redesigned to make it fit for the annual PGA Tour's Greater Milwaukee Open (GMO). Since 1994, the GMO has been at Brown Deer Park, its fourth venue. The GMO started in 1968 at the North Shore Country Club in Mequon, and Dave Stockton won the inaugural event. Eventually it moved to Tuckaway Country Club in suburban Franklin before going to Brown Deer.

Those who polished up the tarnished jewel had a gem of a course to work with. First credit George Hansen, the longtime county parks superintendent who designed five of the county courses in the early twentieth century. Hansen was a young pro at Racine's public course when the Milwaukee County Park Commission hired him in 1919 to lay out the county's first course, Grant Park, overlooking Lake Michigan in South Milwaukee. Appointed parks superintendent in 1926, Hansen followed through with four other 18-hole county courses— Greenfield in West Allis, Currie in Wauwatosa, Whitnall in Hales Corners, and Brown Deer, the best of the lot.

The course was built in the late 1920s on former farmland and opened in July 1929. The Brown Deer Park setting is a spacious piece of rolling parkland with open grasslands and tall trees. Hansen worked with what Mother Nature gave him and crafted a course that hosted the USGA Public Links Championship in 1951, 1966, and 1977 and was ranked among the top 10 public golf courses in the country. But a recession and the failure of the original clay drainage system sapped course maintenance, and it fell into disrepair.

A facelift costing more than $2.25 million over a decade starting in 1987 returned Brown Deer Park to its former glory. The course's infrastructure has been fixed now. In addition, Hansen's design was tweaked by the design team of Andy North, the two-time U.S. Open from Madison, and Roger Packard. The most noticed change: shortening number 18, an uphill par-five with a 220-yard carry over a pond from the tee, to 557 yards. A new location for the 18th green eases congestion near the handsome Tudor-styled clubhouse during tournament time, tempts the pros to try for eagle, and creates dramatic TV finishes.

Other major changes included rebuilding greens, changing tee locations, adding bunkers to holes including 18, converting some outdated bunkers into grassy mounds, and redesigning the fifth hole, one of three par-threes on the front nine. The 170-yard fifth hole now plays uphill to a small green guarded by three big bunkers. The course also boasts an excellent practice area.

The pros generally like the course and its sloping, undulating greens. In 2000, in the 33rd annual GMO, Loren Roberts shot a final-round 66 to set two tournament records—the 24-under 260 total for four rounds and the eight-shot margin of victory over Franklin Langham. The course was set up at 6,759 yards and par-71.

Despite the short overall length in comparison to newer courses, Brown Deer challenges any golfer because of its long par-fours—five of them over 400, including the 447-yard 1st hole and the 461-yard 10th hole. The 10th hole is rated by some pros as the toughest hole on the course; trees line both sides of the dogleg right, a pond is located at the outside bend of the leg, and a heavily bunkered green is set back into the trees.

Brown Deer has several tough par-threes. The 215-yard par-three number seven hole features a long shot to a narrow, bunkered green often swept by a crosswind. Others are the 171-yard number three hole with woods and a deep-faced bunker guarding the severely sloping green and the 196-yard 11th hole with water and sand along the left.

One more par-three note for golf history buffs: Tiger Woods made his pro debut here in 1996. In the final round of the 1996 GMO, he recorded his first pro hole-in-one with a 6-iron at number 14, which was set up at 202 yards.

You may not be able to hit a 6-iron that far or compete directly with Tiger. But you can try to match his hole-in-one at the muni course the pros play.

*6,716 yards/par-71/72.6 rating/132 slope*
*Architect: George Hansen*
*Fees: $$$*
*Call: 414/352-8080*
*Directions: Exit Interstate 43 at Good Hope Road and go west to Range Line*
*    Road; turn north to the course.*

# The Bog
*Saukville*

Arnold Palmer's firm designed two courses in Wisconsin—the Palmer course at Lake Geneva National and The Bog. Which one's the best? Play them both, and you decide. But by all means don't let the fact that *Golf Digest* ranked The Bog as the seventh best in the state in 2000 influence your vote..

Number 11 at The Bog.

Palmer's design firm built the course in the early 1990s for Terry Wakefield, a golf traditionalist who made his money in the mortgage finance business while dabbling in high-end residential subdivisions in suburban Milwaukee. Wakefield began his search for the right piece of land in 1990 and finally settled on a 297-acre tract abutting the great Cedarburg Bog. The 1,700-acre bog on the course's western boundary is billed as the largest peatland in southern Wisconsin. And it dominates the course (hence the name) but not so much that the design is monotonous.

Palmer and lead designer Ed Seay carefully used all of what Mother Nature gave them—lovely wetlands and ample uplands with natural groves of leafy trees and wildflower-filled meadows. Wakefield wanted a simple design that emphasized the land, and that's what he got. Deep-faced sand traps—traditionally edged bunkers done in the old Scottish way—were added to define the firm consistent fairways. More than a hundred bunkers dot the course, and about 15 are revetted in the old style. The 530-yard, par-five first hole, for example, has 20 traps. You might think at that point that The Bog should be called The Trap!

But nothing is overdone here. The par-four, 470-yard 15th—the longest par-four on the course—has no sand traps. But Wakefield calls it the hardest hole on the course. This hole goes gradually uphill in the direction of the prevailing wind. You need two very good shots to make it home in two.

The result of this balanced design is one of Wisconsin's most beautiful and challenging courses—it's right up there with the Blackwolf Run courses in Kohler to the north. Few can say they've conquered The Bog. But Dave Spengler, a Wisconsin pro and frequent competitor, scored a record 65 during a U.S. Open qualifier in May 2000.

Palmer, back when he was still competing on the Senior Tour, shot a 74 from the back tees after the course opened in July 1995. And the King made triple-bogey seven on one of the trickiest par-fours in Wisconsin. The 318-yard 12th hole, a dogleg right, makes you think before you blast away, a quality lost on many new courses.

On this hole, you encounter a narrow fairway, fairway sand, a creek in front of the green, and hazard areas around the green. Try to drive over the pair of small traps on the right to set up the best approach. Even if you make the perfect drive, you've got one of the toughest shots in golf—a 60-yard pitch to a shallow green over water. Hit two irons and hope you make it. Next is number 13, a nasty 195-yard par-three with a lovely view overlooking Mole Lake (which comes into play on number 18).

The Bog finishes in fine form. After the number 15 backbreaker mentioned earlier comes the 439-yard 16th. It doglegs 90 degrees left around water and brushy wetlands. The best drive is a draw. The approach must fly bunkers right and avoid a lateral hazard to the left.

Number 17, a 593-yard par-five, also doglegs left, preventing all but the King in his prime from reaching the green in two. The longest of The Bog's par-fives, it's also deemed the toughest. Once you reach the corner, two straight and uphill shots are needed to get there in three. But most of us end up in one of the many water or sand hazards.

Take a breath on the 18th tee, and enjoy another nice view. Then try to figure out how to make par. This 430-yard par 4 offers a sampling of The Bog's charms—Mole Lake to the right, fairway sand to the left, plus sand and an out of bounds left of the green. You'll feel like royalty if you shoot close to par on one of the King's finest designs anywhere.

*7,110 yards/par-72/74.9 rating/142 slope*
*Architect: Arnold Palmer and Ed Seay*
*Fees: $$$$*
*Call: 800/484-3264*
*Directions: Take Highway 33 off Interstate 43. Go west to County I and then*
*    south 0.25 mile.*

# Country Club of Wisconsin
*Grafton*

Y ou can't afford to belong to a private country club, and you can't afford to play The Bog or the Kohler courses? Then try the Country Club of Wisconsin (CCW). The fees are lower, and the semiprivate course, situated on more than 200 rolling wooded acres a short drive from downtown Milwaukee, off Interstate 43, is as fine as many country clubs.

The course, which opened in 1994, also has an interesting history. The $4 million–plus course was financed through a public stock and bond offering; a small number of individual, family, and corporate memberships were set aside to provide cash flow; and the idea for the course began with Edgehill Consulting Group (which included some notable names in Wisconsin golf—Tony Coleman and Dennis Tiziani). Edgehill supervised design and construction of the course, laid out by Kerry Mattingly and Greg Kuehn, landscape architects from Grafton.

Despite some early opposition from neighbors and environmentalists, CCW has succeeded in providing great golf at a fair price. Four ponds, numerous wetlands, tall natural grasslands, abundant trees, and a rolling landscape of bentgrass turf provide a perfect setting for golf. The course matured quickly and got notice at the time for being the first daily-fee, championship course built in metro Milwaukee in 60 years.

One of the best holes is the par-four dogleg right fifth hole, measuring 397 yards from the back tees. Water and wetlands narrow the landing area from both sides, and the approach is to a sloping, elevated green.

The 405-yard ninth hole has a block of leafy trees to the left. But it gets really tricky on the second shot, because the fairway falls over a grassy ridge to the trap-protected green. The 532-yard 10th doglegs slightly right. A good drive will tempt the big hitter to go for the green in two, but a pond lies in what could be the landing area for those trying to roll it up with a fairway wood. Our advice: Lay up.

Numbers 17 and 18 are pretty—and pretty tough. The 17th is a 176-yard par-three with wetlands to the right and behind the green. The 18th, a 412-yard par-four, doglegs sharply around a wetland and meadow. The second shot is uphill over a rocky ravine to a green perched on a wooded ridge. After this, you could get used to country club golfing.

*7,049 yards/par-72/74.5 rating/136 slope*
*Architect: Kerry Mattingly and Greg Kuehn*
*Fees: $$$*
*Call: 262/375-2444; Web site: www.ccwgolf.com*
*Directions: Exit 93 from Interstate 43. Go west on County W 2 miles.*

## Other Area Courses

Brown Deer Park is the best and most famous of the 16 Milwaukee County courses. But at least three other 18-hole courses are rated at a level just below the course where the GMO is held. Call 414/257-8024 for information about Milwaukee County golf courses. Here are three to consider:

# Dretzka Park

*Milwaukee*

Heavily wooded and similar to Brown Deer Park but newer. Opened in 1964. The ninth, a 428-yard par-four, and the 18th, a 480-yard par-five, are tough.

*6,830 yards/par-72/72.3 rating/124 slope*
*Architect: R. Mikula*
*Fees: $$*
*Call: 414/354-7300*
*Directions: One mile north of Highway 41/45 off Highway 145.*

# Oakwood Park

*Franklin*

This is the newest of the 18-hole regulation courses, opened in 1971. It's also the longest course. Fairways have tightened as trees have matured. Number 12, a 430-yard par-four, doglegs right and goes uphill, and number 18, a 401-yard par-four, is narrow and uphill to a small hole guarded by a deep bunker.

*6,972 yards/par-72/72.8 rating/125 slope*
*Fees: $$*
*Call: 414/281-6700*
*Directions: South on 27th Street and then west on Oakwood Road.*

# Whitnall Park

*Hales Corners*

When George Hansen designed Whitnall Park, which opened in 1932, it was far away from city lights. Now the area is smack in the middle of suburbia. Towering trees make playing this parkland course a pleasure.

*6,335 yards/par-71/69.6 rating/118 slope*
*Architect: George Hansen*
*Fees: $$*
*Call: 414/425-7931*
*Directions: Take Highway 100 south to Rawson Avenue and then go east to*
*92nd Street. Look north for the park entrance.*


# Hawthorne Hills
*Saukville*

This fine Ozaukee County municipal course is a good warm-up course for The Bog. Opened in the mid 1960s, the hilly layout usually is in good shape.

*6,657 yards/par-72/70.8 rating/119 slope*
*Fees: $*
*Call: 262/692-2151*
*Directions: Take exit 96 off Interstate 43 and then go west on Highway 33 to*
*County I. Go 4 miles north on CR I.*


# The Squires
*Port Washington*

This course, built in two stages (Depression era and late 1950s), features beautiful views of Lake Michigan. Wind and terrain make this a sporty course. Two holes are most often talked about: the 555-yard fifth, a par-five with a big ravine in front of the severely sloping green, and the par-three 17th, which features glimpses of Lake Michigan over the treetops. At 250 yards, it's said by the owners to be the longest par-three in Wisconsin.

The term *taking a snowman* (an 8) takes on new meaning at Forest Ridges near Cable. The 15th green, called the "Snowman" because of its three-level shape, is 140 feet deep.

*5,791 yards/par-70/67.3 rating/112 slope*
*Fees: $*
*Call: 262/285-3402*
*Directions: 3.5 miles north of Port Washington on County LL.*

**Best Nine-Hole Courses**

# Missing Links
*Mequon*

If you're an avid player with little time, try the nine-hole championship par-three in Mequon. Missing Links opened in 1984 for use with the Cayman golf ball. The Cayman ball is designed to fly only half as far as the normal golf ball; operators of these courses found out that people actually wanted their golf balls to fly twice as far as the normal golf ball, so Missing Links became a heckuva par-three executive course. The course is a good workout for your game, and it takes about an hour and a half to play. You'll get to use all of your irons and an occasional wood to negotiate the hazards, which include water on six of the nine holes. One water hole, the 136-yard third, conjures up visions of the island green at the Tournament Players Club at Sawgrass in Florida. Call 262/243-5711.

# Milwaukee County Parks

A good way for beginners and high-handicappers to get into the swing is by sampling Milwaukee County Parks courses. Good beginner's courses include: a regulation nine-hole course (Lincoln Park), two 18-hole par-three courses (Hansen Park and Warnimont Park), and six nine-hole pitch-and-putt courses (at Dineen Park, Doyne Park, Lake Park, Madison Park, Noyes Park, and Zablocki Park). Call 414/257-8024 for information about all the Milwaukee County golf courses.

**Practice Facilities**

No matter what the weather, you can practice indoors and actually see how the ball flies. At least three inflated "domes" with inside golf ranges and other practice facilities are in Milwaukee County: Golf Park, 11027 S. 27th St., Franklin (414/304-2700); Currie Park Golf Dome, 3535 N. Mayfair Road, Milwaukee (414/453-1742); and Family Golf Center, 8500 N. Granville Road, Milwaukee (414/355-3500).

Young people interested in the game can get a primer at the Golf Foundation of Wisconsin Learning Center at Noyes Park in Milwaukee. There's also a nine-hole pitch-and-putt at Noyes Park, located on the same side of the city as Brown Deer Park (414/353-6323). Contact the foundation at 414/365-4470.

## More Fun Things to Do

Let's start with Ozaukee County, now a part of the Milwaukee metro area. The county seat is Port Washington, a pleasant city with an interesting maritime history. Visit the Lightstation Museum, in a restored 1869 lighthouse.

Three miles inland at Saukville, on the upper Milwaukee River, is Pioneer Village, a "living museum" of 17 buildings from the nineteenth and early twentieth centuries. Call 262/377-4510. You might also come across a stone marker noting the crossroads of two great Native American trading routes—the Green Bay and Dekora trails. Saukville is located at the site of a major Potawatomi village and trading post.

Now to Milwaukee, the state's largest city with the attractions to prove it. But where to start? How about the parks? Milwaukee County has one of the nation's best urban park systems—more than 150 parks and parkways on nearly fifteen thousand acres of land. One of the park system's many jewels (in addition to the golf courses) is Lake Park, planned by Frederick Law Olmsted's firm, which also designed New York's Central Park. Lake Park on the East Side has an added attraction—a gourmet French restaurant called Lake Park Bistro.

Whitnall, the county's largest park at 660 acres, is home to the Wehr Nature Center in Franklin (go to www.uwm.edu/dept/biology/wehr/ or call 414/425-8550), where nice hiking trails can be found, and to the Boerner Botanical Gardens (go to www.uwm.edu/dept/biology/boerner or call 414/425-1130), where 50 acres of indoor and outdoor gardens attract plant lovers year round.

When it's too cold to play golf, warm up at the Mitchell Park Horticultural Conservatory, where three domes house different ecosystems—all warm. Go to www.uwm.edu/dept/biology/domes/ or call 414/649-9830.

Call the parks at 414/257-6100 or go to www.countyparks.com for more information about all their attractions.

Milwaukee has a rich variety of performing arts staged at the Pabst Theater, the Marcus Center for the Performing Arts, and other, smaller venues. Consult the *Milwaukee Journal-Sentinel* (www.onwisconsin.com) for ongoing performances.

The Milwaukee Art Museum (414/224-3200) soon will open a stunning new $100 million, 142,000-square-foot addition designed by Santiago Calatrava. The museum houses more than twenty thousand fine works, including *Poppies,* by Sun Prairie-born artist Georgia O'Keeffe. When you're done inside, stroll to the lake and along the paved path toward Bradford Beach and the city marina.

Other stops for the art lover: the Pabst Mansion, a cultural museum in one of Milwaukee's most splendid buildings (414/931-0808); the Charles Allis Art

Museum, an Edwardian mansion with exhibits by Wisconsin artists (414/278-8295); and churches such as St. Josaphat Basilica (414/645-5623). The Annunciation Greek Orthodox Church in Wauwatosa, designed by Frank Lloyd Wright, is at 9400 W. Congress, but there are no tours.

The Milwaukee Public Museum, a massive building on the west side of downtown, specializes in walk-through exhibits such as one replicating a Costa Rican rain forest. It's always doing something exciting to augment its permanent exhibits, so check it out (414/278-2700). A sobering history lesson is in store for those who visit America's Black Holocaust Museum (414/264-2500), where shocking photos of lynchings can be seen. The founder is Milwaukee author James Cameron, an African-American who survived a lynching attempt.

Car buffs shouldn't miss the Brooks Stevens Automotive Museum in Mequon. It features vintage cars such as rare Packards, Cadillacs, and Excaliburs—part of the collection of the late Milwaukee industrial designer Brooks Stevens. Among other things, he designed the Oscar Mayer Weinermobile.

Speaking of hot dogs, why not munch on one while watching a sporting event? The Milwaukee Bucks play at the Bradley Center downtown into late spring if they advance in the playoffs (414/227-0500). And the Milwaukee Brewers, now in the National League and in a new home, play baseball at Miller Park just west of downtown (800/933-9000).

Wash that dog down with a beer at the game or take the Miller Brewing Company tour in nearby "Miller Valley" (414/931-BEER). Or tour another local institution, the Harley-Davidson plant (414/535-3666). And if you feel lucky after winning at golf, you might try your luck at the Potawatomi Casino, which features high-stakes bingo, slot machines, and entertainment. Go to www.pays big.com or call 414/645-6888. Look for the 95-foot-high torch.

If you're holding a torch for a loved one, treat them to a Lake Michigan cruise. Three cruise operators are worth a try: Celebration, at 414/278-1113; Edelweiss, at 414/272-3625; and Iroquois, at 414/332-4194. Or hold hands and walk around Cathedral Park, a pleasant city square on the north side of downtown surrounded by a cathedral and trendy cafés.

The big city has plenty of kid stuff, too. First on anybody's list should be the Milwaukee County Zoo, featuring a great collection of animals in a lovely setting west of downtown near Miller Park (414/771-3040). Cool off at the Lake Michigan beaches or ice skate at the Pettit National Ice Center, an Olympic training complex with daily public skating. Go to www.thepettit.com or call 414/266-0100. Hike near the lake and have the kids do hands-on projects at the Schlitz Audubon Center in Bayside, a 225-acre nature sanctuary. Go to www.asapnet.net/audubon or call 414/352-2880. Or tour a 137-foot, three-masted schooner at the Milwaukee harbor. Go to www.execpc.com\~schooner\ or call 414/276-7700.

Little kids like the Betty Brinn Children's Museum. Go to www.bbcmkids .org or call 414/291-0888. Bigger kids will like the James Lovell Museum of Science, Economics and Technology, featuring scores of interactive displays. Go to www.braintools.org or call 414/765-9966. And kids of all ages will like the huge screen at the 275-seat Humphrey IMAX Dome Theater. Go to www.humphrey imax.com/pages or call 414/319-4629.

## For More Information
Milwaukee: 800/544-1448; www.milwaukee.org/visit.htm
Port Washington: 800/719-4881
Ozaukee County: 800/403-9898

# 16

# Kettle Moraine Country

Only a little inland from Lake Michigan lies a four-county area studded with glacial ponds and lakes, emerald green hills, and vast cattail marshes. If it sounds like a good place for golf, you're right.

From Waupun at the northern edge of the Horicon Marsh, the largest freshwater cattail marsh in the eastern United States, to Eagle, in the midst of the southern unit of the Kettle Moraine State Forest, lies some of the best golf terrain in Wisconsin. You can credit the handiwork of great glaciers, which pushed and molded and shaped the landscape more than ten thousand years ago.

Good golf courses have been in Dodge, Washington, Jefferson, and Waukesha counties for decades. The Eagle Springs Golf Resort, a one-of-a-kind nine-hole layout in the old Waukesha County resort community of Eagle, dates back to 1893. That makes it one of the oldest in the state. The late twentieth century saw a boom in golf course construction, adding several very good courses to an already impressive list of places to play.

This area boasts some of the prettiest inland parts of Wisconsin, where healthy dairy farms abut sod farms, charming small towns, and fish-filled, bird-drawing waterways. The annual fall flight of Canada geese to the Horicon Marsh is a sight to behold, though the presence of the stately bird does demand careful walking on some golf courses in these parts. While some courses have recruited man's best friend to scare off the geese, a pooper scooper could come in handy. But that's a minor annoyance for access to great golf!

Though some small farming hubs have been rapidly suburbanized and transformed into Milwaukee commuters' bedroom communities, playing golf here often takes you to some of the most sedate, out-of-the way places in the state. On the way, you can experience varied slices of Wisconsin history: prehistoric Indian culture (at Aztalan State Park), religious culture (at Holy Hill), Old World ethnic heritage (at Wales, Erin, Watertown, and Germantown), dairy farming (at Fort Atkinson), and old resort areas (Oconomowoc and Eagle) where golf was one of the main attractions.

This is an area often passed through quickly by travelers driving on Interstate 94 or Highway 41. You can see a fair amount of decent golf holes right from the freeway. But a golfer would be wise to get off the four-lane roads and wander a little. You'll be pleasantly surprised by what you find.

# Bristlecone Pines
*Hartland*

Upscale golf course living isn't just for those who winter in Florida, Arizona, and the Carolinas. It's as close as Hartland, in the middle of the pretty lake country of Waukesha County. That's where developer John Malec created Bristlecone Pines, a golf course and residential development that definitely didn't spare expense when it came to the former.

Residents of fancy single-family homes and luxury golf villas not only get the country club ambiance—and often a view—they also get one of the area's premier golf courses. Residents make up the membership at Bristlecone Pines; they get reduced green fees, lockers, and advanced tee times. But at least the rest of us get to play this Scott Miller design.

In 1995 Miller laid out a course that can be a monster from the way-back tees; Malec and head pro Brien Paquette tweaked it in 1998. Par-71 at 7,005 yards is very hard to achieve. It's not just the length that provides difficulty. Numerous, large sandy waste areas sprawl around the meticulously maintained fairways and greens. Conventional sand bunkers are quite common, too. And since you're in lake country, water is no stranger.

The good news is that the driving areas at Bristlecone Pines are very generous. The bad news is that the second and third shots often must be placed inside an increasingly tight target as you approach the hole. A case in point is number three, a terrific 613-yard par-five that gets narrower and narrower. The landing area for the second shot is pinched by sand and mounds. And the third shot must fly a quartet of little bunkers in the front to a green backed by five more sand traps.

Number four is the first of several fine par-threes. The 199-yard hole has water along the entire right side. Two sand traps—one on the righthand peninsula could save your ball from getting wet—fill out the hazards.

Numbers six and seven are highlighted by the sandy waste areas. On six, a downhill 218-yard par-three, golfers see a large flat green nearly surrounded by sand. A semicircular waste area with trees nearly rings the green; a conventional sand bunker at the right front is added for good measure. Rolling it on is tough, because there's only a very slight opening to the green. Number seven, a 509-yard par-five that doglegs slightly right, is pure target golf. Waste areas cross the fairways at the midsection and about fifty yards from the green, hemming in the big hitters.

The 474-yard eighth is another one of those holes that narrows as it approaches the green. Sandy areas lie along the entire lefthand side of this straight hole. And after the drive, trees come into play on the right. The two-tiered green is backed by a grove of trees and is guarded by a bunker on the right-front side. A pin placement on the upper tier to the right makes a difficult hole even more difficult.

Water is the bane of the inaccurate golfer on the back nine. Water comes into play on all but the 582-yard par-five 11th hole. Only those hitting from the back tees on the 430-yard par-four 10th hole must contend with water, however.

But from number 12 on, wetlands, ponds, and streams make you yearn for more of those sandy waste areas. The two par-threes—the 178-yard 12th and the 146-yard 17th—are dandies. The tee shot on 17 is pretty much all or nothing. Here, golfers hit over a big wetland to a green with a ridge running from the top to the left-front corner. On the right is a creek, two traps guard the front, and a trio of pot bunkers are dug into a mound on the left.

Number 18 provides a memorable finish. Golfers hit over a big sandy area to a big landing area pinched by sand traps and wasteland. A rock-strewn creek runs along the second half of this 402-yard par-four, and trees provide the backdrop. One of the green's three corners juts into a wide section of creek on the right, providing no room for error if the pin is placed on that narrow spit of green.

Whew! After a round here, you'll wish you had a villa so you could take a quick rest. But the well-appointed clubhouse provides a nice respite for the weary. Do yourself a favor and play Bristlecone Pines from the short tees the first time.

*7,005 yards/par-71/74.1 rating/138 slope*
*Architect: Scott Miller*
*Fees: $$$*
*Call: 262/367-7880*
*Directions: From Milwaukee, go west on Interstate 94 to Exit 184 (Highway*
*    16) at Pewaukee. The course is 0.5 mile north on the left.*

# Koshkonong Mounds
*Fort Atkinson*

This course has character—and history—to spare. Koshkonong Mounds is located on the southeastern shore of Koshkonong Lake, a dammed-up part of the Rock River where Native Americans have gathered since 300 A.D. The Woodland Indians, the first known inhabitants, built mysterious effigy mounds, ranging from 20 to 140 feet long, in the shapes of turtles, birds, and tadpoles.

The Winnebago tribe came much later, and the name they gave to the wide lake stuck. *Kosh-kon-ong* meant "the lake we live on" because tribal members relied on it for wild rice, fish, and other things they needed for sustenance. But the "meadow of rice" disappeared when a dam was built on the south end of the lake in about 1850. Wonderful views of the lake are available from the first tee, 18th green, and the comfortable clubhouse, where old photos show a glimpse of the history.

After the dam came a resort. In 1870, a hotel was built overlooking the lake to accommodate hunters who came to sample what was advertised as some of the finest duck hunting in the country. A Chicago family held the property for a time until just before the turn of the century, when local businessman Art Hoard bought the property and converted it into a 30-room resort.

Hoard's cottages and hotel—called Koshkonong Place—did so well that he decided to build a golf course. He had 5,000 trees and stumps cleared and built the 3,056-yard, nine-hole course on a design that incorporated some of the ancient mounds. It opened in 1924. The current 18th green, old number nine, is surrounded by mounds including "Big Chief," the big one to the left. Pick up a brochure at the pro shop to take a self-guided tour. The Jefferson County Indian Mounds and Trail Park, at the entrance to the club, preserves more mounds.

A local group of golfers and businessmen bought the place in 1944, after the death of Hoard, and created a stock corporation, Koshkonong Mounds Resort. In 1973, the old Hoard hotel was knocked down, and a new clubhouse was built.

The old holes feature big oaks, dramatic elevation changes, small ponds, severely sloped and fast greens, and fairways that give you awkward lies. The newer holes, designed by Art Johnson, opened in 1981; these are generally longer and lie mostly on a flatter plateau inland from the big lake.

The two nines are meshing better as trees on the newer holes mature. Major improvements also have occurred at the course, including new tee boxes to lengthen certain holes, installation of a new watering system, and improved maintenance.

The toughest hole, frequent players agree, is the 531-yard, par-five fifth hole. It's a dogleg left that starts on the plateau and then dips into a narrow wooden chute that cants hard to the right. The drive goes over the hill to a spot you can't see. Then you try to hit your next shot to the only fairly level spot on the fairway— the corner of the dogleg. From there, it's dramatically uphill to a tiny green guarded by trees all around and a sand trap on the right. Par here is to be treasured.

That's followed up by a difficult par-four, which doglegs sharply right. You hit from elevated tees providing a good view of the trouble—trees and water right and out of bounds left. If you get to the dogleg, it's still a long shot to the elevated green guarded by sand on the left.

Hole number eight is a driveable 300-yard downhill par-four if you have the wind behind you. Careful, big hitters; you can't see the green from the tee. Number nine is a longer and much more interesting 349-yard par-four. It's also down-hill but has trees right and sand and a swamp to the left.

Number ten is a tough 186-yard par-three with trees all along the left. You hit from an elevated tee to an elevated green. Don't miss the green; there's nothing but high scores from the downslopes. The eleventh hole gives number five a run in the "toughest hole" category. This is a 444-yard par-four all uphill with woods on the left and trees on the right to a small green that slopes hard right.

The best of the newer holes (12 through 17) is the 528-yard uphill par-five. A big trap pinches the landing area from the left, pushing many golfers to hit their tee shots into the trees on the right. The green lies at the end of a fairway that hooks sharply to the left at the top of the hill; the green is guarded by three big bunkers. Few will be able to reach this smallish, usually windswept green in two shots.

Number 18 is intimidating until you see that it's a 451-yard par-five. Even with the extra stroke, it can pose a lot of grief. The tee lies far below the putting surface, and the golfer sees three tiers of fairway rising between thick woods on the left and water, sand, and more trees on the right. "Big Chief" awaits you at the hilltop green, and it could prevent a hot shot from going down over the hill toward the big lake.

*6,431 yards/par-71/70 rating/121 slope*
*Architects: Art Hoard/Art Johnson*
*Fees: $$ with mandatory cart on weekends*
*Call: 920/563-2823*
*Directions: Traveling about 1 mile south of Fort Atkinson on Highway 26, go*
*    west on old Highway 26 and take the first right following signs to the*
*    county park. It's at the end of the dead-end road.*

# Naga-Waukee

*Pewaukee*

Waukesha County officials showed a high degree of foresight in 1958 when they bought 200 acres of the old Audley farm for $55,000 back before Pewaukee was considered a Milwaukee suburb. The course, which opened in 1966, is still one of the state's best municipal courses. Naga-Waukee's appeal is such that it's also one of the most heavily used golf courses in the state.

Though the traffic is heavy and the tee times sometimes hard to secure if you're not a county resident, Naga-Waukee is a joy to play. As designer E. Lawrence Packard once said, "It's a very, very lovely place."

You know what he means when you step to the 14th tee. Spread out before you is a 542-yard, double-dogleg par-five that winds down a wooded hill toward gleaming Pewaukee Lake, which is often dotted with sailboats. Regardless of your score at this point, the exhilarating view makes you feel as if you can hit the drive of your life. Even if you don't, stroll down the fairway and relish the view. Holes like that are why golfers never get tired of playing Naga-Waukee, which got its name for the nearby lakes of Nagawicka and Pewaukee.

A course that attracts more than sixty thousand golfers a year must be doing something right—like managing to maintain nicely landscaped grounds and smooth greens. Course maintenance and improvement is a priority at Naga-Waukee. The 15th green recently was rebuilt, and new tees were added or rebuilt on the eighth and ninth holes. The managers here also put a premium on speedy play. The course promotes its own David Letterman–style top 10 ways to speed up play. Examples, "No. 10: Forget about honors; hit when ready"; "No. 1: take up tennis." But if you played tennis, you might never play Naga-Waukee. And that would be a shame.

Packard took a great piece of land and designed a course that is challenging for low-handicappers without being punishing to the high-handicappers. Most holes have wide landing areas for drives, big rolling greens, and places to bail out.

At Timber Terrace golf course in Chippewa Falls, watch out for the sawdust trap on the third hole. The century-old wood shavings in a pit are all that remain of an old riverside sawmill.

Good shotmaking is rewarded here. Position your drives correctly, and you'll find open avenues to the greens. But trouble lurks for those who don't find the fairway. The trouble is water on the tough fourth hole, a 427-yard dogleg right, which has a pond stretching along most of the right side. Two traps on the outside part of the dogleg make drive placement crucial.

On the fifth hole, the trouble is sand. This 362-yard, right-angle par-four has three big traps at the corner, including two on the inside corner to prevent big hitters from taking a shortcut. Two more traps guard the big green. There's more sand on number eight, a tricky 144-yard par-three with three large greenside bunkers. Trees are the trouble on holes like the uphill par-four number seven, a ticklish 365-yard dogleg right with woods along the entire right side.

On the backside, things really get interesting. You get the sense of things to come on the 411-yard, 10th hole, a downhill dogleg right bounded by trees. To achieve par, you'll need to place your drive on the flat, open landing area in the left-center fairway about 190 yards from the hole; big hitters looking to fly the trap on the right have to lay up because of looming trouble. There's only a very narrow fairway through the ravine that lies between the landing area and the green.

Drives also are key on 14 and 15. Number fourteen, the downhill par-five with the great view, is a potential birdie hole—if you set it up with a drive to a level spot on the left side. But slice into the woods to the right off the tee, and it's bogey or worse. Number 15, a 362-yard uphill par-four, becomes much easier with a drive to the level spot at the dogleg's left-hand turn. But hit into one of the three deep sand traps at the corner, and you're looking at a potentially big number.

The finishing holes wrap up nicely. Club selection is paramount on the 16th hole, a 179-yard par-three. The tee boxes offer a grand view of Pewaukee Lake. The green lies on a ledge far below tee level. Use a couple of clubs less than you normally would for the distance, and hope your shot lands on the putting surface instead of in the two big sand traps. The 17th is a long, testy par-four dogleg right of 427 yards with traps at the corner and at the green.

The 18th hole is considerably shorter at 358 yards. But don't let down your guard. It's tempting to try to cut the dogleg, but let the green and the trees deter you. Hit to the corner, which will give you a decent approach to the green at the top of the hill.

Atop the hill is the pleasant clubhouse, which has a pro shop, snack bar, locker rooms, and a display of golf antiques in the trophy cases. There's also a driving range.

*6,795 yards/par-72/71.9 rating/126 slope*
*Architect: E. Lawrence Packard*
*Fees: $$*
*Call: 262/367-2153*
*Directions: From Interstate 94, exit at Highway 83. Go north 1 block to Golf Road, turn east and go 1 mile to County E, then north 0.5 mile.*

This is a good place to mention that Waukesha County has two other golf courses of note: the 18-hole Wanaki Golf Course along the Fox River in Menomonee Falls (opened in 1971 on a design by Billy Sixty Jr.) and the nine-hole Moor Downs in Waukesha (built in 1915 as an addition to the renowned Moor Bath Hotel and Spa). For more information on Wanaki, call 262/252-3480. For more information on Moor Downs, call 262/548-7821.

# Old Hickory
*Beaver Dam*

We've all played nine-hole courses that were expanded to 18 holes with little thought to continuity. You abruptly go from the old to the new.

Old Hickory is one of those "blended" courses that works. Maybe it's the big trees, including hickory, of course. Or maybe it's the serene setting, located between the sleepy community of Beaver Dam (the hometown of actor Fred MacMurray) and the Horicon Marsh (site of awesome bird migrations during the fall and spring). Or perhaps it's the great care given to this manicured course, which didn't open to the public until the 1970s.

For whatever reason, Old Hickory is a joy to play. Heck, it'd be a joy to walk without the sticks. But take the clubs along, because you'll want to play holes like number seven. Off to the right is a pond covered with floating lily pads. The single blue heron that sometimes claims this spot as home seems oblivious to the intrusion of golf carts or the thwack of Ping against Titleist. Grass in a nearby meadow moves softly in the breeze. And trees of numerous leaves, still wet from an evening rain, shimmer in the morning sun.

While the pond lies between you and the green, it's not a frightening hazard. The carry is a little more than 100 yards from the back tee on this 158-yard par-three. The land around the green rises gently, forming a pleasant outdoor amphitheater. And just beyond is a barbecue pit—a reminder that this would be a wonderful spot for a picnic. Hit away and thank the golf gods for places like this.

Forest Point Resort and Golf Course near Gordon has proof that there's water on Mars. Actually, the owner claims that one of the water hazards on the course was created long ago by the impact of a meteor.

Old Hickory opened as a nine-hole course in 1920 on the design of Tom Bendelow, a Scotsman who had a hand in several fine Wisconsin courses. According to a 1995 club history book, the first season family membership was $10.

Over the years the course was tweaked, changed, and improved. By 1927, when local golf legend Norbert Hammer was winning his first series of club championships during brief time-outs from his farming chores, the course measured 2,849 yards and played to a par-36.

The "old nine," as it's known today, was forged in 1936 with the addition of the course's first water hole (today's number seven). Then in 1937, Billy Sixty Sr. set a course record of 31 for nine holes and 66 for 18 holes. Sixty, the longtime bowling and golfing columnist for the old *Milwaukee Journal,* occasionally played good golf at and wrote good prose about Old Hickory.

When it came time for a new nine, Billy Sixty Jr. laid out the routing, and Robert Greaves of Milwaukee did the engineering work. The 18-hole course, spread out over nearly two hundred acres, officially opened on July 7, 1968. Wisconsin Lieutenant Governor Jack Olson handled the formal dedication with a drive off the number one tee. Bobby Brue, the Ozaukee Country Club pro and trick shot artist who later played on the Senior Tour, shot a two-under 70.

The new nine, measuring 6,688 yards, was built partly on farmland that contained several rock fences made from remnants of the last glacier. Course developers left the one on number four to add a different kind of hazard on the 510-yard par-five. Other stone fences were buried or pushed into piles and covered with dirt to create grass bunkers or mounds, course members recall.

The 1968 revision also created the longest hole on the course—the 577-yard 18th. The expansion combined two short par-fours from the original layout into one great par-five. The fairway on the newer 18th is level for the first half of the hole and then slopes severely from left to right the rest of the way to the green near the remodeled clubhouse. Staying out of the right rough and the trees in that rough is key to conquering this hole.

The 16th is another good par-five, measuring 540 yards. The hole takes a sharp left turn about two hundred yards from the tee, tempting the big hitter to fly small trees and three sand traps at the corner. It's possible to cut off some significant yardage here, but out-of-bounds markers on the left could make the risk not worth the reward.

Numbers 10 and 11 are a pair of tough par-fours. Number 10 features a green high above the fairway, giving golfers only a glimpse of the flagstick. A high soft second shot from the right-center fairway is necessary. Number 11, a 421-yard hole, starts next to the number 10 green. From this elevated tee, you need to hit a long and straight tee shot to the tree-lined fairway. From there it's a long, uphill iron shot to another hard-to-see green.

Perhaps the course's most difficult hole—and certainly one of the most scenic—is number 14, a 419-yard par-four. The tee shot is from an elevated tree down a wooded chute to the 90-degree lefthand dogleg, which is backed by a pond that stretches the length of the second shot and wraps around the green.

Cutting the corner with a wood is tricky because of the high trees to your left. It's more prudent to hit a mid-iron straight-away, stopping short of the pond. From there, it's 200 yards to the water-protected green. Good luck.

But even if you plunk it into the water, look around and savor Old Hickory.

*6,721 yards/par-72/72.6 rating/129 slope*
*Architects: Tom Bendelow/Billy Sixty Jr.*
*Fees: $$*
*Call: 920/887-7577*
*Directions: Take Highway 33 from Highway 151; 2.5 miles east of Beaver Dam.*

# Rainbow Springs
*Mukwonago*

One headline writer once dubbed this "The Resort that Wasn't" because of perennial financial problems and an abandoned lodge and convention center that still haunt the place. But one of the toughest and most unusual golf courses in Wisconsin has survived the ordeal in good shape and with green fees at bargain rates.

Rainbow Springs has been a hard-to-beat track since its earliest days, despite the absence of sand traps. That's right. No sand traps. But once you've run dangerously low on golf balls, you might come to pine for the relative comfort of sandy bunkers. At Rainbow Springs, water and marsh provide more than enough trouble—for amateurs and pros alike. Fifteen of the 18 holes feature water or marsh. The Women's Western Open, once a regular stop on the LPGA Tour, was played here in 1966. Hall-of-Famer Mickey Wright won the $1,500 first prize with a four-round total of 302—the highest winning total by far on the tour that year.

Since then, a lot of golf balls have been lost in the water, woods, and wild brush at Rainbow Springs. And a lot of money and speculation have chased the dream of Francis Schroedel, a wealthy Milwaukee developer who hoped to build a complete and luxurious resort on land he and his buddies had used for a hunting and fishing retreat.

First came the Rainbow Hunting, Skeet and Trap Club, which featured an indoor pool. It opened on New Year's Day, 1959. Then came the golf course, built in the breakneck pace of 143 days, according to course historians. On the heels of that came a 756-room hotel and a 90,000-square-foot convention center—all built with the finest of materials.

But by 1966, Schroedel's grandiose project began to slide because of mounting debts. He died in 1976 at the age of 67, still dreaming the dream. On eviction day in 1973, he was said to vow: "My ghost will haunt Rainbow Springs after I'm gone." Don't believe in ghosts? The string of successors who have unsuccessfully tried to resurrect the resort may convince you otherwise. So will a look at the shuttered buildings, occasionally used for Halloween "haunted houses."

But don't let all this scare you from trying "Big Mo," as the main 18-hole course is called. (Rainbow Springs offers an 18-hole 4,253-yard par-60 executive layout called "Little Mo." It's just as tough—with seven par-threes of 200 yards or more.)

The front nine of Big Mo is relatively open, but water is present on all but one hole—good for the plentiful waterfowl but bad for those who spray the ball. After a long but fairly docile par-five 10th hole, you travel into golf wilderness for a set of testing holes that have caused even good players to wave the white flag.

Number 11 is a 215-yard par-three with little room to maneuver. Hit the ball straight or write down bogey or higher on the scorecard. Number 12 is a 440-yard par-four that evokes cries of "unfair" from many. But you'll rejoice if you somehow achieve par. The blind tee shot requires a long draw for righthanders over and around a steep, tree-covered mound left by the glaciers. But it's such a tight turn, and the landing area is so small, that few land the ball on the fairway. If you miss, you'll likely end up in the creek that runs along the right side or in a nasty spot on the hill. Even if you find a flat, playable lie, the second shot to the slightly elevated green still requires a mighty effort. All of which is why the flagstick on this hole has flown the skull-and-crossbones from time to time.

> At George Williams Golf Course, Williams Bay, part of the course runs through University of Chicago property occupied by the world famous Yerkes Observatory. Dr. James Naismith, the inventor of basketball, laid out the course.

Numbers 13 and 14 are relative breathers but not so much that par is guaranteed. Then comes 15, a 518-yard par-five. Like number 12, the drive is all-important here. It requires a 240-yard blast to clear the creek that crosses in front of you and continues down the right side. If you bail out far enough to the right, you could find the landing area you should have played on number 12. The rest of number 15 is uphill to a green that has brush and woods to the left and rear.

After 16, another tough par-three with a pond on the right, you'll emerge to play the more open and conventional two finishing holes. And you'll finish with a few stories to tell.

The Rainbow Springs golf experience is an unusual one that will bring you back—if for no other reason that to see if any resort owner can overcome Schroedel's curse.

*6,914 yards/par-72/73.4 rating/132 slope*
*Architect: Francis Schroedel*
*Fees: $$*
*Call: 262/363-4550*
*Directions: West of Interstate 43, 5 miles west of Mukwonago on Highway 99.*

# Washington County
*Hartford*

When you first look at this course, you might mistake the long, continuous ribbon of black asphalt as some sort of paved nature trail. No, it's all part of Washington County Golf Course, opened in 1997 on 175 acres of former farmland. This smooth surface for cart-riding golfers is one of the extras you get at this most upscale of municipal courses. It also boasts great practice facilities—three full practice holes, a driving range, two practice bunkers, and two practice greens.

The county also picked the right place for an airy, well-appointed clubhouse, which includes a snack shop and locker rooms. High atop a hill north of Hartford, the clubhouse offers a great view of the course and another hilltop landmark to the south—the National Shrine of Mary at Holy Hill.

If that isn't enough to inspire you, the challenge of conquering this windswept golf course will. Despite a virtually treeless landscape, Arthur Hills designed a memorable course that will test every facet of your game. Let's hope they never plant a lot of trees on this course. There's already enough trouble: more than 50 sand traps; four big water hazards; many mounds topped with high grass; three walls made of boulders gathered during the $7 million construction process; and the wind, which always seems to be a factor.

Here's hoping your tee shots are always downwind at Washington County. Because if they aren't, long par-fours—such as numbers one (417 yards from the back tees), two (449 yards), nine (450 yards), 12 (455 yards), 15 (411 yards), and 18 (405 yards)—can be awfully tough. The ninth and 18th holes can be especially difficult because they're uphill doglegs with plenty of sand.

The par-threes can be tough, too, especially the 197-yard 14th hole, which has a pond flanking the left part of the green. Hills also placed big ponds on numbers seven and eight. The latter is a 334-yard par four that doglegs left around water in the lowest part of the course. Those willing to drive over water can significantly shorten the approach shot.

But number seven is almost everybody's choice as the toughest hole on the course. It certainly deserves its 1 handicap rating. This sweeping dogleg left has water from the landing area to just before the green. Mounding creates problems on the right side, but at least that's dry land. And at 545 yards, three good shots are required to get home in regulation.

*7,007 yards/par-72/73.1 rating/130 slope*
*Architect: Arthur Hills*
*Fees: $$$*

*Call: 888/383-4653*
*Directions: From Highway 41, take Highway 60 west to Hartford; turn north*
*on Highway 83 and go 1 mile to Clover Road.*

## Other Area Courses

# The Golf Club at Camelot
*Lomira*

This pretty course is known for its steep and fast greens, built that way in 1966 to toughen up a short course on 120 hilly acres. Plenty of water and mature trees add to the challenge. This is a must stop for the traveling golfer in search of nice views of rural Wisconsin. Two of the course's best views are from two downhill par-threes, the 179-yard number two hole, and the 195-yard 13th hole.

*6,046 yards/par-70/68.8 rating/124 slope*
*Architect: Homer Fieldhouse*
*Fees: $$*
*Call: 800/510-4949*
*Directions: Take Highway 41 to Highway 67. Go east 1 mile.*

# Deertrack
*Oconomowoc*

Depending on how you're playing, you might think this course, on the edge of Alderley Lake, should be named for ducks, not deer. Water comes into play on 12 of the 18 holes at this well-maintained family course that features flowers, numerous waterfalls, and fountains. A creek and a pond challenge golfers at the 171-yard 17th, a par-three that's all carry.

*6,313 yards/par-72/71.9 rating/127 slope*
*Architect: Donald Chapman*
*Fees: $$*
*Call: 920/474-4444*
*Directions: From Interstate 94, take Highway 16 to County P, turn north, then*
*go 7 miles to County O; turn east.*

# Ironwood Golf Club
*Sussex*

This course, opened in 1996, offers a nice alternative for those who can't get on nearby Naga-Waukee. The course has a good variety of holes cut over more than three hundred acres north of Pewaukee Lake. A practice facility and full-service clubhouse complement an increasingly popular venue featuring two distinct nines.

*6,412 yards/par-72/71 rating/125 slope*
*Architect: Jim Ceman*
*Fees: $$*
*Call: 262/538-9900*
*Directions: Take Interstate 94 to Highway 16; then take Highway 16 to County KF. Go north on CR KF for 2 miles to County MD and then turn left.*

# Kettle Hills
*Richfield*

This family-run golf complex, established in 1987, offers friendly service and two good 18-hole courses set on hilly terrain near Holy Hill. Two ranges, two practice greens, and two fun courses are found here. The Ponds/Woods layout is tougher and more mature than the newer Valley course and features a tough three-hole finish—a double-dogleg par-five, a steep uphill par-three, and a 90-degree-angle par-four.

*Ponds & Woods: 6,787 yards/par-72/72.6 rating/129 slope*
*Valley: 6,455 yards, par-72/70.9 rating/122 slope*
*Architect: Donald Zimmerman*
*Fees: $$*
*Call: 262/255-2200*
*Directions: Take Highway 41/45 to Highway 167. Go west 1.5 miles.*

# Kettle Moraine
*Dousman*

On the edge of the southern Kettle Moraine State Forest, Kettle Moraine is a scenic, fun, often challenging course that uses the hills, dales, woods, and wetlands that Mother Nature presented. Starting in 1968, it was built a few holes at a time by the architect and original owner, Dewey Laak. The full 18 opened in

1978. Use your head more than your driver, and you'll do okay here. One of the area's best par threes is number seven, a 178-yard beauty that demands a shot over a wide, rough valley to a green protected by a deep-faced bunker in the front.

*6,406 yards/par-72/70.3 rating/118 slope*
*Architect: Dewey Laak*
*Fees: $$*
*Call: 262/965-6200*
*Directions: Take Highway 67 off Interstate 94 and go 7.5 miles south. The course is on Highway 67.*

## Mayville Golf Club
*Mayville*

Bob Lohmann improved this course, which dates back to the 1930s. It's a pleasant, sporty course on the edge of the great Horicon Marsh where water comes into play on five holes. Number 10, a 384-yard par-four dogleg left, demands a long carry over water to the green. Watch out for the par threes—ranging from 128 yards to 212 yards.

*6,173 yards/par-71/69.5 rating/119 slope*
*Architect: Bob Lohmann*
*Fees: $$*
*Call: 920/387-2999*
*Directions: In Mayville, east of Main Street on German Street.*

## Meadow Springs
*Jefferson*

This old nine-hole course, dating to 1920, was expanded to 18 in the 1990s. Ken Killian did the honors, designing 13 new holes and changing the rest (numbers one, two, 16, 17, and 18). His re-creation opened in the spring of 1998. This is the sister course of Meadows of Sixmile Creek in Waunakee (see p. 285).

*6,375 yards/par-71/70.7 rating/119 slope*
*Architect: Ken Killian (redesign)*
*Fees: $$*
*Call: 920/674-6858; Web site: www.madisongolf.com*
*Directions: In Jefferson, 3 blocks east of Main Street off Washington Street.*

# Muskego Lakes

*Muskego*

Another friendly design by E. Lawrence Packard. Once a private club, this 1970s vintage course went public in the 1980s and has a reputation for being a well-maintained family-run course. A lot of water and nice terrain typify this layout, which has some very tough par-fours. At the top of the list is number 10, a 443-yard hole with a creek in the landing area; the second shot is to an elevated green guarded by traps.

*6,517 yards/par-71/72 rating/129 slope*
*Architect: E. Lawrence Packard*
*Fees: $$*
*Call: 414/425-6500*
*Directions: On Highway 36/45, 3.5 miles southwest of Highway 100, south-*
*west of downtown Milwaukee.*

# Olde Highlander

*Oconomowoc*

This golf course is probably best known for the big mound that's visible from Interstate 94. It's not a glacial feature but a manmade ski hill made from the dirt and rocks unearthed during construction of the golf course and the old Olympia resort–conference center.

The course and resort are under separate ownership now, and the well-maintained course has received a recent facelift on a redesign by former owner Randy Warobick. Some old-fashioned bunkers were added. And the tough back nine was softened to remove some long carries and make it more playable. For example, number 17, which had been a 430-yard par-four, was made into a 485-yard par-five with four tees set into the base of the ski hill. The location and the changes make this a good place for a business round of golf.

*6,458/par-72/70.5 rating/118 slope*
*Architect: Randy Warobick (redesign)*
*Fees: $$*
*Call: 262/567-6048*
*Directions: Exit Interstate 94 at Highway 67. Go 1 mile and then turn left at*
*the Olympia Resort entrance.*

## Rock River Hills

*Horicon*

The name gives you a hint of the great scenery you'll find at this pretty layout near the Horicon Marsh, a bird lover's paradise. The course opened as a nine-holer in 1967, and Bob Lohmann designed the second nine, which opened in 1988. Small landing areas, tight fairways, water hazards, and up-and-down greens typify this course.

*6,243 yards/par-70/70.5 rating/127 slope*
*Architect: Bob Lohmann (second nine)*
*Fees: $$*
*Call: 920/485-4990*
*Directions: Take Highway 33 to Horicon. Take Main Street south 1 mile to the*
*course.*

## Tyranena Golf Club

*Lake Mills*

Gilmore Graves handled the expansion of this course, which dates from the 1920s. The new holes were mixed with the old, providing a nice variety. And the new holes were updated and in many cases improved. The three finishing holes are dandies: the new 449-yard, par-four 16th; the revamped uphill 184-yard par-three 17th; and the improved downhill dogleg right 361-yard, par-four 18th that ends at the edge of a pond. Nearby is lovely Rock Lake and the Tyranena Brewing Company.

*6,885/par-72/72.9 rating/127 slope*
*Architect: Gilmore Graves (redesign)*
*Fees: $$*
*Call: 920/648-5013*
*Directions: Two miles south of Interstate 94 on Highway 89 past the business*
*district.*

## Western Lakes

*Pewaukee*

The name tells you all you need to know—lots of water. This course, an E. Lawrence Packard design from the early 1960s, is seen to the north of Interstate 94 and used to be called Tumblebrook. Whatever you call it, bring a lot of golf balls.

*6,587 yards/par-72/71.2 rating/124 slope*
*Architect: E. Lawrence Packard*
*Fees: $$*
*Call: 262/691-1181*
*Directions: Exit Interstate 94 at County SS. Go north about 3 blocks and then*
*turn left on Oakton Road.*

## Willow Run
*Pewaukee*

This 1960s course also can be seen to the north of Interstate 94 going west out of greater Milwaukee. Water is present on 16 of 18 holes.

*6,384 yards/par-71/71 rating/119 slope*
*Architect: Dewey Slocum*
*Fees: $$*
*Call: 262/544-8585*
*Directions: Interstate 94 to County T. Go west on Golf Road 0.5 mile. Next to*
*Country Inn Hotel and Convention Center.*

**Best Nine-Hole Courses**

## Eagle Springs Golf Resort
*Eagle*

No golf trip to the area would be complete with a journey to Eagle Springs Golf Resort, one of the oldest and quirkiest courses in the state. Between the Rainbow Springs course and the town of Eagle, set on the shores of Eagle Spring Lake, this memorable course has a century-old apple tree growing up through the roof of the clubhouse. The clubhouse once served as the headquarters for the Eagle Springs Yachting Association, a group of elite Chicago residents who found relaxation at the family resort.

The course, dating back to 1893, has some holes that look like they were conjured up by a fantasy golf artist. The glacial landscape provided the raw material for a resort course to remember.

The 134-yard par-three number two hole—dubbed the "volcano hole" or "eagle's nest"—features a tee shot from an elevated tee to a glacial drumlin shaped like an upside-down ice cream cone. A big tree and pot bunker on the right help make this one of the toughest par-threes anywhere. Score three or 13, the locals joke.

The first two holes—and only those, for some reason—were designed by Chicago's A. G. Spaulding, the founder of the sporting goods company that still bears his name. The course was 18 holes at one time, but during World War II it was made into a nine-hole course. The course is run by descendants of the same family that started it all. Luckily for us, they're in no hurry to change this charming antique of a course.

*2,814 yards/par-35/33.2 rating/111 slope*
*Fees: $$*
*Call: 262/594-2462*
*Directions: From Interstate 94, go south on Highway 67 and then 2 miles east on County LO.*

# Spring Creek
*Whitewater*

For a quick outing on a newer layout, try the Spring Creek executive course between Fort Atkinson and Whitewater on County N. It's billed as Wisconsin's premier championship par-three, and we can't disagree. Water, deep traps, and hilly greens make this par-27, 1,644-yard course a worthy challenge. Call 920/563-4499.

## More Fun Things to Do
Even if you don't golf, there's plenty of outdoor fun and scenic beauty in Waukesha, Washington, Jefferson, and Dodge counties. The highlights—for those who like to hike and bike—are the Horicon Marsh and the southern unit of the Kettle Moraine State Forest.

During the spring and the fall, you can view thousands of geese making their annual migrations through the Horicon Marsh. Four good venues are

- Wisconsin Department of Natural Resources Headquarters, Horicon, featuring an education center, observation windows, and exhibits. Go to www.dnr.state.wi.us or call 920/387-7860.
- Horicon National Wildlife Refuge, Mayville, featuring trails, an observation area, and displays. Call 920/387-2658.

- Marsh Haven Nature Center, Waupun, featuring a trail, observation tour, and exhibits. Call 800/937-9123.
- Wild Goose State Trail, a 34-mile state bike trail from Fond du Lac to Juneau. Call 920/386-3700.

The Kettle Moraine—a north-south glacier-made corridor of hills, ponds, and ridges—is best viewed by hiking or mountain biking on numerous trails. The best entry point is the state forest headquarters in Eagle, which offers information on twenty thousand acres of prime land less than an hour from Milwaukee. Call 262/594-6200. Another good venue is the Lapham Peak Unit of the forest, near Delafield. Here, you can climb a 45-foot observation tower atop the highest point in Waukesha County. Hiking trails, too. Call 262/646-3025.

Eagle also is the site of Old World Wisconsin, a 600-acre "living history" museum where "residents" tell modern-day visitors what Wisconsin was like back in the good ol' days. The museum features 65 historical buildings (one is the church that once stood on Cathedral Square in Milwaukee) grouped according to immigrant groups, such as the Finns, the Irish, and others. Call 262/594-6300.

Elsewhere in Waukesha County, look to Waukesha and Oconomowoc for a little slice of old small-town life. Oconomowoc, in the heart of this lake country, is smaller than Waukesha and has managed to preserve a larger part of its resort town past—mansions, a train depot, and band shell, for example. Nearby Watertown has a similar feel; visit the pre–Civil War Octagon House, next to the first U.S. kindergarten (call 920/261-2796). Waukesha has a nice downtown and a nice stop for nature lovers—the Retzer Nature Center (call 262/896-8007).

West Bend, the Washington County seat and home to the appliance company of the same name, sits on the southern edge of the Kettle Moraine State Forest's northern unit. West Bend has worked hard to restore historic buildings, including the former Romanesque Revival–styled courthouse. That nineteenth-century cream-brick building now houses the Old Courthouse Square Museum, where local history is detailed (call 262/335-4678). West Bend also has a fine art museum specializing in early Wisconsin art dating back to 1850 (call 262/334-9638).

Germantown, in southeastern Washington County, is one of several communities settled by Old German Lutherans seeking their religious freedom. The old country influence is evident in the downtown and in the community's Dheinsville Historic Park (call 262/628-3170).

Religious influence is evident at the Holy Hill National Shrine of Mary atop one of the highest points in southeastern Wisconsin. Tours are available upon request. Call 262/628-1838.

Nearby, in Hartford, car buffs will appreciate the Hartford Heritage Auto Museum, featuring an extensive collection of Kissel and Nash automobiles made in Wisconsin. Hartford was the home of the Kissel Motor Car Company, which made custom cars until the Great Depression. Call 262/673-7999.

If shopping is your thing, drive your museum piece on over to the Brookfield Square Mall or the outlet mall at Johnson Creek. Both are just off Interstate 94.

Live theater on your list? Try the Fireside Restaurant and Playhouse in Fort Atkinson, Jefferson County. Musicals are the specialty of the house. Go to www.firesidetheatre.com or call 800/477-9505.

Fort Atkinson also has a rich history on the Rock River, which provides a pleasant backdrop to several city parks. Gen. Henry Atkinson built a fort on the river here in 1832. Later, another settler, W. D. Hoard, became governor and the father of Wisconsin dairy farming. See the Hoard Museum and dairy shrine in his 1860s mansion. Call 920/563-7769.

For a little refreshment and a tiny bit of state political history, stop at Bienfang's tavern, a Fort Atkinson fixture since the 1930s. It's always been a hangout for local pols, but the story goes that Richard Nixon made a brief stop here in 1960 during his unsuccessful campaign for president.

In terms of longevity, nothing compares to the history at Aztalan State Park, near the charming Victorian-styled community of Lake Mills. Aztalan preserves an archaeological site showcasing a twelfth-century Indian village. Call 920/648-8774.

A microbrewery named Tyranena after the lake of the ancient people has built on this history to craft "the legendary Wisconsin beers of the Tyranena Brewing Co." Try them out. Or visit online at www.tyranena.com and in Lake Mills on the shores of Rock Lake in Lake Mills.

Got kids? A sure-fire hit for toddlers is the noise and motion of the Kettle Moraine Steam Train, a vintage steam locomotive that takes an 8-mile trip. It's located in North Lake on Highway 83. Call 262/782-8074.

## For More Information

Brookfield: 800/388-1835
Eagle: 800/366-8474
Fort Atkinson: 888/733-3678
Dodge County: 800/414-0101
Germantown: 262/255-1812
Oconomowoc: 800/524-3744
Waukesha: 800/366-8474

# 17

# Lake Geneva, Racine, and Kenosha

The far southeastern part of Wisconsin has a strong Chicago flavor. Many residents work in Illinois and live in Wisconsin. Many people, even the Wisconsinites, root for the Chicago Cubs.

And Lake Geneva—well, that's been a summer playground for the rich Chicago crowd since the 1870s. There's a Wrigley Drive in Lake Geneva. Heck, we once ran into two Chicago sports announcers, the late Harry Carey and "Hawk" Harrelson, at Geneva National Golf Club and shared a friendly round of drinks. In these parts one could imagine seeing posted signs reading "Flatlanders Welcome Here." Chicagoland and Illinois are an integral and recognized part of the economy.

But this part of Wisconsin retains a certain nostalgic flavor that's getting harder to find across the border. Witness the trolleys and Italian clubs of Kenosha; the Wind Point Lighthouse of Racine—one of the oldest (1880) and tallest on the Great Lakes; two strong Frank Lloyd Wright designs in Racine— Wingspread and the Johnson Wax building; the small-town flavor of Waterford; native landscapes at the Bong State Recreation Area and the Chiwaukee Prairie; the circus history of Delavan, where many nineteenth-century traveling circuses stayed for the winter; and the strand of elegant mansions ringing Lake Geneva. Many times you're a mere 90 minutes from Chicago's Loop, but you often feel many more miles and some decades removed.

To make it even better, there's a lot of great golf—some of it still very affordable—in Racine, Kenosha, and Walworth Counties. Some of the golf is played on new courses, such as the 36-hole Hawk's View Golf Club in Lake Geneva (262/348-9900). And some of the golf is played on some very old courses. One such venue is on the property of and next to the Yerkes Observatory, the 1897 University of Chicago facility that houses the world's largest refracting telescope. The George Williams Golf Course, which started in Williams Bay as the Kishwau-ke-toc Golf Club in 1901, was first designed by James Naismith, the inventor of basketball. Unfortunately, the cups on the greens are not the size of basketball hoops. The course now has 18 holes measuring 5,066 yards (262/245-9507).

The best golf courses, not surprisingly, are on the north side of tourist-rich Lake Geneva. But don't limit yourself. Explore a little, with our help, and you'll be rewarded.

The 12th hole at Abbey Springs.

# Abbey Springs Golf Course
*Fontana*

Some of the best views are on the "other side" of Lake Geneva. That's where you'll find Abbey Springs Golf Course. And if all you get for your money are the views, then you've gotten a very good deal. In the fall, which comes rather late in southern Wisconsin, the views will allow you to forget a lousy round. Stand above tree-top level on the 12th and 17th tees. Gaze over the green fairways to brilliantly colored woods and shimmering Lake Geneva. And forget your woes.

But there's more to Abbey Springs than beautiful scenery. There's meticulously manicured grounds. Here's a place that comes as advertised: "A Public Course with a Country Club Atmosphere."

And there's constant variety because of the dramatic elevation changes. The 10th hole, for example, is a backbreaking 545 yards from the championship tee and uphill all the way. Trees and underbrush line both sides of the fairway, and the elevated green rejects shots like a sloping putting surface at Pinehurst, says longtime head pro Jack Shoger.

Conversely, numbers 12 and 17, the lake-view holes, play considerably shorter than their respected measured distances of 347 and 320 yards. Both holes seem to invite an attempt to drive the green. Take our advice—it's not a smart play in either case. Hitting the drive sideways will be penalized, and both greens are small and well protected.

An accurate fairway wood or a long-iron hit down the right side of number 12 will kick the ball toward the middle of the banked fairway, leaving a short-iron to a green protected by traps left and right. The situation is similar on number 17, the designated signature hole with a drop of about 100 feet from tee to green. Our recommended approach: Hit an accurate iron off the tee, followed by a short approach shot. This green has a steep-faced bunker at the front, with a marshy hazard to the left and rear. The 13th hole measures 315 yards but plays longer because it's all uphill to a two-tiered green with as much elevation between the tiers as we've seen.

Want more? The 14th hole is a 520-yard par-five that offers a blind tee shot to a narrow fairway. But take heart. Mounding along both sides of the fairway helps keep the ball in play. The second shot will be a lay-up short of a pond that has a narrow strip of beach along its front edge. The approach is to a shallow green with significant back-to-front slope.

The most difficult hole at Abbey Springs is the par-four 15th, which measures 467 yards from the championship tee. The drive goes into the upslope of the fairway, dramatically reducing any roll. A big drive is needed to get a flat lie for the second shot. Even then, you still have about two hundred more yards to go. Ahead, in front of the green, is a large sand trap—definitely something to consider as you line up that long approach shot.

Designed by the former team of Ken Killian and Dick Nugent, Abbey Springs opened in 1972. Tapping into Chicago visitors seemed a cinch. But despite its beautiful location, Abbey Springs struggled through the 1970s. In 1981, the course was sold to a group of residents who owned land around the course. The new owners' association launched an improvement plan that enlarged tees and greens, added bunkers, and upgraded the irrigation and drainage systems. All changes were made with the original design in mind and with the oversight of Killian and Associates. Recent improvements include a rebuilt green complex on the 358-yard third hole and a new tee complex on number 17.

Visitors are welcome to use the range, putting green, halfway house, and the 19th hole, but some facilities—such as the yacht club and marina—are for members only. So what? The spectacular views come with the green fee.

*6,259 yards/par-72/71.4 rating/133 slope*
*Architects: Ken Killian and Dick Nugent*
*Fees: $$$$*
*Call: 262/275-6113; Web site: www.abbeysprings.com*
*Directions: One and one-half miles east of Highway 67 on South Shore Drive.*

## AUTHORS' FAVORITES: PAR-THREE HOLES

Forest Ridges at Lakewoods, Cable. Number 13 is 181 yards from one ridge to another—all carry over a bottomless bog lake.

St. Croix National, Somerset. Playing the 182-yard, downhill seventh offers all the thrills of ski jumping.

Troy Burne, Hudson. Number 15 is only 144 yards, but don't be short. First a ravine and then a pot bunker with a 7-foot-high face.

White Eagle, North Hudson. The 225-yard third hole features a 70-foot drop.

Wild Ridge, Eau Claire. Of course, the toughest par-three here—the 211-yard 17th—is on a windy ridge.

Wilderness Resort, Wisconsin Dells. The moat hole overlooking Lake Delton is fun, but the 12th hole is much tougher—240 yards over two ponds and a rock wall.

Palmer Course, Geneva National. The King gave us a royal view on the 218-yard downhill 16th that backs up to Lake Como.

Straits Course, north of Kohler. Miss left at the 223-yard 17th, and your ball is with the gulls in Lake Michigan.

Trapper's Turn, Wisconsin Dells. The 158-yard canyon hole is all downhill into the bottom of a beautiful piece of the Dells.

Teal Wing, Hayward. The 149-yard 15th is a great slice of the North Woods, with a placid wetland bordering three sides of the green.

Portage CC, Portage. The 242-yard third hole sits along lovely Swan Lake.

SentryWorld, Stevens Point. The 173-yard 16th flower hole is a work of art by Robert Trent Jones Jr.

Lawsonia Links, Green Lake. The "boxcar hole," the 161-yard seventh, is only slightly easier than landing a ball on a moving train.

The Irish Course, north of Kohler. Pete Dye, in a tribute to the great Irish courses, gave golfers a blind 183-yard hole from the upper tees.

Peninsula Park, Door County. The number eight cliff hole, only 69 yards in all, has delighted vacationers for decades.

The Squires, Port Washington. The 250-yard 17th claims to be the longest par-three in the state.

Naga-waukee Golf Course, Pewaukee. The 179-yard 16th provides a great lake view and a difficult shot from the elevated tees.

Eagle Springs Golf Resort, Eagle. You won't believe the number two "volcano hole" until you play it.

The Highlands, Lake Geneva. Redesigners showed good judgment in preserving the pretty little 17th hole at the old Briar Patch, which features a shot over a lovely wetland to a green backed by giant willows.

# Geneva National Golf Club

*Lake Geneva*

Let's do some name-dropping. Arnold Palmer, Lee Trevino, Gary Player. What do you get when you bring those three famous golf names together? Three very good Wisconsin golf courses, and as the publicists say, "54 holes of legendary golf."

The original developer, Illinois-based Anvan Development Company, built a 1,600-acre residential and recreational community on some wonderful terrain. The location takes advantage of lakefront and low marshes around the *other* big lake in these parts, beautiful Lake Como. It also uses the wooded and sometimes hilly uplands that rise some three hundred feet above the lake. Maple, oak, walnut, and hickory trees stand next to manicured bent-grass fairways and shade placid streams, ponds, and marshes. Sections of prairie wildflowers remain amid the condos, houses, and golf courses on this glacier-carved terrain. Each course has five sets of tees, providing ample flexibility for skills within your foursome.

Members at the club (base memberships for nonresidents were $13,500 in 2000) get a private course at their disposal six days a week. The private course for

One of the many scenic holes on the Palmer course at Geneva National.

the day rotates among the three courses. In addition to the golf, the development—owned since the mid 1990s by San Diego-based Paloma Golf Group—has a hunting club, a racquet and swim club, tennis courts, and an impressive three-level clubhouse. Not all of that is open to the public golfer, but the most important thing—the golf courses—are. And guests are treated well.

The Palmer and Trevino courses opened in August 1991, and the greats were on hand for a well-publicized grand opening. Lee Trevino christened his course by shooting a six-under-par 66. The next day Arnold Palmer played an exhibition on his course and shot an even-par 72. "I heard what he shot on his course, and that must be a lot easier than mine," Palmer quipped.

Now Geneva National's promise finally has been realized. The 2000 golf season saw the opening of the final nine holes of a splendid 54-hole complex. The final nine of the Gary Player course was delayed because of concerns about the Lake Como wetlands. But now it's open for business, providing the perfect golf trifecta.

## Palmer Course

This was Palmer's first Wisconsin course. His design firm later added another great track, The Bog, north of Milwaukee.

This Palmer course begins in a heavily wooded area before opening up on the eighth hole, a difficult par-three of 227 yards from the long tees. If length weren't enough of a challenge, the green is tucked behind the corner of a pond, making the direct route all carry. Large sand traps discourage bailing out to the left.

Palmer immodestly calls the 393-yard, par-four 15th "just a tremendous golf hole." There's a wide-open fairway to the left, which narrows quickly as it reaches a bend to the right that's guarded by a pond. Standing on the elevated tee, "you take off just as much as your guts will let you take off," as Palmer put it, with a gleam in his eye.

Number 16 is another long par-three (218 yards from the back tee) that backs up to Lake Como. It's slightly downhill, and the ground behind the green falls away toward the water. From the tee, it looks as if the lake is right against the back edge of the green.

The 17th is another Palmer favorite. Like the 18th at Pebble Beach, which is bordered on the left by the Pacific Ocean, this 579-yard hole follows the shoreline of Lake Como. You can see the green from the tee, but it looks awfully far away, with nothing but water between tee and green. Golfers with the desire to get home in two may try a dangerous path along the water's edge. It's very risky. Taking the fairway route has its trials as well. There's a large landing area for the second shot, but it's easy to drive through the fairway and into sand traps. The green slopes back toward the lake, and from 100 yards away, the flagstick looks like it's sticking up from the water. They say golf is a mind game; psychologically, this is one tough approach shot.

Number 18, a 435-yard par-four, heads back toward the massive clubhouse and has high grass to the left and a handful of well-placed sand traps guarding the edges of the squiggly fairway. Pick your way through the hazards to the final green.

*7,167 yards/par-72/74.7 rating/140 slope*

## Trevino Course

This course begins and ends in the trees and makes ultimate use of ravines and streams in the forests. In between are several open holes, some of which are bordered by wetlands. It's got the feeling of a mature layout. "When you play the course, you will have thought it was here for 50 years," Trevino once said.

While it has its tough holes, Trevino kept the average player in mind.

Most tees are elevated because, as Trevino said, "I don't know of a soul who doesn't like to stand up on the tee and look like he's shooting down at the whole world." He added, "If you miss a shot, you should have a chance to recover. People will want to come back to our course because they had fun playing it."

Do putts really break uphill at Apostle Highlands in Bayfield? You'll have to see for yourself, and you still may not believe it.

That being said, the Trevino course is no pushover, however. Note that several greens on the Trevino course are cut into the side of hills, meaning they're friendly on the high side, where a shot might kick toward the putting surface, and dangerous on the low side, where a stray shot has a chance of bounding down into a steep bunker or other group. On these holes, take the slope into consideration more than the position of the flagstick.

The fifth hole is recognized as the signature hole. It's a mirror image of the 13th at Augusta National, home of the Masters. The 13th at Augusta is a short par-five that dogs left. The second shot is a lay-up short of Rae's Creek or a daring blast over it. At 520 yards from the championship tees, number five on the Trevino course is a bit longer, and it bends left to right. The challenge on the second shot is the same as at Augusta—the green is potentially reachable in two, but the meandering creek provides a severe penalty if you miss.

The left-to-right movement of the fairway is typical on the course designed by Trevino, who made the fade famous. Eight holes provide an advantage for righthanders who accurately fade the ball.

But there's not much advantage to be had for hookers or slicers on the monster 16th, a 607-yard straightaway par-five with a pond encroaching from the right on the final approach. Nobody but Tiger or his ilk gets home in two here.

*7,116 yards/par-72/74.2 rating/135 slope*

## Player Course

This course opened in two stages: the first nine in 1995 and the second nine in 2000. But it was worth the trouble to meet the environmental concerns, and once you play it, you'll also think it was worth the wait.

Lake Como and its wetlands took priority here, and you can see that they are well worth preserving. Player's course winds around wetlands and uses the hilly wooded uplands to provide great variety, several nice views of the lake, and the opportunity to sight abundant bird life. It's a beautiful place, whether you're shooting birdies or double-bogeys.

The 13th hole on the Player course at Geneva National.

Number two is a fine par-five along the lowlands. This 588-yard hole—the longest of five par-fives—begins with a drive over a wetland and ends with a sharp dogleg left around a wetland. This one wakes you up.

The fifth hole is a neat par-four with relatively modest length. From the back tees, it's 354 yards. But there are choices to make. Pick the wide fairway to the right and play it safe. Or take the shortcut, aim for the smaller fairway to the left, and risk dumping it in a series of bunkers that divide the fairways. Our advice: Take the safe route.

There are two monster par-fours on the Player course—number nine, at 474 yards, and number 12, at 470 yards. Both are right doglegs that demand two good shots to get home in two. Between them is a relatively short par-five, number 10. The fairway slopes to the right, and the hole dogs to the right at the very end around a big pond, making any attempt to hit the green in two shots a risky endeavor.

Number 16 is another good par-five of 556 yards that begins from an elevated tee and proceeds down a narrow, straight fairway to a green flanked by a wetland on the right. This begins a set of fine finishing holes. The 17th is a 223-yard par-three with wetlands and sand along the entire left side of the hole.

And 18 is a 404-yard par-four. The dogleg left requires a drive over a creek to get to the fairway. The creek continues up the right side and in back of a fairway trap. The uphill approach is tricky to the frequently windswept green with two significant traps on the right side.

*7,018 yards/par-72/74.2 rating/139 slope*
*Fees: $$$$*
*Call 262/245-7010; Web site: www.genevanationalresort.com*
*Directions: West of Lake Geneva. Go 4.5 miles on Highway 50.*

# Grand Geneva Resort and Spa
*Lake Geneva*

Bob Hope performed here. So did Henny Youngman and Richard Pryor. Cher tried the putting green while wearing spiked heels. Tony Randall and Sammy Davis Jr. were on hand for the grand opening. In the 1960s and 1970s, many other Hollywood and Las Vegas stars appeared here at the Lake Geneva Playboy Club. The hip nightclub, featuring big-name entertainers and a bevy of beautiful bunnies, provided Wisconsin with the kind of showbiz glitz then not readily available.

The Playboy Club also introduced to Wisconsin the kind of fancy resort golf courses that only frequent travelers got to play. The Brute and the Briar Patch created a buzz in the golf community.

The Playboy bunnies are long gone now, and big Bunny Lake has lost its name. But reminders of their presence—such as the "bunny dormitories" along the left side of the Brute's second fairway—remain.

The Marcus Corporation, the Milwaukee movie, hotel, and resort operation, bought the neglected resort and golf courses and gave them a $30 million facelift in the 1990s. The facelift included a couple of name changes—the 355-room resort became the Grand Geneva Resort & Spa, and the Briar Patch was transformed into the Highlands.

Still, the memories of the Playboy Club linger. Ken Judd was the resort's pro for more than twenty years. "I gave lessons to Christie Hefner [Hugh's daughter] when she was just a little girl," he said before Marcus rescued the resort. Judd watched not only celebrities come and go but resort management as well. "We had 15 general managers in 15 years," he said. "One lasted 48 hours."

But that has changed. Marcus, a stable outfit, has made the 1,300-acre resort and conference center into a place where families, not high-rolling bachelors and bunnies, can get some high-quality R&R. A private lake, ski hill, riding stables, biking and hiking trails, indoor and outdoor tennis courts, and exercise facilities complement the luxurious spa and fine dining. Moms and dads can get some time alone when their children participate in the Grand Adventure Kids Club on site.

## The Brute

The Brute came first, and it has remained the classic course at the property. Designed by an elderly Robert Bruce Harris, it was completed in 1968 at a cost of about $1.8 million—very expensive for the time. It's a long, spacious par-72 layout characterized by elevated tees and greens, massive putting surfaces (averaging eight thousand square feet), 68 sand traps (some as big as a normal green), and plenty of water hazards (yes, even the old Bunny Lake comes into play). It was built to play at more than seventy-two hundred yards long before such long courses came into vogue.

The Brute, especially on a breezy day, still lives up to its name. It's no surprise then, that a concrete sculpture near number 16, a leftover from the Playboy days, is described as an abstract representation of a frustrated golfer on his knees.

If 16, a tough 190-yard par-three surrounded by sand, doesn't bring you to your knees, the 17th and 18th holes may. The 17th, measuring 416 yards, is the signature hole. It starts from a high back tee, providing a picturesque and terrifying look at what's head. The hole calls for a long, precise tee shot to a landing strip with a pond on the right and a sand trap on the left. If you manage that, the second shot is just as demanding—a long shot over a stream and sand to the putting surface.

Now catch your breath. The 18th hole is a monster—464 yards long. Old Bunny Lake to the right isn't really a factor until the second shot, when it sneaks

Number 17 on the Brute at Grand Geneva.

into play just before the bowl-shaped green area that sits below the sprawling hotel.

The tough holes aren't limited to the back nine. The third hole, a 374-yard par-four, requires great care. The fairway slopes abruptly downhill, where two ponds pinch it to a narrow isthmus 250 yards from the tee. It's best to use an iron from the tee. Then try to land another iron shot onto the sloping, highly elevated green.

The 421-yard, par-four ninth hole is a tough finish to the front nine. From an elevated tee, you'll need to hit the ball far enough down the fairway to miss water on the left and right. The big lake stretches along the lefthand side, and a stream crosses in front of the tees and then moves a little up the right rough. The second shot on this slight dogleg right must go uphill past a big bunker. Club selection is tricky here. Take an extra club—or two, if you're hitting into the wind.

Marcus has invested in the Brute, too, tweaking Harris' design for the better and improving the overall look and maintenance of the parklike grounds. On the 521-yard 11th hole, a new bunker has replaced a grove of trees on the right to create a risk-and-reward opportunity for big hitters. The crest of a hill in the fairway of the tricky 370-yard 12th hole has been lowered to expand the landing area and improve playability on the scenic dogleg right par-four, and three new bunkers and more trees have been added to the right side of the fairway to add difficulty.

*6,997/par-72/73.8 rating/136 slope*
*Architect: Robert Bruce Harris*

## *The Highlands*

The old Briar Patch had something of a cult following, but the redesigned Highlands will attract many more fans. The original course, in part because of years of neglect, came to be remembered by most resort golfers not as a pleasant round of golf but more like—well, a walk through a briar patch in shorts.

So Marcus brought in Bob Cupp and spent more than $2 million to overhaul a course that previously had been cursed—or at least cursed at.

The original course, completed in 1971, was built on the design of a couple of guys named Dye and Nicklaus. Jack Nicklaus, then barely into his 30s, already was a golf legend. Pete Dye had been designing golf courses for more than decade, but he was far from reaching the status he holds today.

But Dye doesn't look back on the project with great fondness. He was forced to change the original design several times to accommodate, among other things, an airstrip. "That would have been a nice piece of land," Dye said years later. "Then they decided to put in an airport, a horse farm, a ski hill—all after we started the golf course. So it kind of got screwed up a little." Dye and Nicklaus abandoned the project. Money problems later forced the Playboy staff to build the final 14 holes on the cheap.

The resulting par-71 course was quirky. But it had an untamed feel to it—something that would characterize some of Dye's later, more well-known designs, such as Harbour Town at Hilton Head Island, South Carolina. Dye's penchant for punishing golf holes unfortunately went to an extreme in some cases, resulting in some truly unfair holes. One of them was the old number eight, a short par-four where a golfer could hit a perfect drive over the ridge to a hidden fairway only to never find the ball.

Cupp's redesign—and a lot of earth moving—corrected that and other problems. It's still a par-71, but it's shorter by about one hundred yards. Some long-time visitors may not recognize some of the holes. Number eight is now a 345-yard par-four that doglegs right to a green in the woods. And surprise! You can now see the entire hole. The line of trees in the middle of the number three fairway are gone. The sloping telephone poles that formed the backdrop on the par-four fourth hole? Gone. Number nine, a 461-yard par-four, still is difficult. But the course's longest par-four is a better hole now that the green has been moved about 150 yards to the right above two traps.

In addition, greens have been rebuilt, reconstructed, and enlarged to provide bump-and-run access in many cases. Natural prairie areas have been restored, giving an inland links flavor to the course. The improved course—the Highlands—is friendlier but still different enough from the Brute to entice the traveling golfer. Some of the best of the Dye-Nicklaus design has been largely preserved. Woods and wetlands provide a feeling of seclusion. Thank you, Mr. Cupp.

The double-dogleg 11th hole is still there. This par-five with sand and mature trees has been lengthened more than thirty yards to 594 yards, ending at a small green set into the base of a ridge. Then comes the 217-yard par-three 12th, where golfers hit from one high spot over a big dip to one of the deepest greens on the course. This putting surface used to be shared with golfers on number eight; now golfers playing number 12 have the green all to themselves—a more generous landing area for the long-iron or fairway wood required.

The 17th hole, tweaked only slightly, is a much more delicate par-three of 150 yards requiring a touchy shot over a pretty wetland to a deep, well-bunkered green backed up by tall, full willows. The green also has a big mound in the middle of it, dashing hopes for an easy birdie putt. And the par-four 18th has been appropriately softened. The 18th used to demand a tee shot out of a chute and to the right of a big sandy waste area; the demanding second shot was to a slender green amid terraced sand traps.

Number 18 now is a much more visually appealing 392-yard par-four. You hit over a creek to a wide fairway. Then the hole takes a 90-degree turn to the left. The approach is abruptly uphill to a bigger, reshaped green guarded by three traps. Goodbye Briar Patch. Hello Highlands!

*6,633 yards/par-71/71.5 rating/125 slope*
*Architects: Pete Dye and Jack Nicklaus/ Bob Cupp*
*Fees: $$$$*
*Call: 800/558-3417*
*Directions: Near the intersection of Highways 12 and 50 just east of Lake*
*    Geneva.*

**Other Area Courses**

# Brighton Dale Links
*Kansasville*

Forty-five holes of good golf await you at this Kenosha County muni complex, in a 515-acre county park next to wetlands of the 4,500-acre Bong Recreation Area. It all began in the 1950s, in the midst of the cold war, when the federal government condemned more than five thousand acres of farm and prairie with plans to build a giant air base to protect Chicago. But the advent of ballistic missile defense pushed the air base into the trash bin of history. Most of the land shifted to the state and to school districts in the 1960s. The county, thinking it might build a golf course someday, bought 360 acres from the federal government. And it did build a golf course—27 holes in fact—designed by Ed Ault around 1970. Later it bought 160 acres from a school district for 18 more holes designed by St. Charles, Illinois, designer David Gill.

Gill's hilly White Birch course, which opened in the early 1990s, is a notch above the generally wooded Blue Spruce course. There's also the 3,512-yard, par-36 nine-hole Red Pine course and a driving range.

## *White Birch*

*6,977 yards/par-72/73.3 rating/130 slope*
*Architect: David Gill*

## *Blue Spruce*

*6,687 yards/par-72/72 rating/129 slope*
*Architect: Ed Ault*
*Fees: $*
*Call: 262/878-1440*
*Directions: Ten miles west of Interstate 94, just north of Highway 142 along*
*    Highway 75.*

# Evergreen Golf Club
*Elkhorn*

This course is perhaps best known as the course that never closes. Got cabin fever on a decent winter day? Go to Evergreen, where it may not always be green but where it will be playable.

That may give some a false impression that this is a facility that doesn't care about maintenance. On the contrary, Evergreen's 27 holes—especially the greens—are well maintained and much more difficult than the yardage implies. Local knowledge helps a lot with the blind shots.

*6,531 yards/par-72/71.7 rating/128 slope (North and South Courses, longest*
*    combination of the nines)*
*Architect: Dick Nugent*
*Fees: $$*
*Call: 262/723-5722*
*Directions: Three miles north of Elkhorn on Highway 12/67.*

# Ives Groves Golf Links

*Sturtevant*

It seems like it's always windy on this Racine County muni, built around on a high spot just west of Interstate 94. Big greens, lots of sand, and long holes give these 27 holes a links feel. David Gill, who started in the golf architecture business under Robert Bruce Harris, designed the first 18. His son, Garrett Gill, finished the project his dad started and designed the third nine, which opened some two decades later in the 1990s.

*6,973 yards/par-72/73 rating/131 slope (White and Blue Courses, the longest combination)*
*Architects: David and Garrett Gill*
*Fees: $*
*Call: 262/878-3714*
*Directions: One-quarter mile west of Interstate 94 on Highway 20.*

# Johnson Park Golf Course

*Racine*

This is the more established Racine County muni, in a pretty spot along a river. Severely sloped, fast greens typify this course, which opened in 1931. It's got character—opening with a 602-yard par-five and closing with a 193-yard par-three.

*6,653 yards/par-72/70.8 rating/117 slope*
*Fees: $*
*Call: 262/637-2840*
*Directions: Exit Interstate 94 at County K, go east 5 miles to Highway 38, and then turn right.*

# Petrifying Springs Golf Course

*Kenosha*

This Kenosha County muni is a Depression-era course featuring blind shots, many trees, and undulating greens. Tougher than the yardage indicates, this course lies in a beautifully wooded 360-acre park in the northeastern part of the county.

*5,979 yards/par-71/67.8 rating/119 slope*
*Fees: $*
*Call: 262/552-9052*
*Directions: One block east of Highway 31 on County A.*

## Rivermoor Country Club
*Waterford*

Trees, trees are everywhere on this tight but short course. This course, which dates from the Great Depression, has been owned by the same family since World War II.

*6,255 yards/par-70/70.2 rating/124 slope*
*Fees: $$*
*Call: 262/534-2500*
*Directions: At the west edge of Waterford, 8 miles south of Interstate 43 on Highway 20/83.*

**Best Nine-Hole Course**

## Shoop Park Golf Course
*Racine*

There aren't many places where you can play golf right on the Lake Michigan shoreline for less than $20. But you can do it at the Shoop Park Golf Course, next to the Wind Point Lighthouse and near the Frank Lloyd Wright–designed conference center Wingspread. It's not that much of a course, but who cares? The setting is worth the trip.

Old stone walls, symbols of farmers' backbreaking work, were made part of the course at Devil's Head in Merrimac and Old Hickory in Beaver Dam.

*2,706 yards/par-35*
*Fees: $*
*Call: 262/681-9714*
*Directions: On the coast north of downtown Racine. Take Highway 32 north to County G. Go north and then turn right on Lighthouse Drive.*

# More Fun Things to Do

Most area visitors come to Lake Geneva. And if any community is ready for them, it's Lake Geneva. Tourism has been a staple here since just after the Civil War. There are plenty of nice eateries, art galleries, and shops in the well-kept downtown and plenty of nice hotel-motel-B&B accommodations nearby. But Geneva Lake, a 140-foot-deep spring-fed 5,000-acre body of water, is the main attraction.

Get a glimpse of the past at the Geneva Lake Area Museum of History on Geneva Street (call 262/248-6060). And you don't have to go far to find some beach time. Right off the business district, people play in the water on Riviera Beach next to a Mediterranean-styled ballroom built in 1933.

Walk the more than 20-mile path that circles the lake or take a sightseeing cruise (call 800/558-5911 or go to www.genevalakecruise-line.com) to view some of the elegant mansions that ring the shoreline. It'll also take you to Big Foot Beach State Park, which offers wooded campsites, picnic areas, and a rocky waterfront (call 262/248-2528).

Another great attraction is the Bong State Recreation Area, which preserves some of the wide-open feel once common to the region. It's so big—at 4,500 acres—that public hunting is permitted (call 262/878-5600).

In Williams Bay, see the century-old Yerkes Observatory (call 262/245-5555 or go to astro.uchicago.edu/yerkes). Money for the observatory came from Charles Yerkes, who donated hundred of thousands of dollars to help rehabilitate his image after a stay in prison for crimes tied to a bank scandal. Scientists still are researching the skies here thanks to Yerkes and famed astronomer George Ellery Hale.

On the Lake Michigan coast, visit the revitalized port cities of Kenosha and Racine. You can hire a charter fishing boat, or if you're there in the spring or the fall, fish rivers like the Root for migrating salmon and steelhead. Even if you don't fish, seeing these great creatures will be a thrill. Tour the Root River fishery station, where the state Department of Natural Resources gathers eggs from fish to use for future stocking. You can see fish fighting their way upstream. Call 262/594-6218 for information.

While in Racine, Frank Lloyd Wright fans will want to tour the SC Johnson Wax Building (call 262/260-2154 or go to www.scjohnsonwax.com for tour information). Families will want to visit the Racine Zoo, home to more than three hundred animals and site of a kids' petting zoo (call 262/636-9189). And those with a sweet tooth will want to sample a kringle, the Danish pastry available in many locations.

Kenosha, a little to the south, first was called Southport by its white settlers. And that's not a bad name for the southernmost port in the state. But it adopted the Native American name Kenosha when the city was chartered in 1850.

Kenosha was the birthplace of Orson Welles and Don Ameche of Hollywood fame. And for years it was the auto-making center of Wisconsin, home of the Nash Rambler and later cars from American Motors and Chrysler.

Learn more about the area's history at the Kenosha County Historical Society and Museum in the lakeside Third Avenue Historic District. A new downtown development called HarborPark—on the site of the old Chrysler auto plant—soon will house a new public museum, business, recreational and residential assets. For the shoppers in the crowd, two outlet malls stand ready for you near Interstate 94.

In East Troy, about halfway between Lake Geneva and Milwaukee, music fans rock to tunes at the Alpine Valley stage, and railroad buffs visit the Troy Electric Railroad Museum for an 11-mile ride on the old cars (call 262/548-3837).

## For More Information

Kenosha: 800/654-7309; www.kenoshacvb.com
Lake Geneva: 800/345-1020; www.lakegenevawi.com
Racine: 800/272-2463; www.racine.org
Walworth County: 800/395-8687; www.walworth-county.com

# 18

# Madison and the
# I-90 Corridor

Wisconsin's capital city has four good-sized lakes; a grand Capitol that
mimics the one in Washington, D.C; a world-class university; a Frank
Lloyd Wright–inspired convention center; a thriving economy; and a plethora of
good food, music, and entertainment. It's no wonder that Madison consistently
shows up on lists of the most livable cities.

It could also be hailed as one heck of a golfing city. Madison's fun-loving residents work hard and play hard. And golf definitely fits into the play category—
despite a lot of competition from summertime sports such as sailing, fishing,
waterskiing, and bicycling. If they're not golfing or sporting, they're probably
lounging at the lakeside terrace at the Arthur Peabody–designed Memorial
Union, thinking about having summer fun on the links or elsewhere. Just try to
reach somebody at the office some Friday afternoon in the summer!

Madison golfers are a footloose group, too. They love to travel and explore
golf courses between Madison and Spring Green to the west and between Madison and the Illinois border to the south. From Beloit to Madison—both near and
far from the hum of busy Interstate 90—lie some fine, very playable tracks.

Beloit and Janesville, old factory towns along the I-90 corridor, are revitaliz-
ing and retooling for the new century. Each city is doing better at using its Rock
River real estate, complementing established nongolf attractions.

Beloit College, a private school and the state's oldest college, has a lovely
campus that features two fine museums. Beloit's college often draws top musi-
cians and speakers, and the city's minor-league baseball team—a farm team for
the Milwaukee Brewers—often draws players on their way up to the big leagues.
A new museum houses the largest angel collection in the country, including some
donated by talk show host and film star Oprah Winfrey. We hope the angels
guide you to fewer bogeys and more birdies.

Janesville, perhaps best known as the home to Wisconsin's only remaining
auto-building plant, a General Motors facility, boasts well-maintained parks and
great boating on the Rock River. It also has a fine collection of historical buildings, including the Tallman mansion that hosted Lincoln in the days before
politicians played golf.

# University Ridge
*Verona*

No course shows off the wonderfully varied landscape of this region more than this one—the official University of Wisconsin–Madison layout and home to the Badger men's and women's golf teams. University Ridge also hosted the 1998 National Collegiate Athletic Association (NCAA) women's golf championships. University Ridge, which sits on the cusp of southwestern Wisconsin's nonglaciated Driftless Area, has rolling open prairie, ponds and creeks, and steep wooded hillsides.

You can spy the Driftless Area from the scenic tee on the 191-yard par-three 12th hole. The hole drops dramatically down a hillside, a remnant of the last great glacial period. Beyond the trees is a wonderful western view of the Wisconsin countryside. Club selection is crucial here, especially if the prevailing winds are coming at you.

Wisconsin golfers weren't always sure such views would come from a university golf course. Good things often take time to gel at UW–Madison, the flagship campus of the sprawling University of Wisconsin System. And the University Ridge complex is no exception.

Development of a new golf course was initially talked about in the early 1950s. The first actual plan for a university course was revealed in 1956; it called for an 18-hole course to be located on 150 acres of university land between Picnic Point and Eagle Heights on the Lake Mendota shoreline.

In 1965, prominent Chicago doctor and former UW–Madison athlete Harry Culver died in Scotland on an annual golf outing. He left nearly $1 million to the university for recreational and sports activities. That spurred more talk of a golf course, and 326 acres were bought north of Lake Mendota with money from the Culver estate. A university committee even hired George Fazio to draw up plans for the course. But the site in the town of Westport had problems and was later sold for a big profit.

Then in 1971, the UW Foundation, using the enhanced pot of Culver money, bought 585 acres in the town of Verona far west of campus. And the former Illinois design team of Ken Killian and Dick Nugent was hired to come up with a new plan. The plan included room for new houses, but such development then was barred by a Dane County land-use plan that designated the site as part of a green belt. Golf course planning was shelved once again.

The project was revived in 1983, following a gift from the will of Carl Dietze of Madison, who wished his money to be used for a university golf course. In 1986, yet another committee was formed, and Robert Trent Jones Jr. won the contract. He designed the first 18 holes, which were built at the cost of $5.5 mil-

One of the many challenging holes at University Ridge.

lion, and the course finally opened in 1991. A clubhouse expansion waited until 2000.

And construction of the second 18, envisioned from the start, probably won't start until the fall of 2002—after the opening of an upscale development, Hawk's Landing, next door (608/848-4295). But when the additional $15.5 million UW vision is completed, University Ridge will rate among the top university golf complexes in the United States. It will boast a turf grass research station, a first-class clubhouse, a golf teaching facility, a nine-hole practice course, and an 18-hole putting course.

In the meantime, the remodeled clubhouse–pro shop, the adjacent deck atop a shady hill, polite knicker-clad help unloading your bags, and a free sleeve of logo-imprinted golf balls for every round give University Ridge the feel of a resort. Worth waiting for? You bet.

Playing University Ridge, ranked ninth best in Wisconsin in 2000 by *Golf Digest*, is like playing two courses. The front nine is mostly open, through prairie land. The back nine is cut out of a lovely hardwood forest. The front nine is high-lighted by two holes. The second hole, a par-five, has been tinkered with and lengthened to 546 yards. It's finally matured into a great risk-and-reward hole. Those on the tee face two huge traps and a rocky ditch that handles runoff. Make it over those obstacles and you've got a chance to hit the green in two. The second risk-and-reward comes on the approach, over a rough ravine and past a couple of trees to a small well-trapped green. You can be thinking eagle and take bogey within minutes.

Number four, a 444-yard hole, is one of the toughest par-fours in the state. From the very back tees, you hit uphill over a big marsh, part of Morse Pond to the right. The fairway sits on a ledge between the pond on the right and a thin line of trees on the left. Right is jail. But so is left. So hit it straight. The blind approach is uphill again to a sloping green. Four traps on the right may save you from a double-digit score; beyond that is a golf ball graveyard in the wooded hillside.

The back nine is highlighted by the scenic par-three 12th and a trio of finishing holes that rank among the best anywhere.

The signature hole is a beauty. The 533-yard 16th hole goes down and then up and to the right. It features two routes to a narrow, windswept green. A great stand of trees divides the fairway about where your downhill drive would land. The longer lefthand route is safer off the tee, but the uphill approach still is tough. It's really tough from the righthand approach, which gives golfers the opportunity to get home in two shots. Between you and the green are a dozen traps, including several pot bunkers. Next comes a 199-yard downhill par-three over water to a green set into the trees. Bail out left if you have to.

> Tiger Woods had his first pro hole-in-one at the par-three 14th hole in 1996 during his PGA Tour debut at Brown Deer Park. The six-iron shot traveled 202 yards. Match that!

And then comes the 413-yard uphill par-four dogleg left, which plays considerably longer. Try to cut the dogleg, and you'll likely end up in ankle-deep rough or one of three big bunkers on the inside corner of the dogleg. The best shot is a draw to the elbow. But even then, the long approach to the 40-yard-deep green is difficult.

*6,888 yards/par-72/73.2 rating/142 slope*
*Architect: Robert Trent Jones II*
*Fees: $$$$*
*Call: 800/897-4343*
*Directions: Two miles south on Highway 18/151 from Highway 12/18. Turn*
  *right and go west on County PD. The course is 3 miles on the right.*

# The House on the Rock Resort
*Spring Green*

You can feel the vibes of two great architects here. They are local native and famed building designer Frank Lloyd Wright and legendary golf course designer Robert Trent Jones Sr. They didn't formally collaborate on this work of art (which was formerly The Springs resort). But you can feel both of their influences on 18 golf holes built in a splendid valley near the Wisconsin River named, appropriately, after Wright's uncle, James Lloyd Jones.

Jones, the golf course designer, once said his design "had nothing to do with Frank Lloyd Wright," but he conceded "the association was unique." "I took advantage of the terrain and built a golf course," he said matter-of-factly.

But what a golf course! Jones crafted a beauty that has survived shoestring budgets and many ownership changes. Now it's owned by the folks who operate the House on the Rock, one of Wisconsin's most unusual and most visited tourist attractions. Although some changes to Jones's design have been made—a very un-Jones-like moat was inserted on the third hole, for example—his initial design remains relatively intact.

Even with the new homes on the hillside, there's a wonderful sense of seclusion back in the neck of the valley. Here are two difficult holes on the original 18—the 13th (a par-four doglegging around woods) and the 14th (a downhill par-five with woods and water and subtle hazards along the right side).

Say you're there on one of those bluebird spring mornings. The dew will be heavy upon the grass. A deer or turkey may be picking through the grasses and woods. "It's a wonderful course to play at 5:30 in the morning, when all you hear are the birds," said Robert Graves, a former Wright associate who managed the golf property until the late 1960s. "[Jones] had everything to work with. It couldn't be more unobtrusive than it is. It's something Mr. Wright could have understood very well." Wright, whose Taliesin is close by, liked to blend the natural setting with his buildings. Jones likes to blend his golf holes with the terrain.

Nowhere is that more evident than on the 18th hole, a long downhill par-four with water right and in front of the green and a wooded hillside to the left; it remains one of Wisconsin's great finishing holes.

For years after its opening in the late 1960s under former Johnson Wax executive Willard "Bud" Keland, golfers would pay low green fees at a pro shop housed in a trailer near the first tee. No longer can you play this Trent Jones Sr. course at bargain basement prices. But now there are genuine amenities, including a locker room, fitness facilities, eateries, a hotel, and a new nine-hole course built around a hill that overlooks the original 18.

The North nine, designed by Roger Packard and two-time U.S. Open champion Andy North of Madison, opened in 1994. It has some memorable holes of its own. The sixth through the ninth holes (two par-fours, a par-three, and a dramatic finishing par-five) are quite nice and include a journey through woods and former farmland. An old farmhouse and barn were left on site to remind us of Wisconsin's strong rural heritage—a heritage that influenced Wright throughout his career.

Number nine of the North nine begins with a grand view from a tiny perch in the woods above the Jones course. It doglegs sharply to the right, but a tall tree at the corner blocks most golfers from taking the short cut. North, a Senior Tour player and commentator, had the benefit of local knowledge when he opened the course in May 1994. He shot a 34.

### *Jones Course*

*6,554 yards/par-72/71.5 rating/132 slope*
*Architect: Robert Trent Jones Sr.*

### *North Nine*

*3,262 yards/par-36/36 rating/132 slope*
*Architects: Andy North and Roger Packard*
*Fees: $$$$*
*Call: 800/822-7774 or 608/588-7000; Web site: www.houseontherockresort.com*
*Directions: From Madison, take Highway 14 west to County C, about 3 miles*
*southeast of Spring Green; turn left and go about 2 miles to Golf Course*
*Road. Turn left and follow the road.*

# Riverside Golf Club
*Janesville*

This municipal course on Janesville's northwest side is a gem. It may lack the amenities of newer courses, but this track makes up for the lack of creature comforts with big trees, undulating fairways, and tough holes that set it apart from the usual municipal layout.

The course first opened as a nine-hole layout in 1924. Robert Bruce Harris redesigned it in 1946, adding 11 holes, including the 454-yard par-four 16th. On this hole you have to hit it straight as well as long. The landing area on the dogleg right has a big trap at the corner and pine trees to the right and left. It opens up as you get closer to the tiered green, but it's always a long shot home.

Seven of the original holes remain—albeit with changes. These older holes include the 491-yard dogleg left uphill par-five tenth hole, as difficult as it is memorable. Initially, it was a par-four, and the green was at the top of a steep hill. Golfers now hit their second shots to the base of this steep hill or to the top of it in an effort to get a good peek at a green that now is set back in the woods on a bluff over the Rock River. The other six older holes are numbers eight and nine and 11 through 14.

One of the treats at Riverside is playing among the variety of trees that populate the grounds. Some ancient, regal elms remain. But tall oaks and lindens now dominate—despite a 1993 storm that claimed 84 big trees. "We've still got plenty," said pro Paul Domke.

Golfers will also encounter troublesome bushy trees, flowering crabs, and hawthorns. If you hit your ball under these trees, which line some fairways, your best bet is to bunt it back onto the fairway. Other escape routes are just too risky.

*6,508 yards/par-72/70.7 rating/123 slope*
*Architect: Robert Harris*
*Fees: $$*
*Call: 608/757-3080*
*Directions: Northwest of Janesville on County E (Washington Street). Two*
*miles south of Highway 14.*

# The Meadows of Sixmile Creek
*Waunakee*

Before this course was built, the land upon which it lies would not have been mistaken at first glance for future golf course property. It was a mixture of flat, low-lying wetlands and farmland divided by a single railroad line.

But Ken Killian made nothing special into something very nice. This course, cut through impressive, bird-filled wetlands, is very long and often windswept with hidden water hazards and big, undulating bent-grass greens guarded by deep bunkers.

The layout is a little quirky at times—the front nine finishes with a tough 179-yard par-three over water and a big waste bunker, and there are long walks between the first and second holes on each nine via a short railroad viaduct. But it's a tough measure of any game at 6,919 yards. And when the wind blows, watch out—par-72 seems like a long way off.

That wind brings in migrating birds of great variety—the yellow-headed blackbird for one. And we once played behind two walking sandhill cranes, who allowed us a close look at their feathers for an entire hole before wading into a marsh. Herons of all sorts are present.

The wind also turns relatively benign holes into monsters. And the long holes—well, a bogey seems to be a victory. There's the 596-yard par-five number two, which wakes you up after the 313-yard par-four first hole. Number two is almost always into the wind. This double-dogleg has a pond to the right off the tee, and if you can cut off some of the first dogleg, please do. Then hit between the mounds to the in-fairway 150-yard pole. If you place it to the pole, you can get a good look at the final approach—to a green bordered by water and a beach bunker on the left and another sand trap on the right.

Another tough par-five is the fourth hole. This is target golf all the way. Only the bravest—and most foolhardy—try to launch one to the isthmus between two ponds after the first dogleg left. Hit an iron or fairway wood safely to the first corner before the fairway turns left. Then repeat that club to the flat spot in back of the 150-yard pole, where the fairway turns right. From there, it's easier to avoid the second pond and fly your ball to the green, also guarded on the left by a big trap. Being in the trap is better than being wet, so aim for that on your approach.

There are also two brawny par-fours—the 468-yard number three hole with water right and left and the 449-yard dogleg right finishing hole with marsh all along the right side and sand just about everywhere else. Staying out of the high marsh grass is your biggest challenge at the Meadows. Do that, and you can score well.

The Meadows fast became one of the area's best new courses after it opened in 1997 and became part of burgeoning development that transformed "The Only Waunakee in the World" into a bona fide bedroom community for those working in Madison. It also has a sister course, Jefferson's Meadow Springs Country Club, which has gone from an old hometown nine-holer to an 18-hole course catering to a broader audience. Both are owned by Madison Golf and Development Group, but the Meadows in Waunakee is the more impressive track.

*6,919 yards/par-72/73 rating/125 slope*
*Architect: Ken Killian*
*Fees: $$*
*Call: 608/849-9000; Web site: www.madisongolf.com*
*Directions: Just north of Highway 19 and the main Waunakee business district on Highway 113.*

# Door Creek
*Cottage Grove*

The Bradt family gave up farming near Fort Atkinson and took up golf near Cottage Grove. Thirty-six holes later, you've got to say they made the right decision. This complex, opened in 1990 east of Madison, has a nine-hole par-three layout, 27 regulation holes, a driving range, a pro shop, and a bar and grill amid some well-preserved wetlands.

The new addition (2000 was its first season) is nick-named the Farm; it's a little down the road from the rest of the complex, and it's worth the little detour. There are lots of forced carries over wetlands and a healthy sampling of mature trees (which are lack-ing on the first 18). Number seven, a 541-yard par-five, is a straightaway hole marked by creeks and wetlands throughout. Hit from solid ground to solid ground without straying, and you might find par. Eight is a tough 398-yard par-four with wetlands covering three sides of the fairway. And the ninth hole, measuring 421 yards, is just as tough because of the length and a wetland that sits on the right side near the green. To the right is an old barn, an appropriate land-mark for the Farm.

At Glenway Golf Course in Madison, golfers must get the go-ahead from a stoplight before hitting the blind drive on number nine.

The original 18 make full use of tiny Door Creek and related waters. Water or marshy grass are never very far away on this course. One of the prettiest holes is the 181-yard par-three seventh, which features a 100-yard carry over a wet-land to a severely sloping green guarded by a couple of bunkers. One of the tougher holes is the 419-yard par-four 16th, which requires a long, accurate and sometimes blind second shot to a narrow green flanked and backed by water.

A wild hitter can get away with a few mistakes at Door Creek, but many trees planted between holes will force more penalty strokes as the years progress.

## Original 18

*6,408 yards/par-71/70.5 rating/119 slope*

## The Farm

*3,128 yards/par-36*
*Architects: Jim and Doug Bradt*
*Fees $$*
*Call: 608/839-5656*
*Directions: Located between Cottage Grove and Madison off Cottage Grove Road (County BB) on Vilas Road. The Farm is about 0.5 mile south of the main course.*

## Other Area Courses

# The Bridges

*Madison*

This is the ultimate airport course—right across the road from the Dane County Regional Airport and the Air National Guard's Truax Field. But if you can stand the noise—and the distraction of an F-16 zipping overhead—play the course.

There are some very good holes and—as the name implies—lots of water and wetlands provided by upper Starkweather Creek and various drainage ditches. Water comes into play on 13 of the 18 holes, and seven bridges help you get around. The only hole with a greatly elevated tee is also one of the best. The par-five 15th, 564 yards from the tips, plays to a narrow landing area with a tangle of marsh grass on the left. Hit to the fattest part of the corner on this dogleg left, try to hit a straight second shot, and then go for the approach to a green nearly surrounded by water.

Opened in 2000 on leased county land, the course became popular immediately because of its prime location. It was the first course to open within the city limits in some forty years—since the city-owned Yahara Hills on the far southeast side was annexed in the early 1960s.

*6,888 yards/par-72*
*Architect: Dan Feick*
*Fees: $$*
*Call: 608/244-1822*
*Directions: Located just west of the Highway 30/East Washington interchange at Aberg Avenue and ShopKo Drive.*

# Coachman's Golf Resort

*Edgerton*

This complex has 27 holes, a supper club, motel rooms (some with whirlpools), and an outdoor pool—just off Interstate 90. The appeal here is quick access, reasonably priced packages, and golf holes that are scenic without overly penalizing the high handicapper. A mature 18-hole layout over rolling, often wooded terrain was complemented in 1994 with the addition of nine holes amid woods and wetlands.

*6,423 yards/par-72/70.2 rating/118 slope (longest combination of 18 holes)*
*Fees: $$*
*Call: 800/940-8485; Web site: www.coachmans.com*
*Directions: Exit 156 off Interstate 90 about 20 miles south of Madison.*

# Deer Valley Golf Club
*Barneveld*

This course, opened in 1999 just off Highway 151 between Madison and Dodgeville, is wide open but features some great up-and-down terrain. Homer Fieldhouse had a hand in this design but left the project before completion.

*6,566 yards/par-72/71.9 rating/127 slope*
*Fees: $*
*Call: 608/924-3033; Web site: www.deervalleygolf.com*
*Directions: One mile west of Barneveld off Highway 18/151.*

# Edelweiss Chalet Country Club
*New Glarus*

Located near Wisconsin's charming "Little Switzerland," this course is hilly and fun.

*6,573 yards/par-72/70.6 rating/118 slope*
*Fees: $$*
*Call: 608/527-2315*
*Directions: From Highway 69, take Valley View Road east 1 mile.*

# Evansville Golf Club
*Evansville*

Nine new holes were added to a fine layout in 1993 and jumbled with the old holes. One of the best holes is a golden oldie. That's the 376-yard par-four ninth hole, which requires a 200-yard-plus drive from an elevated tee over a big pond. If you make it over the pond, the second shot is short but tricky—a blind shot up a big hill.

*6,559 yards/par-72/71.2 rating/126 slope*

*Architect: Robert Graves*
*Fees: $*
*Call: 608/882-6524*
*Directions: From Highway 14 north of Evansville, go east on Bullard Road*
*and then south on Cemetery Road.*

# Lake Windsor Country Club
*Windsor*

I f you're looking for a quick round of golf near the
Dane County Regional Airport, this is your
second-best choice. Some nice holes can be
found among the 27 total holes sprawling
east of Interstates 90/94 and metropolitan
Madison. Part of this 1960s layout, using
the upper Yahara River before it flows
into Lake Mendota, was improved with a
Bob Lohmann redesign in the 1990s. Big
oaks and maples dominate many of the
holes, including the 14th hole, a great 156-
yard par-three over a shady pond to a green
ringed with trees on a semicircular ridge.

The
long-ago days of
sand greens haven't
completely disappeared in
Wisconsin. The nine-hole Yellow
Lake Golf Course near Danbury
in the northwest corner of the
state still has its original
1923 putting
surfaces.

*6,154 yards/par-72/69.2 rating/118 slope (red and white nines)*
*Fees: $$*
*Call: 608/846-4713*
*Directions: Exit Interstate 90/94 at Highway 19 and then take County CV*
*north to Golf Road. Go left.*

# Odana Hills Golf Club
*Madison*

T his solid municipal layout through mature trees was updated in the 1990s to
make it even better. For example, the redesigned par-three 161-yard num-
ber four hole over water is short and pretty but requires a lot more precision than
it used to. The third hole, a 454-yard par-four along the Beltline, remains one of
the toughest par-fours in Dane County. This course gets a lot of play, but it's
worth the effort to get on. Jack Nicklaus, in an exhibition, shot 70 here.

The other city complex with regulation golf is Yahara Hills on the far southeast side near the De Jope gambling hall. Thirty-six holes are available on rolling, sometimes wooded land near Interstate 90. Call 608/838-3126.

*6,572/par-72/70.6 rating/117 slope*
*Fees: $*
*Call: 608/266-4724*
*Directions: Between Midvale Boulevard and Whitney Way, south of Odana*
*    Road and north of the Beltline. Entrance is off Odana.*

# Pleasant View Golf Club
*Middleton*

This hilly course received improved maintenance after it was acquired by the city of Middleton. You won't forget the unique par-five dogleg left number 16 hole. The 495-yard hole finishes abruptly at the top of a heavily treed knob. Once there, you have to putt on a steep green. This course's driving range, par-three course, and bar and grill also have one of the best views in greater Madison. Nearby is the Capital Brewery, which sometimes has entertainment to go with its selection of quality beers.

*6,436 yards/par-72/70 rating/122 slope*
*Architects: Carl Schaefer/Art Johnson*
*Fees: $$*
*Call: 608/831-6666*
*Directions: From the Beltline, take Old Sauk Road west to Pleasant View Road*
*    and then turn right. The golf course is on the left.*

# Prairie Woods Golf Club
*Johnstown Center*

It's a little out of the way—let's see, southwest of Milton and east of Janesville and not too far from Whitewater. But this course, which started with nine holes in 1994, is worth a special trip. The course flows through open prairie and rolling hills populated by lovely stands of oak. The Dorr family built a resort-style course that is short but challenging. Fast greens, well-placed traps and water, and tight fairways make for a neat course. A nice clubhouse (with good, fairly priced food and a broad deck overlooking the water-guarded number nine green) and complete practice facilities round out this fine complex.

*6,016 yards/par-71/69 rating/118 slope*
*Architects: Gilmore Graves (front); Kerry Mattingly and Kuehn (back)*
*Fees: $$*
*Call: 800/564-2599*
*Directions: Eight miles east of Janesville on County A.*

# Towne Country Club
*Edgerton*

Edgerton, formerly a tobacco farming center, proclaims itself as the home of author Sterling North. The local golf course rightly proclaims itself as "the home golf course of PGA pro Steve Stricker." Now we know why Stricker is so good. The original nine holes (1920s vintage) measure under six thousand yards at par-70; but it may have the toughest opening three holes in Wisconsin golf. The first hole is an uphill 400-yard par-four followed by a 226-yard downhill par-three and a 233-yard slightly uphill par-three—all to tiny greens. The old, front nine is hilly and wooded. The newer back nine, added in 1997 with input from Stricker, is more open but travels through some nice country close to the Interstate.

*5,913 yards/par-70*
*Fees: $*
*Call: 608/884-8608*
*Directions: From Interstate 90, go south on Highway 51 toward Edgerton.*
*  The course is up the hill from the A&W on the northern edge of town.*

**Best Nine-Hole Course**

# Norsk Golf Club
*Mount Horeb*

To the west of Madison, nearing the charming burg of Mount Horeb, is the Norsk Golf Club (formerly the Norsk Golf-Bowl). Yes, you can do the full Wisconsin—bowl, play nine holes of golf, and finish off the day with a brat and a beer. This course, situated atop a windy knob, usually opens early in the year because it drains so well.

*2,852 yards/par-36/33.2 rating/111 slope*
*Fees: $*
*Call: 608/437-3399*
*Directions: East of Mount Horeb. Take Business Highway 18/151 off Highway*
*151 and then take the first left on County ID.*

The Madison area has a strong municipal course system, and two nine-hole courses stand out—Glenway Municipal on Madison's west side (2,348 yards, par-32; call 608/266-4737) and Monona Municipal on Madison's southeast side (3,183 yards, par-36; call 608/266-4736).

Farther west are a couple of notables: Ludden Lake, Mineral Point, a short nine-hole par-36 course full of sidehill lies named in honor of the late TV game-show host and Mineral Point native Allen Ludden. Built in 1976. (608/987-2888). The Spring Green Municipal, Spring Green, a short nine-hole par-33 course, is a good one for beginners. No phone. On Highway 23 on the south edge of Spring Green.

### Practice Facilities

If you're looking to practice, go where legions of south-central golfers have gone—George Vitense Golfland, a Wisconsin golf institution named after the former Glenway pro and businessman. Golfland, located on Madison's southwest side just off the Beltline, has a driving range; instruction and club-fitting by Fore Seasons Pro Shop; a pitch-and-putt course; and miniature golf for those who like to putt around through and over man-made obstacles. Call 608/271-1411.

Another good place to practice is Bogey's Family Fun Park in Middleton, just west of Madison. Call 608/831-5559.

And now you can practice all year-round at the Urban Links Golf Dome just off Highway 151 going west between Madison and Verona. Call 608/273-3000 or go to www.golfurbanlinks.com.

## More Fun Things to Do

Madison is a city of only some 300,000 people, but the greater metro area has many of the attractions of a much bigger city.

If nongolfers are interested in museums, then Madison has them—from the fine art collection at UW–Madison's Elvehjem Museum (608/263-2246) to the Wisconsin Veterans Museum on the Capitol Square (608/267-1799).

Every summer Saturday morning, the Square is home to a thriving farmers' market (www.madfarmmkt.org). It also is the site during selected Wednesday nights for a Concerts on the Square series attended by devotees who spread elaborate picnics on the Capitol lawn. If you like beautiful gardens, walk the Capitol lawn or take a side trip to Olbrich Botanical Gardens on the near east side across the street from Lake Monona (608/246-4550).

Frank Lloyd Wright, who was born near Spring Green and went to school in Madison for a time, can be appreciated fully in the area. Taliesin, his treasured Wisconsin home near Spring Green along the Wisconsin River, is open to tours (608/588-7900 or go to www.taliesinpreservation.org). So is the First Unitarian Society Meeting House near the university (608/233-9774). And the Monona Terrace Convention Center, inspired by his original designs, sits on Lake Monona in Madison; call 608/261-4000 or check the Web site at www.monona terrace.visitmadison.com. Many other Wright-designed buildings can be found throughout the region.

Live theater is an enduring attraction, especially with the coming addition of a $100 million downtown cultural district. But many visitors focus on the outdoor acting at American Players Theater near the House on the Rock Resort; Shakespeare dominates, but the troupe performs more modern artistic works as well. Call 608/588-2361 or check the Web site at www.americanplayers.org. Those interested in antiques, crafts, and unique gifts should go to Mount Horeb, to the west, and Cambridge, to the east.

If you just want to hang out, nothing beats the Memorial Union Terrace on campus. The terrace overlooks Lake Mendota, the biggest lake in the Yahara River chain and one of the most studied bodies of water in the world. During the summer, Madisonians and visitors listen to good (and free) music; munch on brats, burgers, and pretzels; and sample some of Wisconsin's finest beers.

If the kids are in tow, don't worry. You've got options. Kids who like golf would certainly like George Vitense Golfland. Or you could try the par-three courses at Door Creek or Pleasant View.

Otherwise, in Madison, we recommend the Children's Museum downtown (608/256-6445 or go to www.kidskiosk.com) and the Henry Vilas Zoo (608/266-4732) on spring-fed Lake Wingra, which is also close to nice hiking trails at the UW Arboretum. On a really hot day, nothing cools the family off more than a dip in the lakes or in nearby community pools. Middleton to the west and Sun Prairie to the east have water parks.

Did you say ice cream? The Memorial Union features ice cream made at UW–Madison's Babcock Hall; so does the Monona Bait and Ice Cream Shop southeast of Madison's Isthmus across from Lake Monona. Or try something unconventional. Take the family underground—to the Cave of the Mounds, located west of Mount Horeb. No matter how hot it is on land, the temperature in this well-preserved privately owned cavern is always in the 50s. Call 608/437-3038.

Close to Mount Horeb are several state recreational assets.

- Blue Mound State Park, preserving the highest point in southern Wisconsin. Swimming pool, camping, hiking, and biking. Call 608/437-5711.
- Military Ridge State Trail, between Verona and Dodgeville. 608/437-7393.
- Tower Hill State Park, Spring Green. Preserves a lead-shot-making site on the Wisconsin River. Camping, hiking. Call 608/588-2116.

South of Madison near Stoughton, check out Lake Kegonsa State Park. Camping, hiking, and boating. 608/873-9695.

A little west is the Sugar River State Trail, which runs between New Glarus and Brodhead. Call 608/527-2334.

## For More Information
Beloit: 800/423-5648; www.visitbeloit.com
Janesville: 800/48-PARKS; www.janesvillecvb.com
Madison: 800/373-6376; www.visitmadison.com
New Glarus: 800/527-6838
Spring Green: 800/588-2042

# VII

# Across
# the Borders

Some of the same natural features that make Wisconsin's golf courses great to play also make the courses
near Wisconsin equally inviting. Northern Minnesota and
the Upper Peninsula of Michigan have stunningly beautiful forest courses. Illinois and Iowa have woods, valleys,
and meadows layouts. Of course, the metropolitan areas
of Chicago and Minneapolis–St. Paul have multitudes of
links, including championship public layouts used by the
touring pros. We thought you'd like to know about a few
of the best places to play near Wisconsin. In this case, it's
okay to stray out of bounds.

# Northern Illinois

*The good courses in northern Illinois, especially in the Chicago area, really are too numerous to mention. So we picked an eclectic 11 for their variety, their proximity to Wisconsin, and whether they've hosted PGA events.*

## Chalet Hills Golf Club
*Cary*

This Ken Killian design emphasizes shot making over distance.

*6,877 yards/par-73/73.4 rating/131 slope*
*Architect: Ken Killian*
*Fees $$*
*Call: 847/639-0666*
*Directions: Forty miles northwest of Chicago in McHenry County. 943 W. Rawson Bridge Road, Cary.*

## Cog Hill Golf Club
*Lemont*

Four courses, led by "Dubsdread," site of the PGA Tour's Western Open and other events. Ranked 48th in the United States by *Golf Digest* in 2000.

*6,930 yards/par-72/75.6 rating/142 slope*
*Architect: Dick Wilson; update by Rocky Roquemore*
*Fees: $$$$*
*Call: 630/257-5872*
*Directions: Thirty-two miles southwest of Chicago in Cook County. 12294 Archer Ave., Lemont.*

## Ingersoll Memorial Golf Club
*Rockford*

Tight fairways and small greens characterize this course from the early 1920s.

*5,991 yards/par-71/68.2 rating/108 slope*
*Architect: Thomas Bendelow*

*Fees $$*
*Call: 815/987-8834*
*Directions: Seventy miles northwest of Chicago in Winnebago County. 101*
*Daisyfield Road.*

# Kemper Lakes Golf Club
*Long Grove*

This course hosted the 1989 PGA Championship.

*7,217 yards/par-72/75.7 rating/140 slope*
*Architects: Dick Nugent and Ken Killian*
*Fees: $$$$*
*Call: 847/320-3450*
*Directions: Twenty-five miles northwest of Chicago in Lake County on Old*
*McHenry Road.*

# The Ledges Golf Club
*Roscoe*

This former private club course displays constant variety.

*6,740 yards/par-72/72.5 rating/129 slope*
*Architect: E. Lawrence Packard*
*Fees: $$*
*Call: 815/389-0979*
*Directions: Ten miles north of Rockford in Winnebago County. 7111 McCurry*
*Road.*

# Pine Meadow Golf Club
*Mundelein*

One of the best in the state.

*7,141 yards/par-72/74.4 rating/131 slope*
*Architects: Joe Lee and Rocky Roquemore*
*Fees: $$$*
*Call: 847/566-4653*
*Directions: Thirty miles north of Chicago in Lake County. Pine Meadow Lane.*

# Plum Tree National Golf Club
*Harvard*

This is a solid, traditional course just across the Wisconsin border.

*6,648 yards/par-72/71.8 rating/126 slope*
*Architect: Joe Lee*
*Fees: $$$*
*Call: 815/943-7474*
*Directions: Thirty-five miles northwest of Chicago in McHenry County. 19511*
*Lembcke Road.*

# Sandy Hollow Golf Club
*Rockford*

An old course appropriately named for the more than 50 sand traps.

*6,228 yards/par-71/69.4 rating/113 slope*
*Architect: Charles Dudley Wagstaff*
*Fees: $*
*Call: 815/987-8836*
*Directions: Seventy miles northwest of Chicago in Winnebago County. 2500*
*Sandy Hollow Road.*

# Stonewall Orchard Golf Club
*Grayslake*

This course, opened in 1999, is just 20 minutes west of Great America amusement park.

*7,074 yards/par-72/140 slope*
*Architect: Arthur Hills*
*Fees: $$$*
*Call: 847/740-4890*
*Directions: About 45 miles northwest of Chicago and 14 miles west of Interstate 94 on Route 60 or 1 mile east of Route 12.*

# Thunderhawk Golf Club
*Beach Park*

Just south of the Illinois-Wisconsin border, this 1999 course is situated across 243 acres of the Lake County Forest Preserve.

*7,031 yards/par-72/136 slope*
*Architect: Robert Trent Jones Jr.*
*Fees: $$$*
*Call: 847/872-HAWK*
*Directions: Four and a half miles east of Highway 41 on Highway 173, then*
*    1.5 miles south on Lewis Avenue. 39700 North Lewis Ave.*

# Eagle Ridge Inn and Resort
*Galena*

Galena was a bustling river town in the middle to late 1800s and home to Ulysses S. Grant, the Civil War general and president. Then it became a popular tourist town in the latter half of the 1900s, capitalizing on its historic buildings—such as Grant's home—and antiques shops. Several scenes from the movie *Field of Dreams* were filmed in Galena.

Eagle Ridge is a golfer's field of dreams—a 6,800-acre, year-round resort eight miles from Galena. It has 63 holes of golf—three 18-hole courses and a nine-holer. The resort is best known for The General, a Roger Packard/Andy North–designed course that opened in 1997. True to its name, The General— ranked among the top 20 courses in Illinois—is demanding. It plays along a ridge and valley not far from the Mississippi River and has 250 feet of elevation changes, including a drop of 180 feet on the 357-yard 14th hole.

Packard also designed the rolling North course (1977), the wooded South course (1984), and the par-34 East course (1991). Only The General has bent-grass fairways. After your round, head across the Mississippi River to the real Field of Dreams, the baseball diamond in a cornfield near Dyersville, Iowa, where the movie was filmed.

## *The General*
*6,820/par-72/73.8 rating/137 slope*
*Architects: Roger Packard and Andy North*
*Fees: $$$$ (including cart)*

## *South Course*
*6,762/par-72/72.9 rating/133 slope*
*Architect: Roger Packard*
*Fees: $$$$*

### North Course

*6,836/par-72/73.4 rating/slope 134*
*Architect: Roger Packard*
*Fees: $$$$*
*Call: 800/892-2269; Web site: www.eagleridge.com*
*Directions: From Galena, go east on Highway 20 for 8 miles.*

# Iowa

## The Meadows

*Dubuque*

Bob Lohmann designed The Meadows in Dubuque in 1996 on rolling, mostly open farm land. The course can play nearly 6,700 yards from the back tees. It has water on four holes, including a downhill shot over a pond that angles from tee to green on the 173-yard 11th hole.

Other water holes include nine and 18, guarded by a single pond. Another challenging hole is the 559-yard third, which plays downhill through a neck of fairway between trees and a fairway bunker and then uphill to a well-trapped green. Mounding, 67 well-placed bunkers, a few stands of strategically located trees, and bent-grass fairways make The Meadows a fun round of golf.

*6,667 yards/par-72/72.6 rating/132 slope*
*Architect: Bob Lohmann*
*Fees: $$*
*Call: 319/583-7385; Web site: www.meadowsgolf.com*
*Directions: From Highway 61, take Highway 20 west to Highway 32; and go
    right to Asbury Road and then left 3 miles.*

# Northeast Minnesota

## Giants Ridge

*Biwabik*

About an hour north of Duluth, Giants Ridge in Biwabik opened in 1997 to rave reviews. It was ranked one of the nation's top 10 new upscale courses in 1998, and in 1999 it was ranked number one in Minnesota.

Former PGA Tour star Lanny Wadkins helped design the course, which is adjacent to the Superior National Forest and in the Mesabi Iron Range. The course cuts through stands of towering Norway pine, birch, and black spruce trees. Giant boulders and rocks left by glaciers were used to create rock gardens and hazards on nine holes. The signature hole is number 17, a 226-yard shot over the edge of Sabin Lake. The 16th isn't bad either, a 520-yard par-five with Sabin Lake running the length of the hole on the left side.

Giants Ridge, which has about 80 feet of elevation changes, feature bent-grass fairways, white sand bunkers, and stunning scenery.

*6,930 yards/par-72/73.7 rating/133 slope*
*Architect: Jeffrey Brauer with Lanny Wadkins*
*Fees: $$$ (includes cart)*
*Call: 800/688-7669; Web site: www.giantsridge.com*
*Directions: From Duluth, go north on Highway 53 to Highway 37 at Eveleth. Go east to Gilbert. Go east on Highway 135 to Biwabik and then north on Highway 138.*

# Superior National
*Lutsen*

If northern Wisconsin isn't far enough north, take the 90-mile trip up the North Shore of Lake Superior to Lutsen. It's one of the prettiest roads in the country, with the greatest of the great lakes hugging one side of the road and the boreal forest hugging the other. Where the Poplar River cuts under Highway 61 at Lutsen, you'll find Superior National, 27 holes of mountainous golf with lake views.

The original 18 at Superior National opened in 1992, and a third nine opened in 1999. The River course features a 142-yard hole over a waterfall. The Canyon course has a spectacular par-three 142 yards all downhill to a green hard by the rushing Poplar River. The Mountain course has a 560-yard, uphill par-five across a ravine. While you're roaming the bent-grass fairways at Superior National, keep your eyes open for views of the lake and the occasional black bear or moose that like the area too.

*River: 3,088 yards/par-36/72.1 rating/128 slope*
*Mountain: 3,487 yards/par-36/73.0 rating/133 slope*
*Canyon: 3,281, 3,259 yards/par-36/71.1 rating/127 slope*
*Architect: Original 18, Don Herfort; third nine, Joel Goldstrand*
*Fees: $$$ (includes cart)*
*Call: 218/663-7195; Web site: www.superiornational.com*

*Directions: Follow Highway 61 out of Duluth along the north shore of Lake Superior. The course is on the left, just before the turn to Lutsen Mountain ski area.*

# Grand National
*Hinckley*

Next to but not related to the Grand Casino, the Grand National Golf Club, about an hour north of the Twin Cities, always is bustling with gamblers, celebrities, and special outings. The championship-length course, with bent-grass fairways, has rolling fairways and water on 14 holes. It plays along ponds, marshes, and streams.

*6,894 yards/par-72/73.6 rating/137 slope*
*Architect: Joel Goldstrand*
*Fees: $$ (includes range balls, beverage)*
*Call: 320/384-7427; Web site: www.grandnationalgolf.com*
*Directions: Near the intersection of Highways 35 and 48 in Hinckley.*

# Lakeview National
*Two Harbors*

Less than an hour north of Duluth, Lakeview National expanded and remodeled its original nine into an 18-hole course, which sits about two blocks from Lake Superior. Most of the holes wind through a wooded hillside. Ponds, a marsh, and a stream create water hazards on six holes. On par-four holes six and nine, you'll be hitting your drives right at Lake Superior. Lakeview National is owned by the city of Two Harbors.

*6,773 yards/par-72/72.2 rating/126 slope*
*Architect: Garrett Gill*
*Fees: $*
*Call: 218/834-2664*
*Directions: The course is along Highway 61 on the north side of Two Harbors.*

### Other Area Courses
The city of Duluth operates two courses, the 27-hole Lester Park (218/525-0828) and 18-hole Enger Park (218/723-3451).

# Twin Cities Metro Area

## The Wilds Golf Club
*Prior Lake*

It's advertised as the "crown jewel" of Minnesota golf. With 100 acres of wetlands, 150-foot elevation changes, $100-plus greens fees, and big-name designers such as Tom Weiskopf and Jay Norrish, it lives up to its billing. It also has been ranked the number one course in the state.

The Wilds plays 7,028 yards and has a slope of 140 from the Weiskopf tees. Each nine takes a wide loop around the stylish clubhouse. The Wilds has water on nine holes, more than seventy bunkers (filled with the same white sand as they use for the Masters at Augusta National), and a lovely grove of Ponderosa pines. From the elevated tee on the 440-yard 18th hole, you can see the Minneapolis skyline.

*7,028 yards/par-72/74.7 rating/140 slope*
*Architects: Tom Weiskopf and Jay Norrish*
*Fees: $$$$*
*Call: 952/445-3500; Web site: www.golfthewilds.com*
*Directions: South on 35W or 35E; then go west on County 42 to County 83; and then go south 0.25 mile.*

## Rush Creek Golf Club
*Maple Grove*

In the northwest suburb of Maple Grove, Rush Creek has been one of the high profile Twin Cities metro courses since it opened in 1993. It held an LPGA tournament one year as well as the 1999 World Championship of Women's Golf shootout, featuring 12 of the world's top women players. It is scheduled to hold the 2004 U.S. Amateur Public Links tournament.

The course plays through 260 acres of prairie and marsh on mostly level terrain with water hazards on about half the holes. The 560-yard 18th hole has water down the entire left side of the fairway and in front of the green, making for a fun risk-reward finish to your round.

*7,020 yards/par-72/74.2 rating/137 slope*
*Architect: Robert Cupp*
*Fees: $$$$*

*Call: 763/494-8844; Web site: www.rushcreek.com*
*Directions: Take Interstate 494 to Bass Lake Road; then go west 4 miles to*
*County 101 (Troy Lane) and go right 0.7 mile.*

# Edinburgh USA
*Brooklyn Park*

Some courses are known for their island greens. Edinburgh USA is known for its island fairway. The 17th hole at the Robert Trent Jones Jr. course is only 394 yards from the back tees, but the fairway is surrounded by water. Even though the fairway is 150 yards long and plenty wide, its intimidating appearance—much like Pete Dye's island 17th green at the TPC—has caused many a golfer to flinch and miss the target. Jones designed water hazards on half of Edinburgh's holes, and he carved out about 120 sand traps. Edinburgh USA, owned by the city of Brooklyn Park, hosted an LPGA tournament from 1991 through 1996.

*6,701 yards/par-72/73.0 rating/133 slope*
*Architect: Robert Trent Jones Jr.*
*Fees: $$*
*Call: 763/424-9444; Web site: www.edinburghusa.org*
*Directions: In Brooklyn Park, take County 52 to 85th Avenue and go 1.4 miles west.*

# Prestwick Golf Club
*Woodbury*

Built as part of a housing development in 1985, Prestwick may not be the most scenic course around, but it's popular with weekend golfers because it isn't tight, has large greens, and usually is in good shape with bent-grass fairways. It can challenge the low-handicapper, too, playing 6,723 yards from the tips and often in wind.

Prestwick has 11 water holes, including a 174-yard carry to the green on the par-three sixth hole. Another strong hole is 16, a 569-yard par-five where the third shot—or second if you're long off the tee and bold—must carry water.

*6,723 yards/par-72/72.5 rating/127 slope*
*Fees: $$*
*Call: 651/731-4779; Web site: www.prestwick.com*
*Directions: From Interstate 94, take Radio Drive south to Lake Road and then*
*east to Woodbury Drive.*

# AUTHORS' FAVORITES: FINISHING HOLES

Madeline Island, La Pointe. Par-three. Downhill all the way to get down by the bay.

Spooner Golf Club, Spooner. A picturesque, 396-yard par-four along a wetland. This hole is so good it once was put out of circulation.

St. Germain GC, St. Germain. This 506-yard par-five has it all—two doglegs, trees, sand, and water.

Teal Wing, Hayward. A 544-yard par-five that offers one last chance to be a tree hugger.

Telemark, Cable. It's only a 339-yard par-four—and downhill at that—but a chute of trees and a lovely cedar clubhouse towering over the green make it a fun way to finish.

Trout Lake, Arbor Vitae. At just 260 yards, this par-four can be reached in one—a good place to let it all hang out.

Troy Burne, Hudson. At 470 yards, it's a par-four with enough length and sand to test a champion.

Turtleback, Rice Lake. A 530-yard, dogleg par-five with a big tree, a big pond, and lots of sand.

Wild Ridge, Eau Claire. Drive it down the ridge one last time—435 rolling yards with a pond guarding a two-tiered green.

Brown Deer Park, Milwaukee. Try to eagle this uphill par-five like the pros.

The Springs, Spring Green. Robert Trent Jones created a tough par-four in a pretty part of the lower Wisconsin River valley.

SentryWorld, Stevens Point. Par-four. Uphill, dogleg left first through trees and then to a green surrounded by bunkers. This 448-yard Robert Trent Jones Jr. creation leaves you gasping.

Mascoutin CC, Berlin. E. Lawrence Packard designed this 382-yard hole using woods, water, and the beautiful terrain of the Fox River valley. Number nine on the white nine.

Meadow Valley, Blackwolf Run, Kohler. This 458-yard par-four features one of the most intimidating approach shots you'll find in Wisconsin—over a wide spot in the Sheboygan River.

The Straits, Whistling Straits, north of Kohler. This 470-yard hole heading inland from Lake Michigan features two long carries. Pete Dye may be the only one who knows how to play it.

Horseshoe Bay, Door County. Rocky ridges, trees, and a view of Green Bay complement this 604-yard dogleg right.

University Ridge, Verona. This 413-yard dogleg left on the edge of the Driftless Area is all uphill and rarely yields an easy par.

Devil's Head Lodge, Merrimac. This 448-yard par-four, at the course by the ski hill, might have you wishing for winter.

# Stone Ridge
*Woodbury*

Opened in 2000, Stone Ridge is billed as a heathland-style course with few trees but lots of sand—four acres of it, to be exact. Stone Ridge has large, irregularly shaped bunkers and rolling, bent-grass fairways. Water comes into play on only two holes, but the well-placed bunkers, combined with hard-to-reach pins, make for a risk-reward chess game.

*6,950 yards/par-72/73.3 rating/133 slope*
*Architect: Bobby Weed*
*Fees: $$$*
*Call: 651/436-4653; Web site: www.stoneridgegc.com*
*Directions: From Interstate 94, take Highway 95 south and turn onto the frontage road. Turn right at Neal Avenue. Cross the freeway and turn right on the frontage road again to reach the course.*

# Stonebrooke Golf Club
*Shakopee*

Stonebrooke is one of the big attractions in the suburban city that also is known for Valley Fair amusement park, the Renaissance Festival, and Canterbury Downs horse track. At Stonebrooke, playing the eighth hole isn't quite as thrilling as riding the Wild Thing at Valley Fair, but it's close. The 405-yard hole features a 230-yard carry from the back tees over a lake. Then golfers must take a pontoon boat to the other side. The seventh hole is a white-knuckler, too—a 145-yard carry over the same lake.

The lake and ponds make for water hazards on 13 holes on the rolling, heavily wooded course, which opened in 1989. Stonebrooke also has a par-30 course, The Preserve.

*6,604 yards/par-71/72.4 rating/133 slope*
*Architect: Tom Haugen*
*Fees: $$*
*Call: 800/263-3189; Web site: www.stonebrooke.com*
*Directions: Take Interstate 494 to Highway 169 south to Shakopee, exit on Marshall Road, and go left to County 78. Then turn right on County 79 and then left 1 mile.*

# Willingers Golf Club

*Northfield*

Willingers offers the beauty of a wetland on the front nine and a forest on the back nine, combining for a tight 18 holes that have a slope of 148. The course has more than a hundred sand traps and water on 13 holes. The signature hole is 12, a 445-yard par-four that plays from an elevated tee 40 feet down a ravine and then back up 30 feet to the green. Willingers, which opened in 1991, has been a site of U.S. Open qualifying.

*6,711 yards/par-72/73.4 rating/148 slope*
*Architect: Garrett Gill*
*Fees: $$*
*Call: 952/652-2500*
*Directions: From Interstate 35, go west on County 19 for 1.5 miles and then*
*    north on Canby Trail for 1 mile.*

# Bunker Hills

*Coon Rapids*

At Bunker Hills, you can walk the same sod as golf legends. The course was home to the Burnet Senior Classic on the PGA Senior Tour from 1993 to 2000. From Arnold Palmer to Lee Trevino to Gary Player, most of golf's great names in the last half-century have played a tournament routing of Bunker Hills' 27 holes. Bunker Hills opened in 1968, and a third nine was added in 1990. It has bentgrass fairways, lots of sand and water on four holes.

*North: 3,418; East: 3,381; West: 3,520 yards/par-36*
*North and East: 72.5 rating/132 slope; North and West: 73.4 rating/133 slope;*
*    East and West: 73.5 rating/132 slope*
*Architect: David Gill (original 18); Joel Goldstrand (third nine)*
*Fees: $$*
*Call: 763/755-4141*
*Directions: Take Interstate 694 to Highway 65 north; go to Highway 242 and*
*    then west 2 miles.*

# South-Central Minnesota

## Mississippi National
*Red Wing*

For championship golf or scenic golf, Mississippi National is hard to beat with its 36 holes near the Mississippi River. The Lowlands, an 18-hole course that is plenty hilly, has held regional U.S. Open and U.S. Amateur qualifying. The Highlands is a scenic treat as it climbs two steep, wooded bluffs and dives into the valley between the bluffs along the Mississippi.

Yardage at the Highlands doesn't always mean much. On the 149-yard 17th hole, for example, it's a 150-foot drop from tee to green. Don't take anything more than a wedge, or your shot coming back will be from the Lowlands.

*Lowlands: 6,484 yards/par-71/71 rating/126 slope*
*Highlands: 6,282 /par-71/70.5 rating/121 slope*
*Architect: Gordon Cunningham*
*Fees: $$*
*Call: 651/388-1874; Web site: www.wpgolf.com*
*Directions: On Highway 61 at the southern edge of Red Wing.*

## Cedar Valley
*Winona*

Seven miles south of Winona, Cedar Valley Golf Course opened 18 holes in 1991 and was scheduled to open a third nine in 2001. The course plays along hillsides and through a valley that is bisected by a stream. The stream comes into play on five holes, including two carries over the bubbling brook on par-three holes and one on the par-five 17th.

The most memorable hole is scenic number 14, a 302-yard narrow dogleg along a ledge. Take an iron and hit it straight here. The 18th hole is uphill to an island green. The newest nine will measure about thirty-five hundred yards with two 600-yard-plus par-fives.

*6,218 yards/par-72/68.0 rating/116 slope*
*Architects: Wayne Idso and Frank Ciszak*
*Fees: $$*
*Call: 507/457-3129*
*Directions: From Winona on Highway 61, go south to County 9 and then go*
  *right 3 miles.*

# Michigan's Upper Peninsula

## TimberStone

*Iron Mountain*

In Iron Mountain, Michigan, TimberStone Golf Course is one of the Upper Peninsula's best tests of golf. The course has 310 feet of elevation change, including a 110-foot drop on the par-three, 215-yard 17th hole. Water on four holes, forests, and many natural hazards, including rocks (the 14th green is surrounded by boulders) make TimberStone, designed by Jerry Matthews, a delight to play and one of the best tests in the north country.

*6,937 yards/par-72/75.2 rating/144 slope*
*Architect: Jerry Matthews*
*Fees: $$$ (includes cart)*
*Call: 906/776-0111; Web site: www.timberstonegolf.com*
*Directions: From Iron Mountain, take Highway 2 and follow the signs to Pine*
*    Mountain Ski Area, which is adjacent to the course.*

## George Young Golf Course

*Iron River*

The course opened in 1984 after owner George Young spent about thirty years designing and building the 18 holes one by one. The layout features wooded holes, bent-grass fairways, and several views of Chicagoan Lake. Several holes have great views from the tee, including the 158-yard third hole and 600-yard eighth hole. The course also has a $3.5 million clubhouse and recreation complex and a low, one-price greens fee that lets you play all day.

*7,041 yards/par-72/74.3 rating/130 slope*
*Architect: George Young*
*Fees: $ for all day*
*Call: 906/265-3401*
*Directions: From Iron River or Caspian, take Highway 424 to the course.*

### Other Area Courses

At nine-hole Gateway Golf Course (715/547-3929) in Land O' Lakes, Wisconsin, you can hit a golf ball into the next state. On the third hole, the men's tee is in Wisconsin and the fairway in Michigan. Actually, the clubhouse is in Wisconsin, but the first four holes (minus the one tee) are in Michigan and the final five holes are in Wisconsin. Gateway is par-36, 3,220 yards.

In Watersmeet, Michigan, the Lac Vieux Desert Casino golf course (906/358-0303) has bent-grass fairways and plays a challenging 3,425 yards, par-36 from the back tees. The nine holes are cut from the Ottawa National Forest. The slope is 130 and course rating is 71.2.

# Index of Courses

Index of Courses

# More Great Titles from Trails Books

## Activity Guides

*Paddling Southern Wisconsin: 82 Great Trips by Canoe and Kayak,*
Mike Svob
*Paddling Northern Wisconsin: 82 Great Trips by Canoe and Kayak,*
Mike Svob
*Paddling Illinois: 64 Great Trips by Canoe and Kayak,* Mike Svob
*Wisconsin Underground: A Guide to Caves, Mines, and Tunnels in
and around the Badger State,* Doris Green
*Great Wisconsin Walks: 45 Strolls, Rambles, Hikes, and Treks,*
Wm. Chad McGrath
*Great Minnesota Walks: 49 Strolls, Rambles, Hikes, and Treks,*
Wm. Chad McGrath
*Best Wisconsin Bike Trips,* Phil Van Valkenberg

## Travel Guides

*Great Minnesota Weekend Adventures,* Beth Gauper
*Tastes of Minnesota: A Food Lover's Tour,* Donna Tabbert Long
*Great Indiana Weekend Adventures,* Sally McKinney
*Historical Wisconsin Getaways: Touring the Badger State's Past,*
Sharyn Alden
*The Great Wisconsin Touring Book: 30 Spectacular Auto Tours,*
Gary Knowles
*Wisconsin Family Weekends: 20 Fun Trips for You and the Kids,*
Susan Lampert Smith
*County Parks of Wisconsin,* Revised Edition, Jeannette and Chet Bell
*Up North Wisconsin: A Region for All Seasons,* Sharyn Alden
*The Spirit of Door County: A Photographic Essay,* Darryl R. Beers
*Great Wisconsin Taverns: 101 Distinctive Badger Bars,* Dennis Boyer
*Great Wisconsin Restaurants,* Dennis Getto

*Great Weekend Adventures,* the Editors of Wisconsin Trails
*The Wisconsin Traveler's Companion: A Guide to Country Sights,*
Jerry Apps and Julie Sutter-Blair

# Home and Garden

*Creating a Perennial Garden in the Midwest,* Joan Severa
*Bountiful Wisconsin: 110 Favorite Recipes,* Terese Allen
*Foods That Made Wisconsin Famous,* Richard J. Baumann

# Historical Guides

*Walking Tours of Wisconsin's Historic Towns,* Lucy Rhodes, Elizabeth
    McBride, and Anita Matcha
*Wisconsin: The Story of the Badger State,* Norman K. Risjord
*Barns of Wisconsin,* Jerry Apps
*Portrait of the Past: A Photographic Journey Through Wisconsin,*
    *1865–1920,* Howard Mead, Jill Dean, and Susan Smith

# For Young People

*Wisconsin Portraits: 55 People Who Made a Difference,* Martin Hintz
*ABCs of Wisconsin,* Dori Hillestad Butler and Alison Relyea
*W Is for Wisconsin,* Dori Hillestad Butler and Eileen Dawson

# Other Titles of Interest

*Prairie Whistles: Tales of Midwest Railroading,* Dennis Boyer
*The I-Files: True Reports of Unexplained Phenomena in Illinois,* Jay Rath
*The W-Files: True Reports of Wisconsin's Unexplained Phenomena,* Jay Rath
*The M-Files: True Reports of Minnesota's Unexplained Phenomena,* Jay Rath

For a free catalog, phone, write, or e-mail us.
Trails Books
P.O. Box 317, Black Earth, WI 53515
800/236-8088 • email: info@wistrails.com
www.trailsbooks.com